SEP 1970
OHIO DOMINICAN
COLLEGE LIBRARY
COLUMBUS, OHIO
43219

THE CONCEPT OF MAN IN EARLY CHINA

The Concept of Man in Early China

Donald J. Munro

Stanford University Press
Stanford, California
1969

Stanford University Press
Stanford, California

Printed in the United States of America
L.C. 68-21288

To My Father and Mother

PREFACE

THIS STUDY analyzes two conceptions of human nature that emerged in classical Chinese philosophy. But more than this, it is concerned with the birth of an idea that has had a long odyssey in Chinese intellectual history. The idea is that men are naturally equal, and the end of the odyssey is still not in sight.

Previous commentators on classical Chinese philosophy have been misled by the Confucian assertion that a hierarchical society is justified by the hierarchical character of nature itself, and that men are of unequal merit. It is accurate to associate this assertion with the dominant school in Chinese thought; but the very complexity of the concepts "equality" and "inequality" has blinded many scholars to the essential feature in the early Chinese concept of man. "Equality," as applied to human beings, has two very different broad meanings. The first implies that all men, being of similar worth (the meaning of "worth" varies), should be treated in the same way: they should receive equal political or economic privilege, or impartial treatment before the law, and so forth. In this sense, the dominant Chinese position on human equality has been a belief that men (as adults) are of unequal merit, and that unequal treatment is therefore justified. The second meaning is basically descriptive; it refers to common attributes shared by all men at birth. The present study is concerned primarily with the relationship between equality in this latter sense and the conceptions of man in early China.

The importance of the idea of natural equality lies in the assumption derived from it by the Chinese: that men, lacking innate defects, are perfectible through education. The educational environment determines whether or not men will be good or evil, and educational reform is a key to the solution of urgent social and political problems. Several related assumptions pertaining to the content of that education have important implications for modern educational theory and social control theory, since they concern ways of causing large groups of people to behave in a certain manner. Two such assumptions will be examined in the present study: first, that the primary aim of education and "self-cultivation" is to give men a permanent and correct mental attitude toward certain norms (in other words, social control is to be internalized); second, that people learn through the emulation of models, and that the best way to inculcate any behavior in them is to present them with a model. The idea of natural equality is also significant in that it sets classical Chinese philosophy apart from its European counterparts. For this reason alone the study of the concept of man in early China should be of great interest to a student of cultural history.

My secondary aim in this study is to make the reader aware of a danger confronting any student of early Chinese philosophy—that of injecting ideas that developed at a later time into the interpretation of philosophical terms in the classical texts. For instance, in the Neo-Confucian period metaphysical thought, influenced by Buddhism, had developed to a high degree, and it permeates the numerous commentaries on the classics produced at that time. As a result, old philosophical ideas had evolved and changed their meanings, although the terms employed remain the same. Judging by the extent to which sophisticated Neo-Confucian interpretations of key philosophical concepts (or those from even later periods) are read into the early Chinese texts, many writers have been less than mindful of this fact. For example, two important terms in the present study, [e]*hsing* (nature, as in human nature) and [a]*te* (virtue), have frequently been misinterpreted because of the injection of ideas of a later time into the early texts. The mistake is easy to make when apparently helpful and easily available commentaries are of a much later age. The problems of grasping what was actually being said in the Chou works are enormous, and often insurmountable; but the student should still try to understand these works on their own terms, for the failure to do so has already negated much of the practical value of the scholarship done on the classical period by preventing both adequate description of that period and adequate evaluation of subsequent trends. In our own time an acquaintance with anthropology, though often helpful, has unfortunately produced in some scholars an obsession for reinterpreting classical philosophical concepts to make them compatible with modern generalizations about primitive religion.

One probably should not stop with a criticism of injecting ideas from a contemporary social science into early Chinese thought. There is a general tendency among Western readers, especially those with some philosophical training, to interpret and evaluate Chinese philosophy in terms of familiar categories. For example, they look first for the "argument," or demonstration that the position being advocated in the Chinese work is true; when they find no systematic, step-by-step argument, there is often a feeling of frustration. A new way of viewing Chinese philosophy is essential, and the present study attempts to orient the reader in the new direction.

What were important to the Chinese philosophers, where questions of truth and falsity were not, were the behavioral implications of the statement or belief in question. In other words, the Chinese asked: What kind of behavior is likely to occur if a person adheres to this belief? Can the statement be interpreted to imply that men should act in a certain way? The Chinese thinker's regrettable lack of attention to the logical validity of a philosophical tenet is balanced by his great concern with problems important to human life. There are times when Western philosophy has been characterized by the reverse situation—an enormous interest in epistemological and logical problems and a seeming unconcern with the bearing of its mental labors on the well-being of man.

A word of caution is also appropriate for Westerners who expect the archaic Chinese texts to show the same consistency in philosophical position that Western writings do. Occasionally, a Chinese classic will contain passages on some important topic that seem to contradict other passages in the same work. For example, at the beginning of Section 9 of the *Hsün-tzu* is a reference to some men who are "incorrigibly evil"; this contradicts the Confucian assumption (elsewhere shared by Hsün Tzu) that men are perfectible through education. One must ask whether or not such passages are frequent enough to merit some special explanation (an example appears in this book, in the chapters on the Taoist view of man). If they are not, one had best concentrate on the dominant themes and try to live with the inconsistencies. In many cases they are a product of later additions to the archaic texts; in others they may simply represent the author's lack of concern with consistency, which is so dear to Western thinkers.

For permission to quote from copyright material I wish to acknowledge the following publishers: George Allen and Unwin, Ltd., London, for extracts from Herbert A. Giles's translation of the *Chuang Tzu* (1961) and Arthur Waley's translation of *The Analects of Confucius* (1938); Atherton Press, Inc., New York, for quotations from *Nomos IX: Equality*, edited by J. Roland Pennock and John W. Chapman (1967); Routledge and Kegan Paul, London, and Humanities Press, Inc., New York, for extracts from Francis M. Cornford's *Plato's Cosmology* (London, 1937; New York, 1956); and Arthur Probsthain, London, for extracts from Homer H. Dubs's translation *The Works of Hsuntze* (1958). I am grateful to Bernhard Karlgren for permission to quote material from his translations of the classics, which appeared in *Bulletin of the Museum of Far Eastern Antiquities*, Stockholm, and were published in book form as *The Book of Documents* and *The Book of Odes* by the Museum of Far Eastern Antiquities (1950). In some cases, quotations from these works have been modified slightly (e.g., by the omission of bracketed linguistic information).

I am indebted to the Ford Foundation Foreign Area Fellowship Program for a grant under which part of the present study was carried out. The Foundation is not to be understood as approving by virtue of its grant any of the statements made or views expressed in this work. I am grateful for additional support from the Center for Chinese Studies at the University of Michigan. The actual research was aided immeasurably by several people. Mr. Liu Yü-yün, specialist on Han-hsüeh, enlightened me on the Chou philosophical works and reinforced my enthusiasm for them. In lengthy discussions over a period of several months Professor T'ang Chün-i of New Asia College, Hong Kong, clarified numerous philosophical matters in those works for me. My studies of the oracle-bone and bronze inscriptions were guided by Professor Ch'ü Wan-li of the Academia Sinica in Taiwan and Professor Shirakawa Shizuka of Ritsumeikan University in Kyoto; both gave generously of their time. Professor William Theodore de Bary of Columbia University made numerous penetrating suggestions for parts of the study. I am especially grateful to Mr. D. C. Lau of the School of Oriental and African Studies, London, for taking the trouble to read and criticize an earlier, somewhat different manuscript, parts of which are incorporated in this book.

No less important in making possible the completion of this study has been the stimulation that I have received from a number of friends: Alexander Eckstein, Albert Feuerwerker, Thomas Munro, and Lyman Van Slyke. The degree of one's own enthusiasm is so often a product of the encouragement of one's (frequently captive) audience, and I must record my gratitude to these friends and, most of all, to my wife.

D.J.M.

CONTENTS

THE CONCEPT OF MAN IN EARLY CHINA

Mencius said, "The trees of the New Mountain were once beautiful. Being situated, however, in the borders of a large state, they were hewn down with axes and bills—and could they retain their beauty? Still, through the activity of the vegetative life day and night, and the nourishing influence of the rain and dew, they were not without buds and sprouts springing forth, but then came the cattle and goats and browsed upon them. To these things is owing the bare and stripped appearance of the mountain, which when people see, they think it was never finely wooded. But is this the nature of the mountain? And so also of what properly belongs to man; shall it be said that the mind of any man was without benevolence and righteousness? The way in which a man loses his proper goodness of mind is like the way in which the trees are denuded by axes and bills. Hewn down day after day, can the mind retain its beauty?"

—Mencius

CHAPTER 1

HUMAN NATURE AND NATURAL EQUALITY

TWO THEMES can be found woven through the various poetic, conversational, and prose passages in which early Confucian and Taoist thinkers put forth their concept of man. The first of these themes concerns the presence or absence in nature of a basis for the ethical categories "right and wrong," "proper and improper," and "superior and inferior." The Confucians assumed that nature did reveal these qualities. Certain relationships between natural bodies (planets, rivers, mountains, and so forth) were seen in ethical terms: for example, the "proper" relationship of Heaven to earth was that of superior to inferior, and it was "good" for a planet to move only in its own orbit. Similarly, some human relationships are "proper," and some actions are "good." In short, human society is simply an extension of nature. Taoist thinkers, by contrast, denied that nature revealed any of these qualities. "Superior and inferior," "right and wrong," and "proper and improper," they maintained, were human inventions, which should be "forgotten" by men when in contact with their fellows and should never be read into nature as a whole.

A similar controversy exists in Western philosophy, e.g. between the Platonists (on the Confucian side) and the sophists, over such questions as whether "justice" is a cosmic virtue or simply an arbitrary label. What is unique about China is the agreement on all sides that men are naturally equal. This is the second of our two central themes. Both sides were quick to dismiss as unimportant the objective differences between men; both tried above all to establish a quintessential equality. This second theme, the natural equality of all men, is a major topic of the present study.

As I shall use the expression, "natural equality" is a descriptive term; it refers to the common attributes or characteristics with which all men are born. It is to be differentiated from "equality" in the evaluative sense, which carries the suggestion that men are of similar "worth" or deserve similar treatment. The two senses, descriptive and evaluative, can be related, but they are basically different (see p. 179, footnote †).

Why Natural Equality?

Why did the idea of natural equality arise in China when it did? The answer doubtless lies in the increasing opposition to hereditary privilege among thinkers of the Chou period.* Indeed, opposition to hereditary privilege is the single theoretical position common to all the philosophical schools of the Warring States era. In spite of their clashing views on other issues, they could agree on this. To be sure, one finds occasional favorable references to people with hereditary claims to high position.† The prevailing view was not so much that such claims should be ignored, as that other claims to preferment be given equal recognition. In my subsequent references to "the rejection of the hereditary principle" in early China, these qualifying remarks should be remembered.

All Confucian writings make it clear that birth should not be the exclusive criterion for preferment. Disciples came to Confucius for training in the refined arts (ritual, poetry, writing, numbers) and in the art of government. He claims to have accepted all without regard to their background, and at least one of his students, Tzu-kung, is said to have achieved official position though of humble origin.[1] Mencius (c. 372–289 B.C.) stated that the sage emperors Yao and Shun "were just the same as other men," and that any man, no matter what his background, might by diligence achieve their status.[2] Hsün Tzu (c. 298–238 B.C.) began his chapter on "kingly government" by stating: "Do not regard seniority

* The classical period of ancient Chinese philosophy was from roughly 550 B.C. to roughly 250 B.C.—i.e., from late in the Spring and Autumn period (770–481 B.C.) to almost the end of the Warring States period (480–222 B.C.).

† In *Mencius* i.B.7, for example, Mencius is reported to have told the king of Ch'i that a ruler gives office to "worthies" only if he cannot help doing so, since he will thereby "cause the humble to pass over the honorable." Actually, Mencius's position on hereditary claims vs. merit in this chapter is far more complex than this well-known passage suggests. See Note 2 to this page.

but advance the worthy and able; dismiss the incompetent and incapable without delay; ... develop the common people without waiting to compel them by laws. ... Yet, although a man be the descendant of a king, duke, prefect, or officer, if he does not observe the rules of proper conduct [*li*] and justice [*i*], he must be relegated to the common ranks."[3]

Mo Tzu (fl. 479–438 B.C.), who is believed to have lived a century after Confucius, disagreed with a number of central Confucian principles. The Mohists opposed the depersonalization of the supreme deity, Heaven (*ᵇt'ien*), that they felt had occurred in Confucian thought, and they rejected Confucius's religious skepticism. Moreover, since men should model themselves on Heaven and since Heaven was impartial in its love toward all men, they advocated universal love in contrast to the Confucian dictum that kin are entitled to preferential affection. However, the Mohists concurred in the Confucian opposition to hereditary privilege. They believed that good government required the standardization of rank and monetary reward in accordance with individual virtue. This meant that ordinary farmers and artisans should have the same opportunity as the sons of nobles to achieve high position. According to Mo Tzu, "The sage kings of ancient times ranked the virtuous high and honored the worthy, and although a man might be a farmer or an artisan from the shops, if he had ability they promoted him."[4]

The Lord of Shang or Wei Yang (d. 338 B.C.) and Han Fei-tzu (d. 233 B.C.) were concerned with two characteristic problems of the Warring States period: how to extend a state's control to adjacent territories, and how to organize a society to repel attacks by other states. Their doctrine, known as "Legalism," advocated the universal standardization of behavior by explicit laws impartially applied. No philosophy could be more remote from Confucianism, which advocated "government by men, not by laws," and rated the family's rights at least equal to the state's. And yet the Legalists, like the Mohists, agreed with the Confucian belief that no man had special privilege as a birthright. Law is the means for enforcing this principle, because it knows no favorites. Han

Fei-tzu said: "The law does not fawn on the noble; the [carpenter's] string [when stretched] does not yield to the crooked. Whatever the law applies to, the wise cannot reject nor can the brave defy. Punishment for fault never skips ministers; reward for good never misses commoners."[5] The wise ruler estimates men's abilities and then appoints them to office. He uses ranks and rewards as a means of encouraging the meritorious.

In Taoism we find still another version of the same theme. According to Taoist thinkers, all men, including the ruler, should model themselves on the Tao. Since all things are the same from the standpoint of the Tao, all men should be regarded as equals. The Taoists rejected Confucian distinctions between noble and base, right and wrong, as artificial standards for preferring some people to others. In Taoist thought egalitarianism was carried to its ultimate extreme. Taoists dismissed the very concept of social rank with the observation that he who was superior in the eyes of man was mean in the eyes of the Tao.

The Repudiation of Hereditary Privilege

The repudiation of hereditary privilege had two sources: a religious idea of the West Chou (1111–771 B.C.) and the changing social conditions of the Spring and Autumn and Warring States periods. The religious idea was that Heaven was impartially receptive to virtuous behavior and had no prejudices in favor of certain men or tribes; any man whose behavior was virtuous might be noticed by Heaven and elevated to the ruling position. The Chou house made good use of this idea in their attempts to legitimize their claims of conquest over the Shang, but this expedient use did not detract from the lasting strength that the idea took on in early China. Since Heaven was considered impartial, and since merit was the criterion for occupying the top position, one could infer that the same should hold true for all other positions.

The social conditions behind the general rejection of hereditary privilege are a good deal more complex. Basically, there seem to have been two factors involved: the gradual weakening of the tight clan system once dominant in China, and the appearance of new posts open to men of lower rank. Obviously, there was considerable interrelationship between these two factors, but they can be distinguished for purposes of analysis.

The Breakdown of Tight Clan Ties

In the Shang period (1751–1111 B.C.) there was a fairly strict practice of exogamy. It was believed that sickness would visit those who violated the prohibition: "Those of the same clan do not marry" (*t'ung hsing pu hun**).[6] The expression "same clan" (*t'ung hsing*) possibly included the meaning "same blood."[7] In Shang times the royal house generally practiced exogamy, although there were some exceptions.[8] Much of the realm was ruled by nobles who belonged to the same clan as the king; however, other clans, whose leaders had been enfeoffed by the Shang king, were accepted as part of the Shang group.[9]

By the early Chou period, internal disorders and the consequent population movement may have weakened the blood tie somewhat; many knew only to which family ([a]*shih*) they belonged, not to which clan ([a]*hsing*).[10] Well into the Spring and Autumn period, however, the social structure was still one based mostly on clans, which were fairly strictly organized. Noble clans generally traced their descent to a god or a deified ancestor. The Shang house, for example, was founded by a person hatched from a swallow's egg at the command of a deity; and Prince Millet, the founder of the Chou royal family, came into this world after his mother walked on a toeprint made by the Lord-on-High. Clan life centered on the ancestral temple, where all important ceremonies were carried out, and where significant events affecting the clan were reported to the deceased.

The peoples of China at the beginning of the Spring and Autumn period can be divided into three groups. One group was a confederation of Chou states, whose inhabitants lived in walled cities; people of a given area often bore the same surname (i.e., were at

* Characters for most expressions given in romanization will be found in the Chinese Characters section, pp. 198–202. When two different expressions have the same romanization, they are distinguished by superscript italic letters.

least nominally descendants of a common ancestor), and married people of different surnames from other areas. The second group, the non-Chou states of Ch'u, Wu, Yüeh, Pa, and Shu, were at first outside the Chou cultural area, but were gradually drawn into it. The third group, tribal peoples like the Jung and Ti in the north, the Man and Yi in the south, roamed the grasslands of the Yellow River Basin and the jungles of the Yangtze Valley.[11]

During the late Spring and Autumn period there was incessant warfare between the aristocratic clans and between the clans and the rulers of states. At this time we find signs of a general weakening of bloodline clan barriers, notably an increase in marriages between members of the same clan and a new phenomenon of people born of the same bloodline but belonging to different clans.[12] On scholar feels that in time even the meaning of [a]*hsing* changed, from denoting exclusively bloodline to denoting also an esteemed rank;[13] *hsing* was increasingly used to distinguish the clans of the king and nobles who were his kin from those of the chief ministers, and the original meaning of *hsing* was taken over by [a]*shih*.[14] There are references from the Warring States period to mendicant knights released from former clan ties who were taken in by local feudal lords seeking to gain power.[15] The regional feudal unit, obviously more capable of admitting outsiders than a clan unit, replaced the bloodline group as central.[16] With the loosening of clan barriers during this period, family links became less important in securing office, even high office.

More than 130 states are mentioned in Chou documents. In the West Chou a sizable number of the states in the Yellow River Valley were ruled by lords with some blood tie to the Chou king. The regional rulers were addressed by the king in familial terms; for example, those of the highest rank and with the same surname as the royal house were addressed as paternal uncles.[17] Somewhat later, after the decline of the Chou house, the hereditary principle was applied in awarding the higher posts in individual states. In the early Spring and Autumn period, chief ministers were often brothers of the state rulers; younger sons of the ruler also received high ministerial positions, and their sons in turn were given somewhat lower offices. Ministers of the ^a^*ch'ing* grade were rulers' sons who had been enfeoffed; those of the *tai fu* grade were other sons of the ruler or children of a ^a^*ch'ing*-grade minister. Sometimes the *tai fu* position became hereditary.[18]

By the middle of the Spring and Autumn period certain families had achieved the power to pass on ministerial positions exclusively to their own kin.[19] Their power had often been increased by the award of lands for success in military campaigns; and, of course, the stronger these families became, the weaker became the state ruler. According to Hsü Cho-yün, no ruler's son served as a chancellor after 513 B.C., and no sons of rulers who reigned after this time were able to set up powerful enclaves.[20] In sum, in the middle of the Spring and Autumn period the hereditary principle was still in operation, only in a new form: the family-state had given way to a multitude of aristocratic families, each with its own power center.

In time, however, the constant warfare destroyed the great hereditary clans. Over 110 states disappeared in the bloody wars of the Spring and Autumn period, and when they fell their noble families lost power, some to the point of accepting plebeian status; it was these aristocratic families that had perpetuated the hereditary assignment of offices. By the fourth century B.C. only the state of Ch'u had its chief ministers furnished by hereditary noble families.[21]

New Paths Upward

Before turning to the new channels of upward mobility during the late Spring and Autumn and Warring States periods, a word about the social strata prior to that time. For years there has been a steady stream of partisan works on this subject by Chinese writers. Those eager to affirm a quasi-Marxist portrait of Chinese history, such as Kuo Mo-jo and Ch'en Meng-chia,* have been at pains to prove that the society of the Shang and early Chou was

* Although Ch'en's historical interpretations sometimes reflect a Marxist viewpoint, he has never been identified closely with the party, and in 1957 he was declared a "rightist."

a slave society. The evidence offered to support this view is threefold. First, certain characters on oracle bones are interpreted as "slave." Kuo considers [a]*chung* ("multitude," also appearing as *chung jen*) to be a picture of three men working under a sun (slaves toiling).[22] Among the other characters mentioned are *ch'en* (a "subject" of a ruler) and [a]*nu* (today translated as "slave"). Ch'en admits that there were also freemen commoners, termed [a]*jen* or *hsiao jen*. Second, we are told of skeletons, some headless, that show signs of having been killed for ritual burial along with prominent nobles, and certain expressions on oracle bones are said to refer to human sacrifice. Third, there are various phrases on oracle bones, such as "The [a]*chung* ran away" and "The king goes to repress the disorders of the *chung*," that supposedly indicate the existence of a slave class.[23] Several equally distinguished scholars have rejected the slave society thesis: Tung Tso-pin, Hu Hou-hsüan, and Shima Kuniyo.[24]

For our purposes it is enough to recognize that in the Shang and early Chou there were at least two broad classes, the ruling and the ruled (the third type of evidence—the *chung* running away and the king repressing their disorders—without question refers to a subject people). The majority of the "ruled" were peasants who did not own land but were attached to it and would be tied to the land when it changed hands. They were mostly agricultural workers, except in time of war, when they could be conscripted as foot soldiers to accompany the aristocrats' chariots. Slaves in the strict sense of the term doubtless existed, but they do not seem to have amounted to a large percentage of the population.

By the fifth century B.C. a number of states, having defeated their weaker neighbors, were consolidating their rule and seeking the means to build strength and stability within their boundaries. In these circumstances, new opportunities for advancement became open to the lowborn. Talent brought its own reward, and one of the important places where it was rewarded was the battlefield. By the end of the Spring and Autumn period, the aristocrats' chariots—having proved ineffective in hilly areas and before city walls—were giving way to infantry and cavalry, both drawing men from the lower classes. Soldiers who distinguished themselves were promoted, and by the early Warring States period there was a distinct class of professional soldiers of non-aristocratic stock.[25]

Another development was the emergence of a class of wealthy merchants. Interstate trade was facilitated by the construction of roads and canals, and by the introduction of metal coins, possibly in the sixth century B.C. and certainly by the fourth century. The demand for craft goods, which led certain areas to specialize in the production of specific items, caused the status of urban craftsmen to rise and contributed to the prosperity of merchants who dealt in their wares. Merchants transported goods from Inner Mongolia to the south of the Yangtze, and from Szechwan in the west all the way to Manchuria and Korea.[26] Wealthy merchants were able to buy land and move into official position.

Some peasants benefited from new opportunities for land ownership. Probably during the sixth century B.C. peasants in certain states were freed of substantial obligation to their noble landlords in return for a land tax paid directly to the state.[27] In effect, peasants were elevated from serfs to landowners. This arrangement not only improved the peasant's social position, but offered him a chance to improve his holdings—in some cases by reclaiming unused land. Many landholders, among them merchants, acquired huge tracts.

Finally, men with special skills were needed. Rulers sought to strengthen their states by increasing their wealth, and this meant making better use of existing lands, bringing additional territories under their sway, and promoting commerce. They sought to consolidate control over the population within their boundaries, and they needed strong armies. There were irrigation problems stemming from the monsoon season and Yellow River flooding, and there were canals to be built. A bureaucracy was needed to plan all these tasks and to supervise their execution. Skilled officials were needed to handle economic problems arising from interstate commerce. Active diplomacy between states, including the negotiation of multistate treaties, required personnel trained in governmental procedures, ritual, and writing. The men for all these tasks came increasingly from the low-ranking nobility or from non-aristocratic classes. By the fifth century B.C. the promotion of talented commoners to high office was not an unusual occurrence.

Most of these skilled men were [a]*shih* or "knights," the lowest in the category of "rulers." Men of this rank had been serving as state functionaries throughout most of the Spring and Autumn period. The [a]*shih* included people with writing skills and a knowledge of the ritual and administrative practices required for official service; by the fifth century their functions, once purely military, had become almost purely administrative. The ranks of the *shih* were swelled by the numerous younger sons of the nobles, most of whom practiced polygamy, and by aristocratic victims of the continual warfare. Many *shih* knew the ritual codes and became specialists in them, peddling their talents from state to state; and some, like Confucius, became professional teachers of these skills.

The *shih* often took over positions formerly occupied by nobles on a hereditary basis, for example a magistracy in charge of what had once been a lord's fief. In addition, toward the end of the Spring and Autumn period (around 550 B.C.), as the responsibilities and authority of the *shih* were broadening, talented commoners (including *shu jen*)[28] rose to become [a]*shih*.[29] Their careers were furthered by a new class of teachers like Confucius and Mo Tzu, who offered training in statecraft and the associated arts to all comers.[30] During the Warring States period the state of Ch'in introduced a new form of political organization by dividing its territory into prefectures (*chün*), each under a governor, and districts ([b]*hsien*), each under a magistrate. These administrators were not in any sense feudal nobles having a claim on a certain fief; commoners were eligible for both ranks, and so were men from other states.[31]

Men hired for their competence could be fired for incompetence, and so we find new systems for evaluating the performance of officials, including the practice of yearly reports from district magistrate to governor and from governor to ruler.[32] In short, the whole relationship between ruler and official had changed. Ability was at a premium, and the best rulers were those who exerted themselves to find and keep able subordinates. The social effects of this change are familiar, for example in seventeenth-century France. Historical records of the Warring States period cite marriages between aristocrats and commoners,[33] and recently excavated commoners' tombs from that period have contained ritual vessels of the type formerly found exclusively in the tombs of the aristocracy.[34]

This, then, is the background to the general sentiment that hereditary privilege must be rejected: the religious heritage from the early Chou conquest (Heaven has no prejudice in favor of certain men or tribes), the loosening of the tight clan relationships that perpetuated the hereditary principle, and the gradual appearance of new channels of upward mobility in the late Spring and Autumn and Warring States periods. The emergence of the idea of natural equality in China owes much to this opposition to hereditary privilege, since the claim of human equality is a powerful weapon with which to oppose that privilege. This book will consist in large part of an examination of the belief in natural equality found in the early Confucian and Taoist conceptions of man.

Confucian Man

The Confucians held that all things in nature, including human beings, stood in certain definite relationships to other things, and that there were natural rules dictating the actions of those things. In their view, the social order had three components: a specific number of role positions, a hierarchical relationship between these positions, and a code of conduct governing this relationship in the interest of certain social values or virtues. As we have seen, the Confucians regarded these three components as human counterparts of equivalent phenomena found in nature. It follows, in their view, that at least some men are born with a mind that can distinguish between the naturally noble and base positions and the naturally proper and improper actions of things. Since to hold that the superior-inferior and right-wrong distinctions exist naturally and then deny that any men can discover them would remove from man the possibility of moral conduct, at least some men must possess from birth an ability to interpret nature's ethical signals. These matters are discussed in Chapter 2.

Some men or all men? Mindful of the fact that the claim of special wisdom is all too easily passed on by individual families, the Confucians could only answer "All men." Specifically, they maintained that all men are equally endowed at birth with an "evaluating mind," a capacity for making the discriminations in question. In the words of Mencius, "The sages only apprehended before me that of which my mind approves along with other men."[35]

In Chapter 3 it will be shown that according to the Confucians, the content of human nature is threefold: first, a number of constant activities that man shares with other animals (eating, drinking, sleeping, sex); second, certain social activities unique to man (the statement of what these are varies from thinker to thinker); and third, an evaluating mind that can assess the natural nobility or baseness, rightness or wrongness, propriety or impropriety of an object, act, position, or event. Man can use his evaluating mind to guide his innate social tendencies along the proper lines. These three components are shared by all human beings and make them biologically equal.

The primary interest of the Confucians was in social behavior, and the precise nature of people's social behavior was believed to depend on the degree to which they used the evaluating mind. The Confucians never maintained that all men were identical at birth; rather, they held that people's natural differences had little effect on their future performance as members of society. Thus Mencius states:

> In good years the children of the people are most of them good, while in bad years most of them abandon themselves to evil. It is not owing to any difference of their natural powers conferred by Heaven that they are thus different. . . . There now is barley. Let it be sown and covered up; the ground being the same, and the time of sowing likewise the same, it grows rapidly up, and, when the full time is come, it is all found

to be ripe. Although there may be inequalities of produce, that is owing to the difference of the soil, as rich or poor, to the unequal nourishment afforded by the rains and dews, and to the different ways in which man has performed his business in reference to it. Thus all things which are the same in kind are like to one another; why should we doubt in regard to man, as if he were a solitary exception to this? The sage and we are the same in kind.[36]

Hsün Tzu felt the same:

Everyone has characteristics in common with others. When hungry he desires to eat; when cold he desires to be warm; when toiling he desires to rest; he wants what is beneficial and hates what is injurious—with these attitudes a man is born; he has them without waiting to learn them. . . . A person can become a Yao or a Yü; he can become a Chieh or a Chih;* he can become a day laborer or an artisan; he can become a farmer or a merchant; it depends on what training he has accumulated from his ways of looking at things and his habits.[37]

The point is summed up in the *Analects*: "By nature, men are nearly alike; by practice, they become very different."[38]

Confucian writings also held men to be naturally equal in that they share the same responses to the same situation (e.g., to injury, deceit, kindness, lack of food and water). Furthermore, all men love their kin and act so as to care for them. Certain ethical principles follow from this equality, among them the rule, "Never do to others what you would not like them to do to you"; in other words, one's own feelings were the best guide to the treatment of others.[39] In Confucian thought, from the fact that men equally feel pain and hunger, or equally enjoy music and tranquility, it did not follow that all should have their needs equally satisfied; instead, the principle of "reciprocity" ([a]*shu*) was often used to encourage rulers to share their wealth and pleasures with their people.† Clearly, strict reciprocity was impossible; the idea was

* The rulers Yao and Yü were symbols of good, the rulers Chieh and Chih symbols of evil.

† In some respects the Mohist doctrine of universal love seems to be a logical extension of the Confucian virtue of *shu*. Not only should men treat other men as they would want to be treated, but also each state should regard other states as it would want to be regarded (obviating warfare).

that rulers should measure their subjects' needs by their own and act accordingly. From the fact that all love their kin and try to care for them, it follows that a person's affection for kin can and should be extended to other people. More will be said in Chapter 3 about the social virtue [b]*jen,* which arises when this extension of affection occurs.

Obviously, the Confucians were mindful of the ways in which men do objectively differ from each other. Some are clever, others stupid; some are strong, others weak.[40] In the Confucian view, people are not attracted to such non-moral qualities as strength and cleverness, and so these qualities are unimportant. Men are drawn to virtuous models alone, and social stability results from their emulation of those models. In Chapter 4 arguments are presented to support the thesis that virtuous models are those who utilize their evaluating minds, and that people are necessarily attracted to and emulate them.

The doctrine of natural (biological) equality gave the Confucians the strongest possible argument to support the contention that merit should be the sole criterion in awarding political and economic privileges. Since they also believed that a social hierarchy was natural, their demand was for an aristocracy of merit. If all men possess an evaluating mind, privilege should go to the person who best uses the discriminations made by that mind to guide his conduct. Such a person was called, among other things, a "worthy" ([b]*hsien*). In Chapter 4, where the path to privilege is examined, the discussion focuses on the technique for bringing an evaluating mind into operation and for developing the attitude that obedience to its dictates takes precedence over all other considerations.

The Chinese were not alone in advocating an aristocracy of merit; Aristotle, among others, had very similar ideas. The crucial difference between the Confucian and Aristotelian positions was that whereas the Confucians believed in the natural equality of all men, Aristotle believed that men were born unequal. In the Greek view, a real, continuing aristocracy of merit is hard to imagine; in time, some families or tribes will inevitably acquire the honor of being hereditarily meritorious, and others will be relegated to hereditary natural slavery. The Chinese view offers no such difficulty.

As a result of the belief in man's natural equality, Confucianism came to focus on the here and now—on the environmental factors that cause differences in moral excellence among men, and on the training techniques that are available to correct bad habits. Two environmental factors were particularly stressed: economic well-being and education. Following Mencius's observation that men whose livelihood is insecure are not likely to perceive and perform the "right" actions, Confucian works occasionally suggest that the government intervene in the economic life of the country, purportedly to guarantee the people the economic security necessary to reliable moral discrimination. For example, Confucian officials sometimes urged that the government attempt to buy up produce in times of plenty and sell it cheaply in times of need (protecting the people against speculating merchants), and that the government correct the unequal distribution of land. The focus on education was far more significant. The idea of natural equality reinforced the Confucian belief that men are malleable, since none of them have innate defects; hence the direction of a man's moral growth depends very much on education.

This notion of plasticity has had a tremendous impact on Chinese social and political behavior. It has its origin not just in the idea of natural equality, but in the Confucian treatment of human nature in general. The Confucians distinguished between these aspects of human nature that man shares with other animals and the social tendencies unique to his species, which they considered the essential aspects of human nature. Often this "essential nature" was then confused with human nature in general: Mencius, for example, confused the idea that man's essential nature is [b]*jen* (humanheartedness) with the idea that "man is *jen*" (*jen che jen yeh*); the second phrase implies that "animal" needs, instincts, and reflexes are not the essential part of man. Obviously, from a factual standpoint, a person's "social nature" is more susceptible to environmental influence than are his "animal needs"; the confusion of the two meant that physical demands, limitations, and defects were often ignored, whereas the facility of molding man's (essentially social) nature was overemphasized. As a result, the Confucians expected miracles of moral education. Confucians were active as teachers and vocal in their demand for state-supported schools, the first of which were established in the Han dynasty. They also undertook historical projects, one aim of which was to discover suitable moral exemplars from the past. On the theoretical side, they produced endless writings on how to teach the cultivation of proper habits. The Confucian view of education simultaneously stressed introspection (to discover the innate evaluating mind and social tendencies that are equally possessed by all) and the emulation of models (to develop the habit of using that mind to make suitable decisions about conduct). Teachers were to serve as models for their students, and Confucian officials (including the ruler) were to serve as models for the people as a whole.

There is no need to romanticize China. Government intervention in economic activities was often a means for officials to rake off profits that had previously gone to merchants, and the number of peasants personally affected by Confucian teachers or schools was very small. Nevertheless, there are certain qualitative differences in Chinese culture stemming from the ideas just described that mark it off from European culture. The natural-equality doctrine produced a tendency to regard changes in educational technique as the solution to urgent social and political problems; and its contention that "any man can be a Yao or Shun"* if only economic and educational conditions are adequate helped produce some of China's unique cultural institutions, among them the civil service examination system (formally institutionalized in the early T'ang dynasty, i.e., the seventh century A.D.).

Taoist Man

The Taoists also believed men to be naturally equal, but in a radically different sense, one having nothing to do with ethical

* Sage-rulers in the distant past.

qualities allegedly found in nature. Taoism asserts that a Unity, Tao, underlies and is present in the many particular things in the world. Being a Unity, Tao cannot be more or less present in one thing than in any other. When individual objects come into being, Tao is found in each one as its [a]*te,* the principle that determines what a thing is like and what changes it will undergo. Taoists concede that some men can be objectively differentiated from others; but they consider the difference ephemeral and hence negligible. Only the "Tao within" is eternal, and hence it is the only essential aspect of man's endowment.

Tao is usually described as "nothingness" or "void," meaning among other things that it has no quality (good or bad, superior or inferior, beautiful or ugly, and so forth). In addition, Taoist writings stress that "Heaven and Earth are not benevolent." Such statements imply that it is wrong to read into nature terms from the human ethical vocabulary. This tenet, which separates the Taoists from their Confucian competitors, has two important consequences. One, which we shall consider in detail in Chapter 5, is the amorality of the universe, and hence the triviality of the Confucians' "evaluating mind." The other, the subject of Chapter 6, is a radical egalitarianism. The Confucians, while affirming men's equality at birth, believed that they became unequal as adults; hence the possibility of an aristocracy of merit. The Taoists, by contrast, repudiated all the categories by which people are differentiated as adults in Confucian thought. It followed that all people were equally deserving; all should be tolerated, none singled out for favor. Here there is a transition from equality in a descriptive sense (the Tao is found equally in all things) to equality in an evaluative sense (impartiality).

With the dismissal of the evaluating mind goes the elimination of the idea of moral preeminence. The Taoist sage has understanding, not moral preeminence, and his understanding permits him to act as a living model of the principle that equal treatment for all must replace unequal treatment for some. He has learned not to consider some men better than others, gold better than dross, power better than impotence. He accepts them all, and thus the idea of privilege becomes meaningless. Indeed, the man best able to discover the Tao within is the man who has most fully thrown off his evaluating mind. The Confucian and Taoist paths to a proof of natural equality are diametrically opposed.

Equality in China and the West

The idea of biological equality was fraught with more revolutionary implications for political and social action than any other early Chinese philosophical idea; and some of the cultural variations it gave rise to set China apart, often brilliantly apart, from her Western counterparts.

There were Greek believers in natural equality, notably the Sophists Antiphon and Alcidamas. The former argued that Greeks and barbarians, being alike in natural endowment, should be treated alike; the latter, a student of Gorgias, supposedly said, "God set all men free. Nature has made none a slave." But this was by no means the dominant position among Greek philosophers. Plato distinguished three major levels of souls: "gold," "silver," and "brass," paralleling the hierarchy of reason, spirit, and appetites in the individual soul. With the proper selective breeding, those with "gold" souls would generally (not always) perpetuate their own kind.[41] In the *Phaedo* Plato rejected the epiphenomenalistic view of the soul as "an attunement of our physical elements at a given tension" on the ground that some souls are better than others.[42] Plato did not totally reject the concept of natural equality, but he maintained that it had existed only in the distant past. In the *Timaeus* we learn that at the "creation" all souls were equal, but that since then there has been a steady change.[43] Aristotle regarded human nature as uneven and held that a majority of men were slaves by nature.* He excluded from his citizenry not only slaves proper, but mechanics, tradesmen, husbandmen, women, and resident aliens. Lacking as they did the "faculty of deliberation," such people were not fit to play any role in political affairs.

* Aristotle stated that "the slave has no deliberative faculty at all" (*Politics* i.13.1260a.12).

Biological or natural equality became strong only in Stoic thought. The Stoics identified reason with God and regarded it as immanent in all things. Since all men possessed reason as the spark of divinity within them, all men were naturally equal. Cicero states:

> For no single thing is so like another, so exactly its counterpart, as all of us are to one another. Nay, if bad habits and false beliefs did not twist the weaker minds and turn them in whatever direction they are inclined, no one would be so like his own self as all men would be like all others. And so, however we may define man, a single definition will apply to all. This is a sufficient proof that there is no difference in kind between man and man.[44]

It followed that slavery violated natural principles. The Stoics made no great effort to put their egalitarian ideas into effect, though some scholars maintain that the Roman "law of the peoples" or *jus gentium* (principles of law and rights supposedly common to all peoples) reflected Stoic influence.

It is interesting to contrast, say, Plato's ideas on hierarchy with Chinese ideas. For Plato, the mechanistic realm of bodies in motion is the servant of Purpose, the mortal is the servant of the divine, and the body is the servant of the soul: those men in whom the soul is too closely tied to the body are the servants of those in whom the rational part of the soul controls the body.[45] In Confucian thought the natural superiority of Heaven to Earth, or of *yang* to *yin*, has no such ready extension to men at birth. This difference had extremely important long-range consequences for the later philosophies of the two areas.

The egalitarianism in Judaism and early Christianity was primarily evaluative.* Judaism spoke of men as equal before God's law; Christianity spoke of the equal worth to God of all his children (and consequently of the hope equally held out to all mankind for redemption). Saint Paul wrote to the Galatians: "There

* The closest the Hebrews came to natural equality was the idea that God endows all men with His image, the *Tselem Elohim.* According to Emanuel Rackman, Jewish scholars of a later time, under Aristotelian influence, identified this with "reason." See Chapter 8, Note 19.

is neither Jew nor Greek, there is neither bond nor free, there is neither male nor female; for ye are all one in Christ Jesus."[46] He meant by this that one need not observe the holy days, be circumcised, or accept the law of the Jews in order to be considered a child of God. One need only have faith in God and accept his guidance, and one can do this regardless of sex or station.[47] But such equality is not natural equality. Equality based on the belief that God considers all his children equally worthy does not mean that all men are born with similar empirical characteristics. A father can love all his sons equally without their having any important natural attribute in common. To be sure, the Christian belief that all men have souls offered a basis for a belief in natural equality, and in fact there was from the beginning a minority stream of Christian thought that emphasized this equality, opposing the classical heritage from Plato and Aristotle.[48] But there can be no dispute that the doctrine of natural inequality was paramount in the West until modern times.*

The Platonic legacy demanded belief in a natural hierarchy in the cosmos, and thus a belief in hierarchical human institutions and in similar relationships between men, who are innately unequal. Saint Augustine confirmed the thesis: "From heaven to earth, from the visible to the invisible, some things are good, others better than others. In this they are unequal, so that all kinds of things might be."[49] The problem, therefore, was how to explain the natural inequalities and offer hope at the same time. The solution was predestination: inequalities among men were determined by God and could be explained as man's punishment for original

* Paul S. Sigmund (in Pennock and Chapman, pp. 142–48) has argued that "the myth of equality began to have institutional implications by the last part of the Middle Ages." He points out that Nicholas of Cusa used the idea of "man's original equality" in his *De Concordantia Catholica* (1433) to demand that government be based on consent. The principles of equality and consent implied that there should be representative councils in church and state. But this "original equality" meant only that no men are endowed at birth with the *right* to more political power than others. This is a far different thing from claiming that men are born naturally equal. Nicholas was still able to maintain that men are born unequal in reason, and that those born superior in reason should rule. His philosophical position is characterized by the attempt to harmonize these two beliefs.

sin. Whatever the future equality of men before God on judgment day, the slave must accept his lot. More fortunate men could pass their time by spelling out the patterns of obedience, humility, and ritual purification that would ensure the slave a favorable seat in the eschatological congregation.

A further discussion of the concept of equality in China and the West will be found in Chapter 8, pp. 178–82.

Conclusion

From a philosophical point of view, the Confucian and Taoist doctrines of natural equality are unstable. Obviously, men are naturally similar in some ways and different in others. If one wants to emphasize natural equality, one stresses certain characteristics: the fact that all men evaluate, the Tao present in all, or the fact that all have certain needs and experience certain feelings. If one wants to take the position that men are naturally unequal, one focuses on other characteristics: some are black, others white; some are strong, others weak. In arguing man's natural equality, the Confucians and Taoists are simply foisting on their readers their own criteria of what is important. There is an implicit value judgment in their arguments.[50]

Another difficulty in demonstrating man's natural equality is that two people may disagree on whether a given allegedly equalizing characteristic is in fact equally present in all men. For example, whereas Aristotle justified his doctrine of natural inequality on the basis of differences in innate rational capacity, the Stoics justified natural equality by the existence in all men of that very capacity.[51] Similarly, the special affection for kin that Confucians took to be universal was an easy target for their opponents.

And yet the idea of natural equality had great and lasting strength in China, not only on the two major schools of ancient Chinese thought but on all branches of Chinese philosophy and political theory down to the present day. It played a role in the sinicization of Buddhism in the seventh century, and in the sinicization of Communism in the twentieth. It helped produce the distinctive Chinese habit of regarding a revolution in education as the cure for urgent political and social problems, and it dictated in part what the content of a proper education should be. Any search for the concept of man in early China will lead at the same time to the idea of natural equality, which dominates that concept. It is a central idea to any deep understanding of the Chinese world view.

CHAPTER 2

NATURAL ORDER AND THE HUMAN MIND

THE EARLY Chinese belief in natural equality is intertwined with the Chinese conceptions of human nature. In Confucianism, both of these ideas derive in large part from the belief that a hierarchical social system and the norms and virtues by which it is maintained have a basis in nature. This chapter will examine the Confucian views of society and natural order in greater detail, and will compare them with some of the major Western ideas on the same subjects. It will conclude by showing how the Confucian conception of man's "evaluating mind," which is at the core of the ideas of human nature and natural equality, is directly related to their view of that natural order.

The Social Order

Three related elements are included in the early Confucian vision of the "social order," and it can be argued that a basis for each of the three exists in nature. The first element is a collection of occupational positions, every one having its own "job description." Second, there is a hierarchical relationship between these positions. Third, a formalized code of behavior, variously affecting the occupants of each place in the hierarchy, ties the whole together; the social virtues are realized by individuals who abide with this code. The social norms set the standard for distinguishing the noble from the base (as between any two social positions) and right from wrong (as regards acts). These two standards are interrelated, and what is right or wrong in the case of an act frequently varies with the relative status of the person affected by the act.

There are several systems of listing the different social positions. One hierarchy included the king, the princes or dukes (who became de facto rulers of many individual states), the ministers, the knights, and the peasants, merchants and artisans; each of these had its job description.* Within the categories of minister and [b]*shih* there were numerous gradations. This classification would adequately describe the social strata of the West Chou until the middle of the Spring and Autumn period, and it was idealized by many later Chou Confucian writers. In fact, the functions, costumes, and protocol of the numerous officials in an idealized early feudal court are described in detail in the *Chou li* (Ritual of Chou). A simpler division of the basic social positions included ruler, minister, father, son, older brother, younger brother, husband, and wife.† The social function of each position was spelled out, and Confucian teachers saw one solution to the political strife of the time in causing people to live up to the ideal descriptions of these positions. "Let the prince be a prince, the minister a minister, the father a father, and the son a son," said Confucius.[1]

One aspect of social function was the famous Confucian doctrine of the rectification of names (*cheng ming*), which had both ethical and logical applications in China. Its original intent was ethical, based on the belief that once names have firm meanings they will almost magically serve as effective standards of conduct. For example, if the meaning of "king" were fixed and changes in its content were impossible, no upstart adventurer would dare to call himself a king, as so many were doing; moreover, a legitimate ruler would be intimidated into acting in accordance with the ideal prescription. The same held for the other social positions. If *cheng ming* could be effectively carried out, the social order would become firmly established. Hsün Tzu even declared that one of a ruler's main responsibilities is to maintain the standardization of names by seeing that no unauthorized distinctions between words are made, and that no new words are created. The Legalists con-

* The *Tso chuan* lists four ranks ([a]*teng*) of rulers: king ([b]*wang*), duke ([a]*kung*), minister (*tai-fu*), and knight ([b]*shih*). It gives six ranks of ruled. The division of manual laborers into six grades probably stems from a desire to pair a total of ten social ranks with the ten time divisions of the day (the text makes clear the influence of this magic number); it does not necessarily reflect the social reality. *Tso chuan*, Chao kung 7.

† The classic formulation of the "five relationships" was: father-son, elder brother–younger brother, husband-wife, ruler-minister, friend-friend.

curred with this, and also with Hsün Tzu's plea for the use of direct, unflowery language by officials in discussing rules of conduct.* Their "laws" contained the job descriptions for each office and occupation, and were the standard against which they proposed to measure right and wrong behavior. One can regard the system of rewards and punishments that they devised as a means of enforcing an exact correspondence of name, function, and actual practice of the function. The Confucian teachers, with their excessive concentration on the ideal functions themselves, had hardly mastered the practical problems of enforcement.

The notion of conformance with one's function also seems to have meant that one should not act outside the boundaries of one's own position or usurp the functions of someone in another position. A dramatic example of this idea is the opposition of Mencius to a group best described as communal agriculturalists (*nung-chia*). Praised by some Communist writers today as having established primitive egalitarian societies, the *nung-chia* tilled their own land, made their own clothes, and generally recognized no division of labor. Their practice was intolerable to Mencius because they did not abide by the functional divisions of social positions, each person performing the actions appropriate to several different positions.

The idea of strict functional divisions probably derived from primitive tribal practices, and the early Chinese thinkers were not the only ones to rationalize it. Plato's ideal state, as described in the *Republic*, is distinguished by a set of distinct social functions, each one the responsibility of a particular social position. "And is this not the reason why such a city is the only one in which we shall find the cobbler a cobbler and not a pilot in addition to his cobbling, and the farmer a farmer and not a judge added to his farming, and the soldier a soldier and not a money-maker in addition to his soldiery, and so of all the rest?"[2] The major division of Plato's society is threefold: philosopher-kings, executives, and pro-

* One wonders how much of Hsün Tzu's interest in standardizing language came from professional distaste for the Logicians (notably Hui Shih), who made men's heads swim with their word manipulations.

ducers. Justice lies in having those in each occupational position carry out only their own functions, doing so for the good of the whole.

The Confucian notion of strict functional divisions does not imply that one cannot move from one social position to another; it simply means that while occupying one position one is not to usurp the functions of another. There is nothing to prevent the virtuous peasant (i.e., one who fulfills his family duties as a father or elder brother and his function as a farmer) from being noticed and elevated to higher status. There was supposed to be a hierarchical relationship between different positions, and it was customary to speak of the positions in pairs, one "high" and the other "low" (e.g. prince-minister, father-son, elder brother–younger brother). Hsün Tzu said that the purpose of names is "to make evident the noble and base." A hierarchy of moral stature was also present, since the occupants of the highest positions were supposed to be morally superior to those in the lower ones.

Thus far we have seen that the Confucian vision of the "social order" includes a number of clearly separated social positions with certain explicit duties, and that these positions are of different distinction, forming a hierarchy. The third and most important element can be described from two points of view. One can speak of "rules of conduct," which determine the concrete relationship existing between two persons in different positions, thus binding the individuals occupying separate positions into one interrelated system. Or one can refer to the social virtues that are realized through conformity to the norms.

The rules of conduct are collectively known as [a]*li,* a term that originally meant "to sacrifice" but later acquired the connotations of "order" and "arrangement." *Li* is usually translated as "rules," "ceremony," "ritual," or "propriety." At first the application of the term *li* seems to have been restricted to ceremonial rites of a religious character; as such, it was narrower in scope than the term [a]*i* (customary code), which frequently appears on bronze inscriptions of the West Chou, although there was some overlap. Later, a whole range of ceremonial activities connected with social procedures such as behavior at court, meetings between ambassadors, or deportment at archery meets and on the battlefield, were governed by *li*. Finally, the term came to denote all standardized customs, especially those covering interpersonal relationships; *li* described "good form" not just in the temple or at court, but everywhere, and it set norms for every daily action of any significance.

Confucius and his followers gave the [a]*li* an ethical significance by regarding them as essential for bringing order into the individual's life and into society. The Master spoke of the necessity of refining a man's natural constitution: "When natural substance prevails over ornamentation, you get the boorishness of the rustic. When ornamentation prevails over natural substance, you get the pedantry of the scribe. Only when ornament and substance are duly blended do you get the true gentleman."[3] The *li* do the blending, by molding natural predispositions into socially acceptable forms and introducing control into all acts. For example, when courage is not under the control of *li*, it becomes blustering recklessness.[4] Moreover, the *li* produce a harmonious relationship between the occupants of differing social positions. Toward the end of the Chou period, when the *li* became the subject of much scholarly study, further attempts were made to explain their precise functions. They were said to regulate and refine the emotions, preventing strife between conflicting sentiments (e.g., between self-interest and family obligation) and confining passions to decent expression.* Specific rites, too, had their own rationalized purposes. Filial mourning rites, for example, gave one an emotional satisfaction and demonstrated gratitude for all one's parents had done; there was less interest, in theory, in whether or not the dead parents actually received the sacrifice.

The term *li* covered a wide range of customs (such as the son's obligations to his father), taboos (such as that against men and women touching hands), and ceremonial practices. The last were the easiest to deal with explicitly, and several works were written to describe what they should be, with reference to the practices of an idealized feudal society. The *Li ching* (Classic of Ritual), one

* Such discussions occur in the *Hsün-tzu* and the *Li chi* (Book of Rites).

of six works accepted as classics by Confucian literati of the Han dynasty, included several Chou works on ritual and related subjects; of these, the *Chou li* (Ritual of Chou), *I li* (Ceremonial and Ritual), and *Li chi* (Book of Rites) exist today. No attempt was made to spell out the infinite number of rules governing various types of interpersonal contact. Usually, one learned general types of responses suitable for general types of situations, and was then expected to make the concrete expression appropriate to the specific conditions.

When asked what submitting oneself to the dictates of *li* involved, Confucius replied: "To look at nothing in defiance of ritual, to listen to nothing in defiance of ritual, to speak of nothing in defiance of ritual, never to stir a hand or foot in defiance of ritual."[5] His followers seem to have carried this to its logical conclusion, with the result that Confucians appeared to their neighbors to advocate a life burdened by strictures on every daily act. In a sense, the utilitarianism of Mo Tzu was a reaction against this concern with "form" and a call for attention to practical matters—the burden that much of the ritual placed on the society's wealth, for instance. The Confucians, he thought, were so concerned with good form that they were blinded to the practical consequences of acts. Similarly, the Taoists' search for spiritual freedom can be viewed in part as a reaction to the oppressiveness of a life in which so many daily acts were prescribed by a fixed code. Some people today associate the ideal of "freedom" from social restraint with Yang Chu (fourth century B.C.?), who is reputed to have advocated making the most of a short life by giving free reign to all desires. Finally, the universally applied law favored by the Legalists totally ignores the customary morality included in the *li*.

The social virtues that arise from obedience to the *li* are: loyalty ([b]*chung*); filial piety (*hsiao*); respect ([a]*ching*); straightforwardness, in the sense of having no self-deception and truly expressing one's beliefs ([a]*chih*); and kindness ([b]*jen* or [a]*te* in the narrow senses of the terms). All of these individual virtues are encompassed in the abstract Virtue of the perfect man ([b]*jen* in the broad sense, or *ch'eng*). The term *jen* (humane, humanheartedness) is all-important in the *Analects*, where it occurs in 58 of the 499 chapters. Most often it has one or the other of two meanings. One of these is "love," which manifests itself in humane treatment of others.[6] Basically, it referred to affection for kin (the early etymological dictionary *Shou-wen chieh-tzu* defines it as *ch'in*, meaning "kin" or "kinship feeling"). Filial piety is spoken of as the "root of *jen*."[7] This affection for kin naturally can and should be extended to all men, and any man is capable of doing so. The other sense of *jen* in the *Analects* is a general virtue comprehending specific virtues, such as filial piety, courage, loyalty, courtesy, diligence, and so forth.[8] In this sense, *jen* stands for the perfect development of a man; it is the highest ideal, something that any man can achieve but few do. In other words, *jen* in one usage is *descriptive* (man is a creature who loves his kin and can extend the sentiment and the humane treatment to all people). The other usage is evaluative, referring to the proper goal for a man; it says what a man should become.

In addition to having a narrow meaning of "true to oneself" or "no dishonesty," *ch'eng* (integrity, sincerity) is also used to denote a generalized virtue. It resembles [b]*jen* in having this broad sense; for example, *ch'eng* like *jen*, comprehends a multitude of specific virtues, such as knowledge, love of others (*jen* in the narrow sense), and courage.[9] It is described as "irrepressible," a description often applied to *jen* in the *Mencius* and elsewhere.[10] Because *ch'eng* has the meaning of Virtue, it is often said to involve simply "understanding, choosing, and holding firm to the good."[11]

The Natural Basis of the Social Order

When philosophical thought is just beginning to emerge in a society there is a tendency to read the human social order into the structure of the universe. The ideas of inviolate social divisions, hierarchy, and the social norms are applied to the different inanimate phenomena making up the cosmos. The advantage of doing this, unconscious though it may be, is that one can then speak of a natural basis for the particular social system one wishes to defend —a system exhibiting those very attributes first read into nature.

This practice was quite common among the pre-Socratics. For example, the four elements (earth, air, fire, and water) are important in the cosmological thought of Anaximander (sixth century B.C.). He held that each element has its own spatial sphere in the cosmos, with boundaries that must not be violated by any of the other elements. "Justice" occurs when each element stays in its own sphere, and the encroachment by one element on the sphere of another is "injustice," the penalty for which is dissolution. The "sphere of influence" of each of the four elements is the counterpart of an individual social position, which Greek tribal custom also recognized as inviolate.[12] In other words, the idea of bounded positions is taken from the human tribal organization and read into nature.* In China, it will be recalled, the doctrine of the rectification of names had emerged, during the transition from religion to philosophy, as a means of rationalizing the earlier belief in inviolable boundaries separating social positions.

Another Greek view of "justice" (*dike*) is found in Hesiod and in Plato's *Protagoras*. Here, we see characters holding that justice does not have any basis in the cosmic structure but is simply a gift of the gods to men, one not given to other beings. Hence the laws men make, though useful, are arbitrary, and there is no universal law affecting all beings. Socrates, on the other hand, is portrayed by Plato in several dialogues as one wanting to reestablish the cosmic significance of justice, albeit in a form somewhat different from Anaximander's; and he finds justice in the principle of all parts of a whole occupying their own positions and doing their own work for the good of the whole.

In early China cosmological speculation centered around the five elements ([a]*wu hsing*): water, fire, metal, wood, and earth. Although the attributes of these "elements" were sometimes described by analogy from the physical materials indicated by their names, it is best to consider them as "forces." As in Anaximander's

* The Greek term *moira* has usually been understood as fate in a temporal sense, a person's cradle to grave "lot." However, F. M. Cornford finds its earliest meaning to be "part" or "alloted portion." Each god has his own province or field of activity, i.e., his *moira*. Thus the earliest meaning was spatial rather than temporal.

system, each element was considered to have its own cosmic boundaries, which must not be violated by any of the other ones. By Chou times the elements were becoming associated with specific spatial regions and seasons of the year. A Han text spells out this spatial phenomenon: "Each of the five elements circulates according to its sequence; each of them exercises its own capacities in the performance of its official duties. Thus wood occupies the eastern quarter, where it rules over the forces of spring; fire occupies the southern quarter where it rules over the forces of summer."[13] In another text we learn what happens when the elements do not keep within their proper "borders": "The five fluids come forward in turn, each of them takes precedence once. When they do not keep to their proper sphere, there is disaster; when they do, everything is well-ordered."[14] To stay within the bounds was "right," to cross them was "wrong." It is not surprising, then, that most of the early words for "wrong" in Chinese carried the sense of "to overstep" or "to transgress" (for example *kuo,* [a]*yü,* and *p'an*).

Two other important concepts in late Chou and early Han cosmology demonstrate the reading of hierarchy into nature—*yin* and *yang*. *Yin* has the connotations of dark, negative, passive, weak, and destructive, and *yang* the connotations of light, positive, active, strong, constructive. In texts of the Warring States period they were associated with the primal ether of which the universe is composed (*ch'i*), either as its two modes or as the forces governing its movement. At first *yin-yang* and the five elements were independent concepts in cosmological speculation, but eventually they were combined. Each element was said to rise in power over all phenomena in nature, and then to decline; the rising and falling were the respective actions of the *yang* and *yin* forces.* The concept of *yang* and *yin* reveals quite clearly the imposition of a hierarchical social pattern on the structure of things. *Yang* is high, *yin* low; Heaven is described as *yang* and noble (*shang*), the earth as *yin* and humble (*pi*). There was thus a model for the distinc-

* There was a good bit of speculation about the relationship between the different elements in their cycle of dominance. The two favorite theses were: first, that each element conquers and destroys the one that precedes it; second, that each produces the next in line.

tion between father and son, prince and minister, and the rest. In the words of one early text, "As high and low are thus made clear, the honorable and the humble have their places accordingly."

From a temporal standpoint it might be most accurate to consider the third element in the Confucian social order as the first to be read into nature. Chou texts saturated with Confucianism (such as the *Tso chuan**) are also full of discussions about the five elements and *yin* and *yang*. But the open merging of these cosmologic ideas with Confucian themes first occurred in the early Han dynasty (for example, in the appendixes to the *Book of Changes* [*I ching*] and in the work of Tung Chung-shu, ca. 179–104 B.C.). In other words, the early Confucians first read into nature certain principles found in the customary norms, as well as the social virtues that are realized through obedience to those norms. More specifically, some of them portrayed [a]*li* as a cosmic principle: since *li* differentiated the noble and the base and determined right and wrong, these qualities must also be present in nature. Other writers made a cosmic principle of the comprehensive virtue *ch'eng* (integrity), which in this context meant single-minded devotion to the good.

A person who realized the social virtues was considered to be acting naturally, and what he did was therefore good. Natural (i.e., good) behavior by man was simply a counterpart in the human sphere of natural (i.e., good) behavior by non-human phenomena:

"Allow me to ask," said Chien Tzu, "what we are to understand by ceremonies [*li*]." The reply was, "I have heard our late great officer Tzu Ch'an say, 'Ceremonies are founded in the regular procedure of Heaven, the right phenomena of earth, and the actions of men.' Heaven and earth have their regular ways, and men take these for their pattern, imitating the brilliant bodies of Heaven and according with the natural diversities of the earth. Heaven and Earth produce the six atmospheric conditions, and make use of the five material elements. Those conditions and elements become the five tastes, are manifested in the five colors, and are

* The *Tso chuan* is supposedly a commentary on the *Spring and Autumn Annals*, a concise yearly record of events in the state of Lu from 722 to 481 B.C. The *Tso chuan* covers the same period and presents a history of China at that time, although some of the material in it is fictionalized. It was probably compiled in the third century B.C. from earlier materials.

displayed in the five notes. When these are in excess, there ensue obscurity and confusion, and the people lose their proper nature. The rules of ceremony were therefore framed to support that nature."[15]

Hsün Tzu, the most prominent Confucian to turn *li* into a cosmic principle, stated:

> *Li* is that whereby Heaven and Earth unite, whereby the sun and moon are bright, whereby the four seasons are ordered, whereby the stars move in the courses, whereby rivers flow, whereby all things prosper, whereby love and hatred are tempered, whereby joy and anger keep their proper place. It causes the lower orders to obey, and the upper orders to be illustrious; through a myriad changes it prevents going astray. But if one departs from it, he will be destroyed. Is not *li* the greatest of all principles?[16]

The *li* dictate that certain phenomena stand in definite relation to others, that the noble and base are distinguished from each other, and that some things should obey other things. There is a right way for one season to follow another and a wrong way, a right way for one natural body (mountain, river, planet, or element) to be related to another and a wrong way. There are antecedently fixed rules dictating which actions by all objects, including man, are good or bad.

Some Confucians who did not explicitly describe *li* as a cosmic principle (although they may have accepted the idea) did treat the comprehensive virtue "integrity" or "sincerity" (*ch'eng*) as such a principle. In this usage, *ch'eng* meant single-minded devotion to the good. Mencius stated, "If a man does not understand what is good, he will not attain sincerity in himself."[17] And the *Doctrine of the Mean** says, "He who attains to sincerity is he who chooses what is good and firmly holds it fast.[18] In other words, *ch'eng* referred to the unwavering attempt to realize the specific social virtues. From other passages in the texts we know that all these actually involved conforming with *li*. *Ch'eng* was then read

* *The Doctrine of the Mean* and the *Great Learning* were not treated as classics by themselves until Neo-Confucian philosophers (in the Sung dynasty, A.D. 960–1279) separated them from the work of which they once formed parts (*Li chi,* Chapters 28 and 39 respectively). But both date from the Chou or Ch'in periods and reflect many of the dominant Confucian ideas of the time.

into nature. Mencius continued: "Therefore, sincerity is the way of Heaven. To think how to be sincere is the way of man." And the *Doctrine of the Mean* speaks of *ch'eng* as "overspreading" and "containing" all things. When natural bodies abide by the "right" (in fact, conform to their customary movements), they are "true to themselves" and "good," just as a man who obeys the dictates of his moral sense ([b]*i*) is true to himself and good.

Subsequently, other social virtues underwent the same transformation. The *Hsiao ching* (Classic of Filial Piety), a Confucian work of the Han dynasty, describes "filial piety" (*hsiao*) as a principle penetrating the universe. In the Sung dynasty (A.D. 960–1279) [b]*jen* (humanheartedness) was said to link all men and things into a harmonious whole, giving a natural justification to the doctrine that all men are brothers; and it was the innate affection men feel for their "brothers" that enabled them to carry the ideal of a one-family world into practice.

It is quite clear that the early Greeks also read into nature principles abstracted from human social organizations and behavior. The word "cosmos," for instance, originally signified proper order in a state or community.[19] When Anaximander stated, "It is necessary that things must pay one another the penalty and compensation for their injustice according to the ordinances of time,"[20] he was applying to nature the human idea of *dike* (justice, the principle supporting the right of a person to his due). According to Anaximander, the causal link between coming into being and passing out of existence is like a lawsuit: time is the judge, and "excessive" things are deprived of some or all of their being. Some Pythagorean thinkers regarded "reciprocity" (willingness to give and take) as the basis of all human virtues and all natural order in the universe.[21] The "give and take" between natural bodies created a balance and harmony, so that the cosmos did not plunge into chaos. "Love" (*eros*) was considered by many scientifically inclined scholars to be the force that produced ordered change in the universe. In Plato's *Symposium* Eryximachus the physician praises Love's power of bringing harmony to the opposing elements in the human constitution.[22]

But generally speaking, in the dominant schools of classical Greece the chief attributes of nature did not stop with these principles drawn from human social life. Even where some such principles are applied to nature, one often finds that the dominant characteristics of the universe are otherwise. Besides being governed by *dike*, Anaximander's universe had a definite geometrical structure built on ideal mathematical proportions: the universe was a sphere with the earth at the center; the paths of the sun, moon, and stars were circular; the course of the sun was 27 times the diameter of the earth; the moon's course was 18 times the diameter of the earth; the diameter of the earth was 3 times its height; and so forth.[23] Some Pythagoreans may have regarded "reciprocity" as the basis of the natural order, or, like the Confucians, emphasized "harmony"; but a definite mathematical structure governed everything.[24] The Confucians, by contrast, paid less attention to mathematical proportion in the universe, and instead emphasized ethical relationships.

Reasons for the Natural Basis

As we have seen, the Confucians read into nature both the principles governing the customary social norms (well-defined relations between things, distinctions of noble and base, obligations and duties) and certain social virtues; by doing this, they could then derive a justification for the particular social system they desired to support. But there were other reasons, of a different sort, for their describing nature in social terms.

First, the [a]*li* were originally religious in essence, and ancestral sacrifices, governed by *li*, had a certain efficacy in bringing about changes in nature. Many passages in the early works describe this magical power of *li*,[25] and Confucius remarked that a man who really understands the ancestral sacrifices can deal with any situation in the world. If the *li* pertaining to human activity could work wonders in nature, there had to be some link between the two spheres.

The second reason was also religious. In China, as elsewhere, the supreme deity (Heaven) gradually became equated with nature or with the natural regularities. When this occurred, the attributes that had been assigned to the deity were in part retained by nature. In early China one strong tradition conceived of Heaven as a semi-personalized deity with moral attributes; the "love of man," a human social virtue, was ascribed to it, as we see in West Chou texts, and Heaven itself was held to decree many of the same social norms involved in the human *li*. Confucius said, "Without recognizing the ordinances of Heaven it is impossible to be a superior man."[26] Of course, this is not the only picture of Heaven in the early texts. Heaven was often described as "unpredictable," and at times seems to have operated in ways quite contrary to man's ways. When his disciple Yen Yüan died, Confucius said: "Alas! Heaven is destroying me! Heaven is destroying me!" Mencius blamed Heaven for the failure of the prince of Lu to put his correct social policies into practice.[27] But in the Confucian heritage the moral Heaven concerned with the moral conduct of each man dominated: "Wherein I have done improperly, may Heaven reject me!"[28] After the concept of Heaven as a supreme deity had evolved to that of Heaven as nature, the virtues that had been attributed to the personalized Heaven were preserved in nature.

The third reason that the social norms were transformed into a cosmic principle is the most important: the *li*, which were no more than the customary norms of the Chinese in the Chou times, were believed to be universally valid. This belief had to precede the treatment of the *li* or a social virtue, as a cosmic principle, since no "cosmic principle" could find expression in just one society. The Confucians viewed the norms of their own society as absolutes. In early Greece, on the other hand, the customary norms were regarded by many philosophers as relative to the particular society in which they were found. Plato, referring to obedience to the customary code as "popular goodness," was well aware that standards changed from country to country; his lifelong search was for an absolute standard transcending this popular morality.

The Greek distinction between popular and universal morality was in large part a product of geographical and economic factors. Many of the Greek city-states were regularly exposed to the influence of distant and diverse civilizations; Persia and Egypt were not far, and even communication with the Indus Valley (with which Greece had contacts by 398 B.C.) presented no huge geographical obstacle. Furthermore, the Greek states lay on the easily navigable Mediterranean and carried on an active sea trade, in part because some areas were not self-sufficient in basic commodities. The Ionian Greek settlements in Asia Minor, which were in physical contact with the non-Hellenic societies, helped facilitate cultural exchange.

The sophists, or teachers of the art of achieving political success, traveled from one place to another in Ionia and in the Peloponnesus, and in their travels they became aware of the vast differences in the norms of the various city-states and barbarian peoples. Naturally enough, many sophists maintained that rules of conduct were not absolute but relative, since they changed from one location to another: "Man is the measure of all things," and men invent their own codes. Plato himself believed that it was ridiculous for the Athenians to consider their mores (their *li*) as absolute in any sense. He contended that the "Forms" of Justice, Temperance, Courage, and so on were transcendent and unchanging; any particular act in any city-state, in order to be considered just, temperate, or courageous in a universal sense, must conform to the criteria defined by the absolute Form in question, and not to the customary local standard. Plato himself saw no contradiction between his applying terms from the human ethical vocabulary to the universe and his rejection of the absoluteness of the Athenian popular norms because he differentiated between the virtues as he defined them and as they were popularly defined in Athens. That is to say, the behavior that would bring about "justice" according to Plato was different from the behavior that would bring it about according to the popular view.

Geography and economic factors played an equally important role in early Confucian thought. North China is cut off by mountains and deserts to the north and west, and by mountains to the east in Shantung province. There are also mountain ranges (penetrated by few passes) running parallel to the coast in southern

China, and oceans lie on the east and south. As a result, the Yellow River culture was relatively isolated from other civilizations during much of the Chou period. Although trade in such commodities as salt, iron, fish, and handicraft articles did develop between individual states during the East Chou, the Chinese areas as a whole were more or less self-sufficient in basic commodities. There was little motivation for these agricultural people to venture into the grassland and desert regions of Mongolia and Sinkiang. Some people have speculated about foreign influences entering China from the Eurasian Steppe during the bronze age; as proof, they point to "un-Chinese" features in art motifs. But recent archaeological discoveries have revealed the Shang and West Chou prototypes of these motifs.[29] China's isolation was very real indeed. Firm contact with the formerly Greek kingdom in Bactria, the civilized nation most accessible to China by land, was not established until the mission (c. 130 B.C.) of Chang Ch'ien, ambassador of the Han emperor Wu; and the first through silk caravan did not go from China to Iran until 106 B.C.

The isolation of the Chou people from cultures with vastly different norms was obviously one of degree in comparison with Greece; it was not complete. There are early references to the people of some parts of China itself as being somewhat uncivilized, and this means that many of their customs conflicted with those of the Chou people. But even within China proper the cultural variation was not as significant as historians once thought. It was once customary to divide the East Chou culture into three subcultures (Ch'in, Yen-Chao, Wu-Yüeh), but archaeologists now find such a uniformity in the three that they refuse to make the distinction.[30] There was considerable continuity from the Shang to the Chou, although these were different peoples. Agricultural techniques, the use of wells, tiled houses, brick-decorated walls, walled cities, two-man chariots, and other forms of material culture were the same in China under both dynasties. The social organization was similar, including the relation between the king and his lords; the same holds for many religious practices. A few differences do exist; for example, the Shang calendar grouped days in units of ten, whereas the Chou calendar divided the month into four parts determined by the phases of the moon.[31]

The early Chinese, without the exposure to sets of mores vastly different from their own that the Greeks had, were not continually reminded that the key rules of conduct change greatly from one area to another, and therefore that they may be relative to the particular place in which they are found. Thus Hsün Tzu could say, "Heaven and Earth gave birth to the *li*,"[32] and the early Confucians could equate what was in fact their "customary" or "popular" morality with a universal absolute morality. It was necessary to do this before they could take the next step and turn the *li* or *ch'eng* into cosmic principles. Taoist writings, especially the later ones, first begin to show an awareness of very different customs, and a consciousness of the error of treating as universal what is true of only the small Chinese corner of the world. A late chapter of the *Chuang-tzu* (entitled "Autumn Floods") asks: "Is not the Middle Kingdom, in comparison with what lies within the area bounded by the four seas, like a small seed in a granary?"

To the Chinese, there was a common principle of order running through Heaven, earth, and human society: "Heaven has its seasons, Earth has its wealth, Man has his government," said Hsün Tzu. Once the principle of order derived from human society had been turned into a cosmic principle tying nature and man together, it was possible to turn around and find in nature a justification for practice of the desired social behavior. Thus, for Hsün Tzu, man's task is to establish the social distinctions that have their counterparts in the natural hierarchical order; this is the first step in government. These social distinctions are implemented by the rules of conduct, *li*. It is "natural" for men to obey the *li*: to abide by them cannot but bring peace and prosperity; violation will bring the opposite. This success or failure is not the result of any magical interaction between human behavior and nature, nor is it due to the willful design of a deity. The social distinctions and the *li* by which they are maintained are simply as natural as the four seasons. Seeds planted out of season will die, and men who ignore the distinctions and the *li* will find chaos. The initial responsibility for insuring that human society accords with nature falls on the ruler, since it is his job to establish and maintain the social distinctions by seeing that the *li* are observed. The ruler who is successful at this forms "a triad with Heaven and Earth."

Comparison and Contrast

The late Chou conception of a cosmological order linking human society and nature can be distinguished from a somewhat later variation on the theme. Two characteristics separate the Han-period cosmology of Tung Chung-shu (c. 179–104 B.C.) from that described above. First, Tung Chung-shu attempted to apply the same numerical division to all phenomena in society and in nature. Second, he reestablished the idea of a moral deity, who causes aberrations in natural phenomena to punish human transgressions of social norms.

In the Han "five-elements" system, all things in the universe were classified into five groups; and those things in each group that corresponded to the same element were interrelated. Corresponding to water, fire, metal, wood, and earth, respectively, are the five activities of man (appearance, speech, seeing, hearing, and thinking), the five directions (the Chinese add "center"), the five musical notes, and the five colors.* The New Text School† (*chin-wen-chia*), of which Tung Chung-shu was a leader, believed that when men did not act in accordance with the natural order of things, they upset the previous harmony between man and nature, and unnatural events followed. In other words, there was interaction between man and nature. To determine which behavior

* Attempts at numerical classification were common in Greece as well. Plato seems to like the number "3": producers, auxiliaries, rulers make up a city; appetites, spirit, and reason make up man; temperance, courage, and wisdom make up justice; music, gymnastics, and dialectics make up education.

† The terms "Old Text" and "New Text" refer to different versions of the same ancient classics; the New Text versions are now considered more accurate. During the Han dynasty scholars associated with the New Text School of thought were involved in a lengthy controversy with the Old Text School of Liu Hsin (c. 46 B.C.–A.D. 23). The latter school was relatively less inclined to deal with portents, astrology, and divination. The interpretations of ritual and of administrative rules differed in the two schools. The New Text School based itself on the *Kung yang* commentary of the *Spring and Autumn Annals*, which portrayed Confucius as having received a mandate from Heaven to rectify the evils of the Chou dynasty; some spokesmen even treated Confucius as a supernatural being. The Old Text scholars generally treated Confucius as simply a teacher.

was in accord with nature, one applied the principle that things belonging to the same class affected each other; the process, however, was not one of mechanical causation, but rather one of "resonance." For example, according to the five-element system, the categories east, wood, green, wind, and spring all affected one another. A change in one phenomenon (for example in "green") would affect all the other phenomena (east, wood, wind, spring) in a process like a multiple echo, without physical contact coming between any of them. So the emperor had to wear the color green in the spring; if he did not, the seasonal regularity might be upset. The main idea in this interaction theory is the influence of human behavior on nature, but the converse was also believed to occur. Cosmological occurrences affect man: for example when the *yin* force in nature is on the ascendency, the *yin* in man rises also, and passive, negative, and destructive behavior can be expected. The concept of interaction between the human and natural realms was facilitated by the belief that both were products of a single primal substance (*ch'i*). Thus there was no physical barrier to their effects on each other.

The doctrine of interaction derived additional strength from the new picture of Heaven that emerged among some Han thinkers. "Heaven," in the naturalistic view of Hsün Tzu, had been just another name for the natural order, but Tung Chung-shu and others once more endowed Heaven with the attributes of a supreme spirit that wills, commands, is conscious, and is "good." One reason for this was the political unification of China then being carried on by the Emperor Wu (140–87 B.C.). The unification of separate regions, each with its own local gods, would be facilitated by the introduction of belief in a supreme spirit whose commands are binding everywhere. In any case, aberrations in the natural order (changes in weather, earthquakes, floods, and so forth) were supposed to occur in response to human transgressions of social norms, and to be willfully commanded by a displeased "good" Heaven. In the Chou Confucian conception of a cosmological order linking human society and nature one finds no such role assigned to an anthropomorphic Heaven.

Among the first major attacks on the Han theory was that of Wang Ch'ung (b. A.D. 27), author of a work entitled *Lun heng* (Critical Essays). He dismissed the notion of interaction between the two spheres: "Cold and warmth are dependent on Heaven and earth and are linked with the *yin* and *yang*. How can human affairs or the administration of the country have any influence on them?" Influenced by the Taoist view that Heaven (or the Tao) does not act purposively, he rejected the portrait of a conscious, willing deity who orders things in man's interest and can produce beneficial natural occurrences to reward man's good behavior. He said that Heaven and earth produce nothing intentionally; rice and wheat, for example, are not produced to satisfy human needs.[33] Nor can Heaven consciously respond to man's deeds or words: "Man is not cognizant of Heaven's proceedings; how should Heaven know what man is about? If Heaven has a body, its ears are too high and far away, to hear what men say, and if it be air (air like clouds and fog), how could such hear human speech?"[34] Wang Ch'ung also compared the relationship between man and Heaven with that between lice on the body and the person who carries the lice.

As we will see in chapter 5, the sharpest division between Confucians and Taoists came when the Taoists denied that human ethical categories had any cosmic significance.* Actually, a similar debate was also important in early Western philosophy. There were no greater intellectual enemies than the Platonists and Epicureans; and the Epicureans, like the Taoists, attacked the tendency of people to apply terms from human social and ethical language to na-

* The struggle against the tendency to apply terms from the human ethical vocabulary to nature was an enduring one in China. For example, in the 18th Century one finds a materialistic philosophy sufficiently consistent to make a clear distinction between the realm of human right and wrong on the one hand and nature on the other; Tai Chen (1723–77) was the spokesman. A previous thinker (Yen Yüan, A.D. 1635–1704), whose categories he partially adopted, had described the original potentiality of the *yin* and *yang* in terms of four "virtues" ([a]*te*): *yüan* (originating growth), *heng* (prosperous development), *li* (advantageous gain), and *cheng* (correct firmness). In man these "virtues" take the form of humanheartedness, duty, ritual, and knowledge. Tai Chen built on much of Yen Yüan's teaching, but he replaced the "four virtues" with the "five elements" in order to get rid of the notion that the universe is permeated by moral principles. (Cf. Fung, II, 653).

ture. Lucretius, for example, maintained that one could not understand things (as Plato wished to do) by trying to see how they were "held together by goodness and moral obligation,"[35] i.e., by looking for their contribution toward the realization of some cosmic good purpose. In explaining any given event or object, Plato rejected "mechanistic explanations," answers stated in terms of physical bodies impinging on each other or in terms of physical events that invariably preceded the event being explained. For example, the early mechanistic explanation of vision was as follows: light rays from the eye meet the light of day; the two lights (formed of physical particles) coalesce, forming a bridge on which physical motions from external bodies can travel to the eye and cause motions in the eye, resulting in vision. Plato's preferred explanation of vision was ethical: it helps us see the heavenly bodies and thus learn numbers and mathematics; we go on to purify our souls with this knowledge; and ultimately we are able to bring a justice into our souls corresponding to the justice we have discovered in the universe. In other words, the explanation of vision was in terms of the purpose it served, enabling man to bring harmony and justice into his soul. Lucretius replied, "You must not imagine that the bright orbs of our eyes were created purposely, so that we might be able to look before us. . . . In fact, nothing in our bodies was born in order that we might be able to use it, but the thing born creates the use."[36]

At the beginning of the modern period in Europe, scientifically inclined philosophers, in their attempts to understand the laws of change, had little use for the doctrine that the universe was a moral one, exhibiting justice, goodness, or design. Descartes, for instance, maintained that one realm of being is mind or soul which has the attributes of thought, feeling, will and desire; these things are not mathematically measurable. The other realm is matter, whose attributes include extension, motion, and size. Within the realm of matter all is mathematically measurable, and it is completely devoid of "justice" or "goodness," virtues that pertain rather to the realm of mind or soul. In time, Western philosophers even hesitated to assign human ethical qualities to God. Voltaire remarked, "It would be as absurd to say of God that he is just or unjust as to say, 'God is blue or square.'" One factor influencing this was the transition, evident in many philosophers of the time, from viewing God as the creator of the mathematical order in nature to identifying God with that order; God then completely lost human moral qualities. Spinoza held that human conceptions of right and wrong are irrelevant to nature (or God). Good and evil are human categories: something is good because we desire it, evil because we do not want it. Good is a human term, and the difference between God and man is as great as that between the constellation "dog" and the animal that barks.

The Attributes of Nature and the Human Mind

The universe is a moral universe, and nature has certain signals to indicate the proper relationship between one thing and another and the proper actions of any given thing. This describes nature: what about man? To complete the picture, the Confucians had to demonstrate that at least some men possess an organ capable of recognizing nature's ethical signals. Otherwise, human moral conduct is impossible. In the next chapter we will see what that organ is, and will examine the Confucian claim that it is possessed not just by a few philosopher-kings, but by all men. It is appropriate to conclude the present discussion by again comparing Chinese ideas with those of early Greece, which will show that generally there is a definite relationship between a philosopher's attributing certain qualities to the universe and his also maintaining that some men have mental faculties specifically adapted to knowing those qualities.

According to certain Greek philosophers, the soul (*psyche*) is the organ that responds to the guiding principles of the universe. This belief had not always existed. In the Homeric tradition, the soul was not necessarily supposed to have any intellectual function at all, and there was no reason to treat it as the most honored part of a man's natural endowment. Souls were portrayed as going to Hades, where they would roam about in the gloom; only rarely, in the case of heroes, did they go to the Blessed Isles. Nor was it always believed that the soul is immortal,[37] although immortality was in time regarded as one of the attributes that this most honored part of man shares with the gods. In the Orphic myths the soul came to be regarded as the highest part of man. Of divine origin, the souls of men fell through some sin from the upper region of light and were subsequently entrapped in the prison of the human body; but they craved reunion with the divine beings among whom they once dwelt. A release from the body and the divine reunion could be achieved through purification rites.

The Pythagoreans were among the first to say that the soul is characterized by a certain kind of intellectual power and to single out this phenomenon as what distinguishes man from beast. To them, the universe was mathematical, and number was the key to understanding the nature of things.* Mathematical truths were eternal truths; therefore, the Pythagoreans declared that the essence of the human soul was an intellectual power of discriminating the mathematical structure of the universe. The soul by itself, without the use of the bodily senses, discovered the mathematical truths, and purification of the soul was a process of scientific training to develop this number-discriminating intellect.

A frequently encountered Greek maxim is "like knows like." Hence the soul of man must be like the external things that become objects of knowledge. Aristotle informs us that philosophers who postulate a discriminating soul

> identify soul with the principle or principles of Nature, according as they admit several such principles or one only. Thus Empedocles declares that it is formed out of all his elements, each of them also being soul; his words are:
>
> For 'tis by Earth we see Earth, by Water Water,
> By Ether Ether divine, by Fire destructive Fire,
> By Love Love, and Hate by Cruel Hate.

---

* The world was made up of atoms arranged in various geometrical shapes (e.g., triangles and cubes), and numbers were assigned to everything: "justice" was number four, ten was a sacred number, and so on. A structure like this may have derived, in part, from the realization that music can be reduced to number (differences in musical intervals or tones depend on numerical ratios, such as the length of a string or the weight of a hammer) and the generalization of this situation to all phenomena.

> In the same way Plato in the *Timaeus* fashions the soul out of his elements; for like, he holds, is known by like, and things are formed out of the principles or elements, so that the soul must be so too.[38]

Platonic ontology fills the realm of being with eternal, unchanging Forms. There are the Forms of Justice, Courage, Temperance, Circularity, Triangularity, Manness, Treeness, Whiteness—in short, one for every general term. These Forms give being to things in the sensible world, and all particular things in the universe participate in a number of Forms (e.g., a given man may participate in the Forms Tallness, Manness, Whiteness, etc.). In the *Timaeus* we learn that this universe to which the Forms give being is a harmonious, ordered thing, and mathematics is the key to understanding how things are interrelated. Physical bodies are composed of elements, which themselves are composed of one of four different geometrical shapes (the pyramid for fire, octahedron for air, cube for earth and icosahedron for water). The quantities of the different elements in an object are in definite geometrical proportion.*

Now this conception of the nature of existence had to be balanced by a corresponding conception of the human soul as an entity peculiarly fitted for "knowing" the Forms and mathematical order of the universe. Moreover, the soul had to be like the things it knew:

> But when it [the soul] investigates by itself, it passes into the realm of the pure and everlasting and immortal and changeless, and being of a kindred nature, when it is once independent and free from interference [i.e., independent of the body], consorts with it always and strays no longer, but remains, in that realm of the absolute, constant and invariable, through contact with beings of a similar nature. And this condition of the soul we call wisdom.[39]

Both soul and Forms belong to the categories of things divine, invisible, invariable, and ruling. The Forms can only be known by the soul, and the soul is drawn by love (*eros*) to seek union with

* This view of the structure of the physical world was in opposition to the concept (popular in the Ionian colonies) of an indefinite quantity of matter that periodically fell into chaos because it was not held together according to any system.

that to which it is akin. Soul, for Plato, is intellect,* and the Forms are the objects of knowledge. When the "Form-knowing" soul functions as such, an order begins to appear in it corresponding to the order of the universe.

In the *Timaeus*, a detailed analysis of the constitution of the soul shows that it is "like" the Forms and the mathematical order in the universe. One can make three basic statements about the Forms: a Form exists, it is the same as itself (i.e., it has self-identity, or it never changes), and it is different from any other thing; these are the basic attributes of the Forms and also the fundamental elements of knowledge. In the same way, the human soul is made up of existence, sameness, and difference; and thus adapted for knowing these attributes of the Forms, the soul can make judgments involving them. Plato then compares the soul to a long strip that has been marked off into intervals like those on a musical scale; this gives mathematical order and harmony to the soul. The human soul, therefore, partakes of the mathematical order that permeates the universe, and is perfectly adapted to knowing it. In sum, the human soul or mind is an entity whose essential function is to know both the Forms and the mathematical truths of nature.

The kind of mind that the Confucians attributed to man also had to be "like" the qualities that they assigned to nature. The Confucians had turned certain aspects of the customary norms (the *li*) and social virtues into cosmic principles. For this reason, nature exhibited relationships like superior-inferior, proper-improper, and good-bad. These characteristics of nature played the same role in dictating what the essence of the human mind would be for the Confucians as did earth, air, fire, water, love and strife for Em-

* *Phaedo* 66e. Actually, one can distinguish two different conceptions of soul in the Platonic dialogues. One is pure intellect, which has roots in the Orphic and Pythagorean tradition. The other is the tripartite soul, consisting of appetites, spirit, and reason; this idea goes back to the association of soul with what moves, and to the belief that what moves is alive (see Aristotle, *De Anima* i.2 [404a]). The three "motions" or activities of man were believed to be the satisfaction of physical desires, the pursuit of honor and ambition, and contemplation. In this sense, soul was also viewed as a principle of life, for knowing and sensing were both regarded as "motions." The tripartite description of the soul occurs chiefly in the *Republic* and *Phaedrus*; the description as pure intellect occurs in the *Phaedo*.

pedocles, number for the Pythagoreans, or the Forms and the mathematical order for Plato. Like the Greeks, the Confucians found it necessary to maintain that at least some men had a mind capable of detecting the natural order; but in China "knowing," the activity of the mind, was not a process of grasping nature's scientific principles or mathematical truths, of knowing for the sake of knowing. The activity of the mind in Confucian thought was a seeking for nature's ethical qualities and relationships; it was knowing for the sake of guiding conduct. In other words, the human mind was an "evaluating mind." (The next Chapter will explore the role of this activity, and of the evaluating mind itself, in the Confucian concept of man.)

The consideration of natural equality also entered the picture, for the Confucians went on to maintain that all men possess the evaluating mind. From a philosophical standpoint, the Confucians would have been on firm ground if they had based their doctrine of natural equality simply on the thesis that all men evaluate and choose; indeed this position is still found in contemporary Western philosophy.[40] But in the Confucian doctrine there was an antecedently determined *content* to the evaluations made by the mind: that is, it was assumed that certain specific things would be judged superior and inferior, proper and improper, right and wrong. It followed that nature demanded a hierarchy of social positions, and the Confucians continued to advocate some kind of social aristocracy, no matter how imbued they became with egalitarian sentiments.

CHAPTER 3

THE CONFUCIAN CONCEPT OF MAN

IT IS remarkable that a belief in cosmic hierarchies did not lead the Chou Confucians to a belief in natural inequalities among men, as it did the Platonists in Greece. For the reasons described in Chapters 1 and 2 the Confucians instead adhered to a doctrine of natural equality, based principally on the argument that all men have an evaluating mind; this is the key to understanding the Confucian concept of man. The Confucians did indeed believe in the naturalness of social hierarchies; but for them, no men were by birth (either through hereditary station or through innately superior ability) more exalted than others and thus entitled to higher places in the social hierarchy. The sole criterion for receipt of political and economic privilege was merit; this was defined, as will be shown in the next chapter, in terms of the utilization of the evaluating mind, which all men possess to an equal degree.

We will begin the study of "man" in Confucian thought with an examination of the evaluating mind. The next step is to demonstrate that the Confucians regarded this mind as something equally possessed by all men. The most convincing approach to this second step is a study of the concept of "human nature" (*jen-hsing*) in the early writings.* The elements of *jen-hsing* are common to every human being,[1] and the evaluating mind is one of them. In the final section of the chapter, this will be illustrated by an analysis of *jen-hsing* in the writings of Mencius and Hsün Tzu. In addition to demonstrating that the Confucians did believe that all men are born with the evaluating mind, this final analysis is important for two reasons: it reveals the remarkable similarity between the con-

* For an analysis of other terms that at times denoted something like "human nature," see notes 44 and 50 to this chapter.

ceptions of human nature of two thinkers whose views have hitherto been considered irreconcilable; and it supplements the initial discussion of the evaluating mind in this chapter with more specific information about the mind's essence and function.

In the early Chinese works, the term "mind" (*hsin*) did not have the Western connotation of an entity distinct from the body and having special metaphysical status.[2] It was understood functionally, with reference to certain types of activity,* such as judging and directing actions. These were supposedly controlled by the heart, which, although different from the other active organs (mouth, eyes, etc.), did not have any special metaphysical status. The mental organ (*hsin chih kuan*) and the sense organs (*erh-mu chih kuan*) were equally gifts of Heaven.[3] According to some early Greek thinkers, mind was associated with an eternal, immaterial soul existing within the body. In early Chinese works, too, there are terms that were associated with mental activity and are translated today as "soul": *p'o,* "sentient soul"; *hun,* "spiritual soul"; and *shen,* "soul." However, they also did not refer to any eternal entity having special metaphysical status, as did the Greek term *psyche* in works reflecting Orphic, Pythagorean, and Platonic doctrines. As far as living man was concerned, the Chinese terms were related to such terms as [b]*hsing* (bodily form) and *ch'i* (ether, matter), which were commonly applied to man's physical constitution. The other uses of these terms concerned the nature of the *deceased*; after death, the *hun* and *ch'i* return to heaven, whereas the body and *p'o* return to earth. Compared with Greek thought, the Chinese view was closest to that of the atomists (particularly those in the Epicurean school), who understood "soul" as vital breath (Greek, *pneuma*; Latin, *spiritus*). This vital breath was material (matter in a gaseous state) spread throughout the body, and in its particularly refined state it became the material "mind" of the person, located in the breast. Even so, the Chinese did not think of "soul" as providing a "ghost in the machine" for the body.[4]

The term "mind" (*hsin*) was used in early China to denote many things, including "intentions," "feelings," the location of the desires, cognitive activity, and evaluative activity. The expression

* For example, it was generally agreed that the mind "moves" (*tung*).

"evaluating mind," as I will use it, refers to functions denoted by either or both of two terms: [b]*i*,* the sense that discriminates what is proper and required as a duty in a given situation; and [b]*chih*, "moral knowing," the sense that discriminates right and wrong (*shih-fei-chih-hsin*) and approves or disapproves.† According to Hsün Tzu, man knows the *li* that define appropriate human and cosmic stations and actions "by using his mind."[5] Once the mind decides that something is right or proper, it commands action in accordance with its judgment. So the mind both *evaluates* the requirements of a situation and *commands* proper action; these are its two primary functions.

The Evaluating Mind

In Chapter 2 it was shown that the Confucians derived cosmic principles from terms originally pertaining to moral conduct: *Ch'eng* referred initially to unwavering dedication to the good, and the *li* were the customary norms dictating human action. The direct consequence of deriving cosmic principles from these terms was that the primary object of knowing became the discrimination of proper from improper in order to guide action. The usual object of studying astronomy, for example, was not to understand when one season begins and another ends, but to know that it was right to plant one's crop, execute prisoners, or change the color of one's clothing at a certain time and wrong to do these things at another time. In education, the Confucians felt that men chiefly needed to learn how to distinguish what should or should not be done in human society. Hence training concentrated on either the imitation of living models of conduct or on the reading of books de-

* According to Tuan Yu-ts'ai, the term that is now expressed with the character 義 was often written as 宜 or 誼 in the classical period; in this form it had the meaning of "appropriate" (Ting, IX, 5705a). Peter Boodberg of the University of California at Berkeley would use the English expression "congruity" to translate it. I feel that the phrase "sense of fitting duty" is more accurate, carrying both the idea of appropriateness and that of awareness of an obligation to abide by that judgment in action (Bodde, p. 237). But in the interest of avoiding cumbersome expressions, I will translate [b]*i* simply as "moral sense."

† In view of the extensive criticism in the *Chuang-tzu* of utilizing the mind that discriminates right and wrong (*shih fei*), it is reasonable to associate concern with this mind with many Confucians, and not just with Mencius.

scribing how models of conduct (good and evil) had behaved in the past; it did not concern itself with the study of natural phenomena and laws simply for the sake of understanding more about them.

A comparison with Platonic thought should illuminate the overriding behavioral concern in the early Confucian doctrine. The order that Plato attributed to the universe bore scant resemblance to the social system in Athens, and its principles were not abstracted from the popular norms of Athens. Plato said that the universe is held together by the Good. He never described the Good exactly, but it seems clear that it involved the principles behind a mathematical order. Pythagoras had contended that number holds the world together, and Plato's Forms are like numbers.* They never change, and they exist independently of their particular manifestations. Numbers exist whether or not anyone thinks of them or sees specific numbers of concrete things; the same is true of the Forms of justice, courage, and the rest.

Plato's portrait of man follows from this description of the cosmic order. Man must possess an organ enabling him to rise above everything human and understand the cosmic order, which is vastly different from what he perceives about him with his senses:

> As concerning the most sovereign form of soul in us, we must conceive that heaven has given it to each man as a guiding genius—that part which we say dwells in the summit of our body and lifts us from earth towards our celestial affinity, like a plant whose roots are not in earth, but in the heavens.[6]

Plato definitely expected man to apply his knowledge of the cosmic order to the betterment of the human condition, as the parable of the cave in the *Republic* makes clear. However, the most divine form of activity is knowing for the sake of knowing, making full use of the mind (*nous*). Man should seek to rise above the mun-

* A Platonic Form (*eidos*) resembles a "universal," that which is common to all members of a given class of things, as "manness" is common to all particular men. It differs from a universal in having a substantial existence in a separate realm of eternal Forms, and in being normative (e.g., the Form "white" is a norm to which white things can be compared). Things can fall short of their Form; they do not fall short of a universal.

dane world and gradually gain an understanding of the cosmic order. The most joyous of all states is the half-mystic, half-cognitive condition achieved when one contemplates Good itself or Beauty itself; then one understands how everything in the universe fits together in a harmonious whole. One can sense this concern with *understanding* from the time of the birth of philosophy in ancient Greece. The earliest philosophers studied Nature for no other reason than to try to comprehend it. Their disregard of family, riches, and status and their unconcern with practical problems generated a whole series of anecdotes that were handed down in the Platonic Academy; Thales, while observing some heavenly event, fell into a well and was criticized by his maid for wanting to watch celestial goings-on when he could not even see his own feet; Anaxagoras, accused of paying no attention to his kin or country, pointed to heaven and said, "There is my country."[7] In the dialogues Socrates is the symbol of this other-worldly orientation—a person who often seems to be possessed, wandering about disheveled and shoeless, as if in a trance. Neo-Platonism, and the early Christianity that was influenced by it, went even further, disregarding Plato's imperative that the philosopher return to earth and realize in a human utopia the eternal order he has known. For them, a knowledge of the eternal did not lead to a bettering of this world; earth was a vale of tears, and men had best prepare for Paradise.

Plato advised the study of mathematics and astronomy as a means of raising the mind above the mundane world. Gymnastics is important in Platonic education, but it is devoted to bodily health and thus is concerned with the world of change. Music can be taught because it introduces harmony into the soul, but it does not give any knowledge. Therefore, arithmetic, the other mathematical sciences, and dialectic (which involves the search for the assumptions on which the other sciences are based, and also the search for the first principle of all) are the tools for purifying the soul and helping the intellect transcend this world. Discussing arithmetic in the *Republic,* Socrates remarks: " 'You see, then, my friend,' said I, 'that this branch of study really seems to be indispensable for us, since it plainly compels the soul to employ pure thought with a view to truth itself.' "[8] Since the conversion of the soul, for Plato, depended on training in mathematics and astronomy, the path was limited to those of high intelligence, the golden souls that are most divine. There was no assumption, as in China, that all could profit equally from training if it were equally available.

Plato was not especially concerned with the Confucian idea of model emulation. Supposedly, a person who had developed the habit of the disinterested pursuit of truth would have the unbiased mind necessary for being a political official; but the political application seems secondary to the joy of knowledge for its own sake. Works of the early Greek poets like Hesiod were essential parts of the Athenian educational system. They contained descriptions of gods and men, some of whose heroic exploits were treated as exemplary by the Athenians, just as the Confucians treated similar episodes in the *Book of Odes* (*Shih ching*). Plato, however, explicitly rejected such works from his educational program.

The difference between the early Platonists and Confucians can be stated as follows: The Platonists were more concerned with knowing in order to understand, while the Confucians were more concerned with knowing in order to behave properly toward other men.*

* There was a certain amount of straight cosmological speculation on the origin and structure of the universe in early China, and a number of theories are contained in the *Chin-shu t'ien-wen chih* (Chin-shu, *Treatise on Astronomy*). There were two major theses dating from the end of the Former Han. One was the "ecliptical theory" of Chang Heng (A.D. 78–139), which regarded heaven as like an egg with the earth as its yolk. The other was the "equatorial theory," which treated heaven as an umbrella and the earth as an overturned dish, both being high in the middle and sloping at the edges. Interest in this kind of speculation diminished after about the fourth century A.D.; it did not arise again until the emergence of Neo-Confucianism in the Sung dynasty (A.D. 960–1279). When cosmological speculation did reappear, interest in it was clearly dictated by two practical considerations. One was an attempt to oppose the Buddhist doctrine that the world of change is illusory (things that change, according to the Buddhists, have no self-essence or *tzu-hsing*). For many Buddhists, the fact that the world was illusory also implied that ethical relations (father-son, emperor-subject) and social virtues (filial piety, loyalty) were unreal. Therefore, there was no need for them to discharge their duties as sons or subjects (marrying, having children, paying taxes, doing military service). The Neo-Confucianists attempted to reaffirm the reality of the phenomenal world and of these social relations and virtues. The other practical aim (as in the case of Chang Tsai, A.D. 1021–77) was to give some cosmological support to the doctine that all men are brothers.

In China, truth and falsity in the Greek sense have rarely been important considerations in a philosopher's acceptance of a given belief or proposition; these are Western concerns. The consideration important to the Chinese is the behavioral implications of the belief or proposition in question. What effect does adherence to the belief have on people? What implications for social action can be drawn from the statement? For the Greeks, study was valued both for its own sake and as a guide to action (after all, Plato did write the *Republic,* and Socrates did maintain that "he who knows the good does the good"); but bliss lay primarily in study for its own sake. In Confucianism, there was no thought of "knowing" that did not entail some consequence for action.

Actually, this special concern with the behavioral implications of a proposition applies not only to the Confucians but to most other early Chinese schools as well—even to the Taoists, whose search for the unity behind the many often makes them seem closer to Plato than any Confucian was. Taoists placed nowhere near the emphasis on social behavior that one finds in Confucian thought, and they certainly rejected the Confucian glorification of man's evaluating mind. But even in their case there was a limit to mystical knowing. In many passages in Taoist works the primary object of knowing is portrayed as knowing how to react properly to other men and things.*

Two examples may help to illustrate this contrast. First, the early Taoists recognized that the qualities one assigns to things of this world depend on one's point of view, and usually on what one is using as a standard for comparison. Thus the same thing can be good from one point of view and bad from another, hard from one point of view and soft from another, tall from one standpoint and short from another. These attributes, then, are relative and have no absolute basis in the phenomenal things themselves. Tao is the Unity behind the many particular things; in Tao opposition disappears, since there is nothing beyond Tao to use as a standard for comparison. For the Taoists the significance of this discovery was *behavioral.* That is, if opposite labels can be applied to any person

* See Chapter 6, pp. 144–45.

or situation with equal justice, depending on one's viewpoint, and if all differences disappear in Tao, it followed that one should adopt an attitude of toleration and accommodation toward all men, ideas, and events. No one thing is absolutely good or absolutely ugly.

Plato also recognized the relativity of descriptive terms: "My good fellow, is there any one of these many fair and honorable things that will not sometimes appear ugly and base? And of the just things, that will not seem unjust? And of the pious things, that will not seem impious?" asks Socrates in the *Republic*.[9] For Plato, since a thing is both hard and soft, beautiful and ugly, it never *is* one thing rather than another.

> Nothing is *one* thing just by itself, nor can you rightly call it by some definite name, nor even say it is of any definite sort. On the contrary, if you call it "large," it will be found to be also small, if "heavy," to be also light, and so on all through, because nothing is *one* thing or *some* thing or of any definite sort. All the things we are pleased to say "are" really are in process of becoming, as a result of movement and change and of blending one with another.[10]

The significance of the relativity of opposite qualities is epistemological for Plato. Since a thing never *is* one thing rather than another, the phenomenal world can never be completely known. We should seek instead to know the basic Forms (Tallness, Shortness, Hardness, Softness), as opposed to particular instances of them; the Forms alone always are what they are and nothing else.

Another contrast between China and Greece centers on the quest for some Unity in diversity, for something linking the multiplicity of individual things together. In Plato's case one can speak of the one-many relationship in two ways. First, each Form is one and yet is present in many particular things: "And in respect of the just and the unjust, the good and the bad, and all the ideas or forms, the same statement holds, that in itself each is one, but that by virtue of their communion with actions and bodies and with one another they present themselves everywhere each as a multiplicity of aspects."[11] One must first know the Form, or what is common to all members of a class; only then can one adequately identify or name a particular. One must first know what is the essence of Justice; only then can one go on to identify any particular act as just.

There is another and more comprehensive way in which one can speak of the one-many relationship in Plato. In the famous cave parable in the *Republic* Plato tried to describe the Good (which is above the Forms in the hierarchy of being) by analogy with the sun. Just as the sun makes all things visible to the bodily eye, so does the Good make all things intelligible to the eye of the soul. As one rises by dialectic up to a vision of the Good, one increasingly finds unity in the many; and as he descends after knowing the Good, he can see the interconnectedness of all things. Plato means that there are certain all-embracing principles like mathematical propositions, which, once known, help a person to explain everything in the universe, since there is a mathematical order throughout it.[12] The Good then stands for the principle of interconnectedness by which things become intelligible. The epistemological significance of this notion of unity in the many can be seen in the *Meno*:

> All nature is akin, and the soul has learned everything, so that when a man has recalled a single piece of knowledge—*learned* it in ordinary language—there is no reason why he should not find out all the rest, if he keeps a stout heart and does not grow weary of the search, for seeking and learning are in fact nothing but recollection.[13]

Thus the significance of the one-many relationship is again cognitive. One can go from learning a single piece of knowledge to learning all of it, since all nature is akin.

The early Chinese were also interested in a unity in the many, but the behavioral implications of the notion, rather than any epistemological implication, were of primary importance. In Confucianism the idea stemmed from a belief that all things somehow derive their being from a common source (Heaven); all, therefore, equally possess a "Heavenly nature" (*t'ien-hsing*). Thus all men are brothers, and present in each man is the ethical imperative to love all men. When a Confucian understood that the one existed in the many, he knew that this required him to treat all men as brothers. The Logicians, who flourished in late Chou times, might have been expected to focus on the logical and epistemological significance of the one-many relationship, but even they emphasized the behavioral aspects. The tenth "paradox" of Hui Shih (fourth century B.C.) is "Love all things equally; the universe is one body"—a blend of the Mohist ideal of universal love and the Taoist idea found in the *Chuang-tzu* ("The heavens, the earth, and I have come into existence together, and all things and I are one").

For the Confucians, the foundations of all human virtues are the *li*, the rites or rules of propriety. The Master said: "Respectfulness, without the rules of propriety [*li*], becomes laborious bustle; carefulness, without the rules of propriety, becomes timidity; boldness, without the rules of propriety, becomes insubordination; straightforwardness, without the rules of propriety, becomes rudeness."[14] For Plato, "wisdom" was the source of all the specific virtues. In the *Meno* Socrates says:

> If then virtue is an attribute of the spirit, and one which cannot fail to be beneficial, it must be wisdom, for all spiritual qualities in and by themselves are neither advantageous nor harmful, but become advantageous or harmful by the presence with them of wisdom or folly. If we accept this argument, then virtue, to be something advantageous, must be a sort of wisdom.[15]

In sum, since the object of knowing, for the Chinese, was knowing *how* to behave, Confucian thinkers defined man as an animal with many of the biological traits found in other animals but also possessing one unique attribute—a mind that discriminated between the natural qualities of "noble" and "base," or "right" and "wrong." In addition, man could take action in accordance with the evaluation made by that mind.

The Commanding Mind

Thus far we have seen that the evaluating mind discriminates the qualities of "proper" and "improper" found in nature (including human society). As its remaining function, the mind commands conformance with its judgments. When a man's action is in accord with the evaluations and commands of his mind, he is able to enter into a kind of communion with heaven. The portrait of the evaluating mind found in the Chou Confucian writings suggests that an internalization of "sovereignty" had occurred. That is to say, whereas the ultimate sovereigns originally (early Chou) were Heaven or the king, external sources of commands, there later developed belief in another sovereign that existed within the individual and commanded from within. Gradually, there developed a correspondence between the content of the internally self-commanded duties ([b]*i*) that resulted from the mind's evaluation and the content of the external decrees (*ming*) that earlier men had believed to come from Heaven to man.* This internalization of sovereignty was a complicated, long-term evolutionary process, which this study can only deal with in broad outline.

External Rulers

In the Shang dynasty it was believed that royal ancestors could visit the region inhabited by the Lord-on-High as guests and be "to the left and right of the Lord-on-High."[16] They served as aides to the deity and carried out various divine tasks, having it in their power to bestow bounties and calamities from the realm of the Lord-on-High.[17] They also served as intermediaries for requests from the living king, such as prayers for rain or improvement of the crop.[18] Because the relationship between worshippers and some of the worshipped was a "family affair," the gulf between terrestrial and celestial was reduced considerably.[19]

Contrary to what has been thought for some time, the religious ideas of the early Chou and those of the Shang were quite similar in many ways.[20] On an early bronze from the West Chou period is the statement, "Wen Wang is above in the center looking down, and next to him the brilliant king does the same";[21] another bronze inscription says that "The majesty of the former kings lies on the left and right of the Lord-on-High."[22] In the *Shih ching* we read: "Wen Wang ascends and descends, he is on the left and right of God."[23] During the sacrificial rites the tablets bearing the names of ancestors were placed after that of the first king and before that of the reigning king, so that their spirits could serve as go-betweens.[24] There were, however, two new developments in the early West Chou regarding the relation between the living king and the deity.

* I am indebted to Professor T'ang Chun-i of New Asia College, Hong Kong, for bringing several aspects of this matter to my attention.

First, the contact between the king and the Lord-on-High (i.e., the contact between man and God) became even closer. The living king did not need to use the intermediary of deceased ancestors in order to communicate with the deity; he could do so directly. By the beginning of the Spring and Autumn period, various nobles and ministers could also claim Heaven-dwelling ancestors, so the same would hold for them. Second, it was no longer necessary to die before one could become an aide to the deity and take part in divine tasks. The Chinese of the West Chou believed that the Lord-on-High issued certain decrees (*ming*) to the king (concerned mainly with the conduct of government, the humane treatment of the people, and feudal social and religious obligations). When the ruler's own commands (*ming*) to his ministers and to the people corresponded in content with those he had received from heaven, he was participating in divine tasks and would be described as exhibiting virtuous conduct (*te hsing*). This virtuous conduct, which involved taking part in divine tasks, was the *sine qua non* for entering into an especially intimate relationship with Heaven. Theoretically, anyone obedient to divine commands could ultimately enter this relationship.

The king who maintained a link with the deity in life by practicing [a]*te* would continue to be in the divine service after death, sitting next to the Lord-on-High. The relationship was denoted by the Chinese expression *p'ei t'ien,* which can be translated as either "to be an assessor of heaven,"[25] or "to enjoy the patronage of heaven," depending on the context (sometimes the term used was *p'ei ming*). The relationship between king and deity implied by the expression included both the contact after the king's death and the contact of the living king who served as counterpart to Heaven in his performance of virtuous acts. The virtuous ruler enjoyed the patronage of Heaven by receiving the kingdom through a divine decree "centered . . . in his person."[26]

This notion of communion between king and deity was reinforced by the belief in the living king's descent from a divine personage. The question of whether or not the Shang people believed in a blood relationship between man and the Lord-on-High has not been settled yet. The first real historical figure in the Shang ancestral tree seems to be Shang Chia, but there were earlier legendary figures. The earliest of all on the ladder was Ti K'u, who came to be identified with the Lord-on-High at a later date, according to one scholar.[27] The second figure on the ladder was Hsieh; a myth from an unknown date states that he was the son of the Lord-on-High, who commanded a mysterious bird (*hsüan niao*) to produce the Shang people.[28] Among the Chou, a myth of definitely early origin relates that a woman named [a]Yüan stepped on the big-toe mark of the Lord-on-High's footprint and then gave birth to Prince Millet (Hou Chi), the agricultural deity who was considered the first ancestor of the Chou people.[29] In the sacrificial ritual Prince Millet's tablet was placed with that of the Lord-on-High, and they were both recipients of the sacrifice, the former assisting the latter. Doubtless this notion of divine descent helped to establish the Chou family's claim to the throne; it also contributed to the Chou conception of the king as the Son of Heaven (*t'ien tzu*).* In the Warring States period many ruling houses traced their ancestry back to a god, such as Huang Ti, the Yellow Emperor. It would probably be inaccurate to say that in the early West Chou only the king himself was held to maintain the intimate relationship with Heaven. The unique contact was shared by the noblemen who were his blood relatives and had a common divine descent.

Internal Rulers

Kings were able to have an intimate link with Heaven when there was a correspondence between their commands to their people and the commands they received from Heaven. Their obedient behavior was virtuous behavior. Gradually, belief in a special relationship between rulers (plus their kin) and Heaven was broadened to include that between all men and Heaven. Any man who was obedient to the Heaven-decreed rules ([a]*i*), i.e., whose behavior was virtuous (*te hsing*), stood a chance of being noticed by

* Of course, among later, more sophisticated thinkers being Son of Heaven meant being "representative" of Heaven, not necessarily having divine descent.

Heaven and given the decree to assume political control. Heaven theoretically had no prejudices in favor of any man.

Toward the end of the West Chou several aspects of the divine contact that earlier had been largely the preserve of the one king and his kin were beginning to appear among other men. For example, a bronze inscription dating from the reign of Li Wang (reigned 878–841 B.C.) speaks of the ancestor of a man named Lu, who was not of the royal house, as existing on high and clearly acting as the aide of Heaven.[30] During the Shang period the expression "I the One Man" (*yü i jen*) was reserved for the king's exclusive use.[31] It was symbolic of the fact that all state activities were termed "the king's activities" on the oracle bones; he was indeed the central figure. In the *Shu ching*[32] and on early West Chou bronzes[33] the same expression is used exclusively by the Chou king. However, from the reign of Ching Wang (reigned 519–475 B.C.) on, the expression began to be used by other politically powerful figures in no way connected with the royal house.[34] In the Spring and Autumn period, the political Heavenly command (*ming*), which the West Chou had viewed as bestowed on the king alone because the king was "enjoying the patronage of Heaven," was believed to be bestowed on nobles who ruled individual states, and also on high officials.[35]

These phenomena were simply signs of the time, but they marked the emergence of a new conception of being a "ruler," which had great importance for philosophical thinking. We have examined the early belief that Heaven commanded (*ming*) certain behavior by men—especially by the ruler, who in turn issued various commands (*ming*) as political decisions affecting the people. When there was a correlation between the decrees of Heaven and those of the ruler, the ruler was taking part in divine tasks and thereby maintaining communion with Heaven. According to the new conception, *every* man was able to "command" and to establish this communion: every man was, in a sense, a ruler, if only of himself. This was the final philosophical development from the very early religious belief that Heaven, in bestowing its decree to rule, was not prejudiced in favor of any one man, tribe, or region. Any person could be a ruler because he had as his innate endowment an internal "sovereign," whose moral commands were like those formerly issued only by Heaven or the acting king. This sovereign could discriminate right and wrong, commanding action accordingly. The moral activities initiated by men's internal rulers involved men quite as much in the Heavenly tasks as had the activities of the Son of Heaven carried out in obedience to the commands of Heaven during the West Chou. Previously, only the actual king had continuing contact with Heaven; now all men, through the dictates of their individual rulers, had this contact.

What were these internalized rulers, found in all men? Mencius spoke of a Heavenly "nobility" (*t'ien-chüeh*), certain innate moral tendencies that should be valued above human nobility (*jen-chüeh*), the actual occupation of a position of great rank and power.[36] Hsün Tzu spoke of the mind as the Heavenly Ruler (*t'ien-chün*),[37] a label that had been used exclusively to designate the reigning king during the West Chou.[38] The innate aspect of Tao present in each individual, according to Chuang Tzu, was his True Ruler (*chen tsai* or *chen chün*).[39] Neither Tao nor the sagely king who approximates Tao was the master of man;[40] man's ruler was to be found in himself. When the internal ruler determined something to be right and a duty, that duty was like a command issued to the self. Thus there was a correlation between the dictates of the moral sense ([b]*i*) and Heavenly injunction (*ming*).[41] The Heavenly injunctions were to practice certain acts, which were identical with the things that man, in the new conception, would command himself to do. I. A. Richards remarked, "It is notable that the mind, for Mencius, is its own law-giver."[42] The individual person who acted in accordance with what his internal ruler commanded was acting with virtue ([a]*te*); this *te*, then, was the means by which he as an individual was able to maintain communion with Heaven, just as it was through *te* that the king had done so in the earlier period. *Te* was the channel for human-divine contact.

From a situation in which only the dead (royal ancestors) had direct contact with the deity there had emerged a belief that the reigning king and his kin could also maintain this contact by performing tasks decreed by Heaven. Then the idea was extended to include all men: since any man could be a "ruler" (because he possessed his own internal sovereign), any man could have direct contact with Heaven by obeying the commands of his internal ruler and acting in accordance with *te*, as the earlier kings had done. Finally, a belief in the physical connection between the king and the deity, stemming from myths of the royal clan's divine descent, contributed to the later belief that all men are children of Heaven.

The early Greek thinkers were also enormously concerned with the idea of man's divine kinship. In certain Orphic doctrines the ancestors of man (the Titans) were held to have dwelt among the gods at one time. Because of a monstrous crime their offspring were condemned to have their divine spark, the soul, imprisoned in mortal bodies on earth. However, it was possible for a man to release his soul from this prison through purification and to reenter the divine realm. For Plato, the intellect became man's divine spark, his instrument of purification and reunion with the eternal Heavenly realm. Through knowing the divine Forms man could become increasingly godlike. In the *Timaeus* Plato said:

> As concerning the most sovereign form of soul in us we must conceive that heaven has given it to each man as a guiding genius—that part which we say dwells in the summit of our body and lifts us from earth towards our celestial affinity, like a plant whose roots are not in earth, but in the heavens . . . if his heart has been set on the love of learning and true wisdom and he has exercised that part of himself above all, he is surely bound to have thoughts immortal and divine, if he shall lay hold upon truth, nor can he fail to possess immortality in the fullest measure that human nature admits; and because he is always devoutly cherishing the divine part and maintaining the guardian genius that dwells with him in good estate, he must needs be happy above all.[43]

But there is an important difference between the Chinese and Greek conceptions of making oneself divine. According to the Chinese, anyone should be able to discriminate the Heavenly norms and act in conformance with them, thus establishing the divine link. According to Orphic myth and to Platonic doctrine, however, the souls of many men (slaves to the senses, tyrants, and other evil persons) are so hopelessly entrapped in their bodies that it is impossible for them to utilize the intellect in order to assimilate themselves to the divine forms. Thus the path to perfection is not equally open to all men.

The Mind Equally Possessed

We must now demonstrate that the Confucians did indeed regard the evaluating mind as something equally possessed by all men. This is best done by examining the concept of "human nature," or *jen-hsing*. Whatever pertains to *jen-hsing* pertains to everyone, and the human mind (whose essence is to evaluate) is part of the content of "human nature."

The Chinese character [e]*hsing* is composed of two elements:[44] the "heart" radical (*hsin*), which by itself denotes "mind" or mental activity; and [a]*sheng*, which by itself has a variety of meanings, including "to produce," "to give birth," "born with," and "life." Although *hsing* does appear in present texts that contain materials dating from the West Chou, there is good evidence that at that time neither the concept nor the character *hsing* had appeared.[45] Rather, the concept of *hsing* seems to have developed gradually over a span of time extending from the end of the Spring and Autumn period through the Warring States period.

Let us first examine the *sheng* element in the character.* *Hsing* evolved from *sheng*, used in the sense of "life" as an endowment received from Heaven.[46] Because "life" implies a vitality or activity that something has had "from birth" in the form of growth and/or response to surroundings, *hsing* retained the sense of activity, of a responsiveness to things.[47] The *Chuang-tzu* says: "*Hsing* is the essence of life (*sheng*); the movement of *hsing* is action."[48] Hsün Tzu, in his most precise definition of *hsing*,[49] says that it involves responsive reaction to things in the environment.† *Hsing*, having

* Details concerning the reason for the addition of the *hsin* element to the character are given in pp. 74–81 and in the notes to those pages.

† Mencius described the *hsing* as a collection of fonts (*tuan*), or aspects of mind, and Hsün Tzu thought that it was composed of desires; in both cases the components of *hsing* were responses to the environment, as will be shown below.

evolved from *sheng*, also retained the sense of a gift from Heaven.[50] Most early commentators agree that *hsing* is "neither learned nor acquired," but instead represents man's innate endowment.[51]

The new term *hsing* differed from the old term *sheng* in that its meaning was, in part, precisely those constantly appearing activities found in life. By describing a creature's *hsing* one described what its conduct in life was likely to be: "That by which life [*sheng*] is as it is called *hsing*."[52] *Hsing* is a being's innate constitution, bestowed at birth by Heaven, and it is made up in part of a variety of regularly repeated kinds of behavior. Generally speaking, *hsing* could be used to refer to the regular behavior of any creature, especially to behavior that was unique to the species in question; by extension, the term could refer to things like the regular "behavior" of a mountain (e.g., growing trees). During the formative period, however, *hsing* was usually used when the topic was "man in general" and attention was being focused on the regular behavior characteristic of a human being. People were primarily interested in the nature of man. This explains why the "heart," or "mind," radical was eventually added to the character *sheng* ("life") to form the combined character *hsing*. Mind was considered to be a unique attribute of man, not of any other "nature."

Before the exact relationship of the evaluating mind to the human *hsing* can be pinpointed, it is necessary to analyze the behavioral content of *hsing*. Two types of regularly appearing action can be isolated: that which man shares with other animals and that which is unique to the human species. The evaluating mind will be found to bear a direct relationship to the latter. Thus it is necessary to go through the following additional steps in order to demonstrate that the evaluating mind was considered to be an equal possession of all men. First, the criteria used by the Confucians to identify "constancies" of natural behavior must be identified. Second, the natural behavior which man shares with other animals must be distinguished from that unique to the human species, since both are part of the human *hsing*. Finally, we will analyze the exact relationship between the evaluating mind and *hsing*, which is the common nature of all men. More specifically, the explanation will turn on the relationship of the evaluating mind to the natural social behavior unique to the human species, as revealed in the *Mencius* and *Hsün-tzu.*

Natural Behavior

It has been stated that *hsing* referred in part to regularly appearing actions. "Constancy" is a convenient word to describe this kind of action when it is repeatedly performed by an individual thing. For example, eating is a constant in every individual man, and growing leaves is a constant of trees. However, in the ancient Chinese texts words indicating constant acts were sometimes preceded by terms expressing desire or ability—e.g., man "desires to eat," a tree "can grow leaves." Use of a term like "desire" was largely a way of indicating potentiality or behavioral tendency, of showing that if the individual in question were unimpeded he would repeatedly perform the action or type of action. In effect, it was a way of indicating that the constancy existed even when not being exercised. An early example of such a constant is the remark in the *Analects* that "Riches and honors are what men desire."[53] Therefore, in a secondary sense, I will use "constancy" to mean the potentiality for repeated action, action that will emerge if conditions permit. Moreover, constants are by definition "natural" behavior.

The early Confucians seem to have used two criteria in characterizing the activities of men as natural (i.e., as "constancies"). The chief criterion was the "joy" or "ease" that a person felt in performing the action.[54] For example, Mencius says that "reason and propriety delight our minds just as the meat of grass- and grain-fed animals delights our mouths."[55] Men naturally delight in eating certain foods, and in the same manner they delight in performing certain natural and virtuous actions; the ability to do these things "with unwearied joy" is man's Heavenly endowment.[56] Thus the ideal virtue of humanheartedness ([b]*jen*) is "man's tranquil abode."[57]

"Ease" or "delight" as a criterion for discovering which behavior is constant or natural has its roots in the earliest Confucian work.

In the *Analects* we are told that the heart finds delight and ease in, among other things, moral acts. The heart can find "delight" in following the true path,[58] a joy not affected by adverse circumstances.[59] It is also pleasant to learn by continuous study and effort. Such virtuous activities are natural, hence effortless, and so the superior man "rests in" them;[60] for example, he would not feel at ease in observing anything less than the customary three-year mourning period.[61]

Another way of identifying innate behavior is to look at a child. Children, whose natural sentiments have not been warped by the environment, demonstrate the innateness of [b]*jen* in their spontaneous responses to their parents and siblings. Thus Mencius said we should "recover the child's mind." In Taoist writings, only the knowledgeless "babe" lives a truly natural life. In Greece, Epicurus justified pleasure as the goal of life on the same basis. Cicero reports him as saying: "Every living creature, the moment it is born, reaches out for pleasure and rejoices in it as the highest good, shrinks from pain as the greatest evil, and, so far as it is able, averts it from itself."[62] The child's responses are spontaneous, and spontaneity is the second characteristic of a "natural" action; it is the operative criterion in the *Mencius* example of an adult who "all of a sudden" sees a child about to fall into a well and immediately experiences alarm and distress.[63]

Thus two criteria—"ease" or "joy" and spontaneity—were used to distinguish the constancies making up *jen-hsing*, or human nature. The next step is to determine exactly what the regularly appearing conduct is, since the evaluating mind will be associated with conduct that is unique to the human species.

Shared Animal Constancies

In the *Mencius* we are told that man's constant behavior of eating certain types of food ("The mouths of all men are like one another"[64]), listening attentively to certain sounds, and looking attentively at certain sights is natural and should be included in the content of the human *hsing*. Hsün Tzu also related certain constancies (hearing, seeing, etc.) to the human *hsing*. In indicating that these activities were constants, he spoke of them as potential; man "can" (*k'o*) do them. So in describing the *hsing* of man one must say he "can see" and "can hear."[65] These natural abilities were found in all men. "Everyone has characteristics in common with others. When hungry he desires to eat; when cold he desires to be warm; when toiling he desires to rest; he wants what is beneficial and hates what is injurious—with these attitudes man is born; he has them without waiting to learn them."[66]

These actions and others like them are characteristic of all living things. To prove that they were human constants Hsün Tzu related them to phenomena permanently present in man, which he called "sentiments" ([b]*ch'ing*). The actual activities were the workings of desires ([b]*yü*), which were defined as "the reactions of the sentiments." Hsün Tzu at times listed six natural sentiments (*t'ien-ch'ing*) that form the *hsing*: love, hatred, joy, anger, sorrow, and pleasure. The list could certainly be extended in accordance with other passages in the work.

The fact that Hsün Tzu spoke of the sentiments as components of the human *hsing* should not lead one to believe that it is a static, covert entity. The sentiments manifest themselves as reactions to things, emerging spontaneously when an object presents itself.[67] The appearance of action was termed "indulging the desires" (as in *ts'ung ch'i yü*)[68] or "indulging the *hsing*" (as in *ts'ung jen-chih-hsing*),[69] and covered a wide range: for example, the purely human act of sacrificing to ancestors was a manifestation of the combined sentiments of devotion and yearning.[70]

But most such acts were not unique to man; an ox or horse also exhibited these kinds of behavioral tendencies—eating, resting, drinking, and so on. There were further aspects of the human *hsing*.

Constancies Unique to Man

Besides taking note of the behavior which man shares with other animals, the early Confucians regarded certain types of social conduct as unique to man. How do we know that this social conduct was considered to be unique to man? One answer is that the term *hsing* denoted, among other things, what is distinctive of the species *qua* species, and that social behavior was said to characterize the human *hsing*. As Tai Chen (A.D. 1723–77) noticed long ago,[71] Mencius, by differentiating between the *hsing* of man and the *hsing* of the dog and the *hsing* of the ox, revealed that *hsing* denotes, among other things, what is unique to a species.[72] Social tendencies were mentioned by Mencius in his discussion of the human *hsing* only because they answered the question, "What is unique about the species man?"

Various early thinkers isolated different types of conduct as distinctive of man. For Mencius, one such activity was giving honor to those older than oneself.[73] Mencius also felt, like the *Analects*, that the exercise of reverence in the support of parents is one attribute of man not found in beasts;[74] another constant was human-heartedness (*ᵇjen*),[75] which in one of its two senses meant the extension to all men of the humane acts seen most clearly in the relationships between family members.* As usual in discussions of *hsing*, these phenomena were described sometimes as overt activities, sometimes as tendencies. They were among the constants characterizing human "life"; but like all constants, their existence was chiefly potential, since, although they were practiced regularly, they were not continually being performed. A constant action distinctive in the life of man, such as "showing honor to the aged," was rooted in a permanent tendency, the "font" (*tuan*)† of reverence and respect.[76] When a man gave honor to another, he could say, "I implement my tendency of reverence" (*hsing wu ching*).[77] I. A. Richards remarks that *ᵇjen* "is more a form of activity or general tendency to act in certain ways than an emotion."[78] Sometimes the term *hsin* ("mind"), when used in connection with the constancies making up *hsing*, also denoted no more than a potentiality for behavior (in this case a tendency to behave respectfully). In the *Mencius*, it is impossible to draw a line between overt social action

* See pp. 28–29 for the other meaning of *jen*.

† The term *tuan* ("font") suggests the sense of "that from which something emerges." Mencius referred to "four fonts" uniquely innate in man as the "minds" (*hsin*) of commiseration, of shame, of respect, and of approving and disapproving.

and covert font, and say that the latter belongs to *hsing* but the former does not. There is an inseparable (though often indistinct) connection between the two, since they are related as tendency and concrete expression of tendency.

[b]*Jen*, more than any other tendency, was viewed as unique to man.[79] In Confucian thought it usually referred to the innate affection for kin manifested in filial conduct and in obedience to parents and elder brothers. It was also considered natural for men to direct this same affection to all people, where it manifested itself in acts of kindness. Since humanheartedness was innate and part of man's *hsing*, there was a close relationship between the conceptions of human nature and the ethics of humanism. According to Confucian thinkers, since all men shared certain attributes, it was right that all should be able to satisfy their common interests. The existence of a common *hsing*, something linking all men as brothers, was grounds for the claim that those who could satisfy their own needs should love all men, i.e. be concerned that all men achieved satisfaction. The innateness of *jen* made the realization of this humanism always theoretically possible. The comparable school in ancient Greece was Epicureanism. A recent writer has said, "It was Epicurus who first extended brotherly love to embrace all mankind and exalted it as the impelling motive for revealing to men the way to happiness."[80] One ancient Epicurean wrote that "the whole earth is just one country, the native land of all, and the whole world is just one household." This love of mankind (*philanthropia*) certainly ran counter to a common Greek feeling of superiority to barbarians, a sentiment especially strong in Athens.[81]

Jen was not the only tendency distinctive of the human species. Hsün Tzu maintained that man, unlike the other animals, could form social organizations.[82] Hsün Tzu also said: "Water and fire have *ch'i* but no life; plants and trees have life but no knowledge; birds and beasts have knowledge but no sense of righteousness; man has *ch'i*, knowledge, and also a sense of righteousness."[83] These two unique traits, forming social organizations and possessing a moral sense (or "sense of righteousness," [b]*i*), are intimately related. Man forms social organizations by establishing social distinctions or social ranks (*fen*), and he implements the social distinctions by means of the specific obligations determined by his moral sense. Even thinkers who differ on as many points as do Mencius and Hsün Tzu agree that man has certain unique traits, and that these traits involve some kind of social behavior. Man is unique because he behaves toward his fellows in certain ways that are not duplicated in the behavior of any other creatures toward members of their own species.

One should not suppose that the meaning of *hsing* was confined to only one of the categories of constancies in man's nature (the animal or the social), an error of many who understand *hsing* only in ethical terms. For example, in the following quotation from Mencius it is clearly not possible to restrict the meaning of *hsing* to man's unique social tendencies:

> Thus, when Heaven is about to confer a great office on any man, it first exercises his mind with suffering, and his sinews and bones with toil. It exposes his body to hunger, and subjects him to extreme poverty. It confounds his undertakings. By all these methods it stimulates his mind, hardens his nature [*hsing*], and supplies his incompetencies.[84]

Mencius is known for stating that "human nature is good," which has tended to hide the complex content of the concept of human nature in his thought; it has caused people to define the human *hsing* in the *Mencius* in terms of one or two factors alone (e.g., humanheartedness). One reason why Mencius held that man's nature is good was his logical confusion of the ideal man with the actual man. In its broad sense the term [b]*jen* ("humanheartedness") indicated what Ts'ai Yuan-p'ei called a "perfect personality embracing all virtues."[85] It referred to a life manifesting the particular virtues of filial piety, wisdom, propriety, courage, and so forth. *Jen* could belong to all men ("Is *jen* a thing remote? I wish to be *jen*, and lo, *jen* is at hand!"[86]), but actually it was an ideal indicating the perfection of man ("The sage and the man of *jen*; how dare I rank myself with them?"[87]). However, in Confucian thought, there was some confusion of ideal man with actual man.

Obviously, the confusion of ideal and actual in the case of *jen* was facilitated by the two senses of [b]*jen*, generalized virtue and kinship affection. *Jen* in the latter sense was believed to be innately present in all actual men (the good and the bad). In the *Analects* is the remark that the man who has *jen* finds his rest in *jen*; the implication is that it is man's natural state, not at all forced. *Jen* in the former sense constitutes a description only of the (ideal) perfectly good man. But the two meanings of *jen* were mixed up, leading to the confusion of the ideal and the actual. When Mencius and the author of the *Doctrine of the Mean* declared, "[b]*Jen* is man,"[88] they were stating that the qualities belonging to the ideal man also belonged to the actual man. This, in turn, led to the remark that those who do not practice the virtues included in *jen* are not men but beasts.[89] The confusion between ideal and actual man is a little like that between the ideal and the actual king in the early Confucian works; *wang* can mean either, and an actual ruler would be denied the title of "king" by a Confucian if he failed to fulfill its ideal attributes.

The possibility of a unique trait in man that distinguishes him from other animals has also been important in Western conceptions of human nature as well. In ancient Greece, for example, the Sophist Protagoras spoke of respect for others and a sense of justice as man's special treasures.[90] Plato in the *Republic* also said that justice is the specific virtue of man, although he used "justice" in quite a different sense. An equally common, but opposing, view was expressed by Callicles in the *Gorgias*: justice is simply a name for the unrestricted right of the strong to take advantage of the weak, and thus it is something that prevails among beasts and men alike. In other dialogues Plato considers intellect to be man's distinct attribute. In the beginning of the modern period of Western philosophy the problem was important once again. A skeptic such as Michel de Montaigne repudiated the idea that human reason is capable of achieving knowledge. He glorified animals, which surpass man in their faculties of sight and hearing and from which we learn arts (weaving and music) and social organization (bees and ants). Man and beast are on a par. Descartes, however, declared that man is unique because he possesses the natural light of reason (and consequently an "awareness" of things) and has a "will."

The Relationship Between Mind and e*Hsing*

The concept of human nature in early Confucian thought included both the behavioral constancies that man shares with other animals (eating, drinking, resting, and so on) and the social tendencies that are unique to man. The next step is to show, by an analysis of the *Mencius* and the *Hsün-tzu*, that the evaluating mind was also linked to the human *hsing*. The major purpose of taking this step is to highlight the early Confucian belief in the natural equality of man. "Human nature" for the Confucians includes the characteristics common to *all* men; and the evaluating mind, which is the most important faculty possessed by men, is one of those characteristics. The precise function of the evaluating mind, as will be shown, is to guide man's innate social tendencies when they take concrete form. That is, the mind discriminates the specific requirements of a given situation and directs the social actions accordingly; furthermore, it controls man's other drives so that the social tendencies may be properly expressed in action.

We will see that there is a remarkable similarity between the conceptions of human nature held by Mencius and Hsün Tzu, two thinkers whose views have hitherto been considered irreconcilable. In addition, the study of mind and *hsing* will throw light on the reason for the eventual addition of the "heart" or "mind" radical to *sheng* to form the character *hsing*.

Mencius

As has been pointed out, the term "mind" (*hsin*) was used very loosely by the early Chinese, and Mencius was no exception. Although *hsin*'s primary application was to the seat of mental acts like evaluating and cognition, it could also refer to other things: to the location of the desires; to "ideas," "intentions," or "feelings"; and to "tendencies" or potential behavior. So it is necessary to distinguish the specific sense of the term when it appears. When Mencius spoke of the four "minds" uniquely innate in man (commiseration, reverence and respect, shame and dislike, and approving and disapproving),[91] he was using the term to refer to two essentially different sets of things. "Mind" in the first two cases denoted potentiality or behavioral tendency, since commiseration and respect both emerge in behavioral forms. Commiseration manifests itself as "humanheartedness" ([b]*jen*) or compassionate activity, such as in governing in a humane manner; respect emerges as "propriety" ([a]*li*). As one of the four "minds," *li* does not refer to the customary rules of proper conduct themselves, but to the *li* in operation, i.e., good form in conduct. From the remarks Mencius made about the font (*tuan*) of *li*, he had in mind modest, yielding, and respectful behavior, especially toward elders. These two tendencies, humanheartedness and respectfulness, are the behavioral constants unique to the human *hsing*.

But the other two "minds" denoted purely *covert* evaluative activity. "Shame and dislike" (the third mind) are associated with [b]*i*, the innate moral sense—that is, the sense of what is proper and improper, together with the feeling of an obligation to act accordingly.* As for the roots of this innate moral sense, "dislike" suggests an innate sense of repugnance at some acts, and "shame" suggests the feelings (considered to be universal) that follow transgressions. Mencius spoke of *i* as man's straight path, meaning that obedience to its judgments keeps a person from abandoning the moral way. The fourth mind, the "sense of right and wrong" (*shih-fei-chih-hsin*), manifests itself as "knowledge" ([b]*chih*).

Obviously, there is a close connection between [b]*chih* (knowledge of right and wrong) and [b]*i* (moral sense). They both involve the evaluating function of the mind—its ability to determine that something is right or wrong, proper or improper. *I*, however, denotes evaluations about events or activities in which the person

* In a number of places Mencius linked the moral sense *i* with obedience or respect for elders (iv.A.27.1, vi.A.5.2, vii.A.15.3). This would seem to contradict his statement that the second of the four minds is that of reverence and respect. But the passages that make the link should be taken as examples of the moral sense in operation. Among other things, *i* dictates what kind of respect is due to a given person in a given instance. Obviously the obligations determined by *i* are much broader in scope than simply right and wrong behavior toward elders. The dictates of *i* were a fixed set of moral rules to which obedience was required, in opposition to conduct guided by considerations of expediency (e.g., "profit" or "utility").

doing the evaluating can be involved; the range of events and activities affected by *chih* is much broader, since many situations can be determined to be "right or wrong" in which the subject cannot possibly be involved (events in other cities, in government, in other lands, and so on). A judgment by the sense of right and wrong that a given course of conduct is right does not necessarily imply "I must act." A judgment by the moral sense (*i*) that "X is right" definitely implies "I must act accordingly."

I and *chih*, the mind's internal evaluating functions, are to be distinguished from *jen* (humanheartedness) and *li* (good form in conduct), which refer to social behavior. However, these two types of activity, the covert evaluative and the overt social, go hand in hand, inasmuch as the evaluations of the mind are necessary to guide the social behavior (commiseration and respectfulness) in specific manifestations. The evaluating mind determines what response is right for a particular situation, and when the behavior actually occurs, humanheartedness and good form are realized. Thus it is that one often finds in the texts phrases combining the terms for the overt social behavior and the covert evaluative sense—*jen-i* and *li-i*, for example. These can be loosely translated as "morality" in the broad sense. "Morality" requires the innate social tendencies to be guided by the discriminations of the evaluating mind.

We can now return more specifically to the question of the connection between mind and the human *hsing* in the *Mencius*. Human nature includes the social tendencies humanheartedness and respectfulness, which are unique to man as a species. These tendencies can be distinguished from the others that man shares with the lower animals because they involve an evaluation of the requirements of a situation, a covert mental (*hsin*) process. A tendency like showing respect to elders, when translated into concrete action, always requires this evaluation; an ordinary biological drive shared with other animals usually does not.* *Hsing* denotes what

* The more highly ritualized the society became, the more various aspects of ordinary biological acts such as eating, drinking, and resting also became subject to judgments of right and wrong. But a difference in the degree to which they were thus subject continued to set them off from the obviously ethical acts involving interpersonal contact.

is unique to the species. The social behavior unique to the human species, which forms an important part of the human *hsing*, is always preceded by a mental evaluation of the specific requirements of the situation made by the moral sense or by the sense of right and wrong. Thus mind is associated with the unique constancies making up the human *hsing*. It sets them off from the common animal constancies, which rarely require the evaluation.

Hsün Tzu

For Hsün Tzu, the starting point for all ethical discussions should be the imbalance between goods available and human desires.[92] Achieving a balance between them through selective desiring by all people is the *sine qua non* of a stable social organization. The balance is made possible by social rank distinctions (*fen*), which formalize selective desiring, the rank distinctions in turn being maintained by the practice of obligations derived from the moral sense (*i*), which man alone has. It will be recalled that Hsün Tzu regarded the activity of forming social organizations as the constant unique to man, a trait closely linked to man's moral sense (something not found in water and fire, plants and trees, or birds and beasts).

If one views this unique trait of forming social organizations as in some way innate, there would seem to be a contradiction with traditional interpretations of Hsün Tzu's conception of *hsing* as qualitatively evil. The traditional interpretations often involve gross oversimplifications of the portrait of *hsing* in the work, generally supported entirely by a few citations from the first part of the chapter "On the Evilness of Human Nature" (*Hsing o p'ien*). The detailed study of the Liu Hsiang text of the *Hsün-tzu* made by Kanaya Osamu has brought forth interesting arguments for viewing at least the first part of that section as composed by later disciples of Hsün Tzu working under the influence of the Han Fei school of legalism.[93] Even in that part the repetition of the statement that the *hsing* is evil is done partly for emphasis in criticizing the *Mencius*. Other facts besides the textual evidence discussed at length by Kanaya should make one extremely wary of attributing great significance to the notion of an evil human nature in any examination of the thought of Hsün Tzu. First, there are no other references to *hsing* as evil in the remainder of the work, which would be unusual if it were such an important idea in the thought of Hsün Tzu. Second, the theme with which Hsün Tzu *is* concerned is quite evident: how to achieve a balance of goods, which are in short supply, and human desires, which are extremely numerous, without demanding asceticism of anyone. Finally, in the rest of the work *hsing* clearly appears not as something evil, but as something undeveloped. A man can be considered "low" (*lou*) or a "lowly person" (*hsiao-jen*),[94] but this does not necessarily mean that it would run counter to his *hsing* to develop into a good man (that is, one who could form or participate in social organizations). Hsün Tzu says: "*Hsing* is the starting point and plain material [*ts'ai-p'o*]; directed action [[a]*wei*] is the refinement and glorification. Without *hsing* there would be nothing to which to attach directed action; without directed action the *hsing* could not become good itself."[95]

Forming social organizations through the sense of individual obligations regarding rank distinctions is unique to the species man. But the undeveloped neutrality of *hsing* in Hsün Tzu would mean that the tendency to act directly in accordance with the dictates of the moral sense is not itself characteristic of *hsing*. One of the key differences between Mencius and Hsün Tzu lies in this fact. Mencius would maintain that certain innate tendencies necessarily lead to the practice of certain moral acts, and that the evaluating mind simply directs these tendencies properly. Hsün Tzu would not hold that the moral acts are *direct* manifestations of innate tendencies; the mind evaluates, but the behavioral drive is not so close to the surface. However, because Hsün Tzu treated the activity of forming social organizations as unique, he definitely believed that certain aspects of *hsing* made it possible. There must be a potentiality in man that emerges indirectly as this activity when one has taken the necessary steps to draw it out; the link between potentiality and activity is indirect, but nonetheless absolute. The unique aspect of *hsing* that permits participation in social groups concerns the function of mind (*hsin*), the nature of the sentiments (*[b]ch'ing*), and the relation between them. With the introduction of "mind" into the picture we come upon the same concept that appeared at this point in the discussion of the *Mencius*: an evaluating mind that can control man's social behavior.

"Mind from birth has the ability to know,"[96] and "the ability to know is present in the *hsing*."[97] The mind can know the norms (*[a]li*) that govern social organizations, and the individual person's mind can know his place in society;[98] hence the mind can know what should be done in any social situation. It is also able to respond to the impression of an external object and know it (*cheng chih*),[99] acting on what the five senses (ears, eyes, nose, mouth, and body) passively record (*wu kuan pu chih*).[100] Hsün Tzu said that the mind "rules" the five senses,[101] and is also "the ruler of the body and wisdom."[102] As the natural ruler (*t'ien-chün*) it chooses, causes, and stops action.* Order and disorder in one's behavior depend on the assent of the mind to a course of action as possible and permissible (*hsin chih so k'o*).[103] The mind can select the sentiment appropriate to a situation and then "move," producing the end-directed action (*[b]wei*) that is to become habitual.[104]

Hsün Tzu accepted the natural sentiments of the *hsing* as innate qualities that could not be eliminated; but he also felt that it was quite natural for them to be regulated in accordance with what the mind knew of the social order and the desired goal in an individual situation.† Hsün Tzu emphasized *[a]li* as the means of regulation: through the *li* control is internalized and made permanent; in our terms, the sentiments are conditioned. This stands in contrast to control through laws or punishments, which merely inhibits actions momentarily.[105] When the *li* are obeyed there is always a

* The necessary role of the mind in correcting what is received by the senses was also recognized by Lucretius in the West. Wang Ch'ung (A.D. 27–c.97) criticized the Mohists for ignoring the mind's function here, and for indiscriminately trusting the sense impressions (see Needham, II, 170).

† Kanaya, "Yokubō no ari kata," p. 173. One finds a similar doctrine in Descartes. A recent commentator has written: "Just as there can be, in Descartes' teaching, no natural passion which does not permit of being rationally regulated, so also is it in the case of the natural beliefs. They vindicate themselves precisely in allowing of this being done." (Smith, pp. 252–53.)

direct relationship between overt behavioral form (*wen-li*) and covert sentiment (*ch'ing-yung*). There is no conflict between natural drive and social action.[106] As is often true in early Chinese thought, the evidence for the naturalness to the *hsing* of regulation by the *li* is psychological, the contentment felt by the mind. Hsün Tzu says, "If I act in such a way because it is prescribed by *li*, this shows that my sentiment is content to abide in *li*."[107]

According to Hsün Tzu, man's unique behavioral constancy, that of forming or participating in social organizations, was based on the three aspects of *hsing* that we have just examined: the mind of man has the innate ability to know what he should do and how to do it; mind innately has the ruling role and can command actions; and it is in accordance with the nature of the sentiments to be regulated with respect to what should be done. However, all three of these traits are in the realm of potentiality; they are only what man *can* do. Hence it is reasonable to say that man's *hsing* is undeveloped, and that he needs teachers and guidance to realize his potential. Only after the "development" of his *hsing* will a person's actual social behavior be guided by the dictates of the mind. The resulting purposive social action is termed [a]*wei*, which Hsün Tzu defines as follows: "By *wei* is meant the direction of one's sentiments as a result of the mind's reflections." Men are born with the equipment to make *wei* possible. But in itself *wei* is not innate; it has to be fostered.*

The portrait of the human *hsing* in the *Hsün-tzu*, in spite of definite individual features, is consistent with that in the *Mencius*. *Hsing* is an innate endowment from Heaven, the same in all men. Generally speaking, it consists of all constancies natural to man (seeing, hearing, eating, resting, retreat from danger, and so forth). In the *Hsün-tzu*, the constancies are expressed in terms of potentiality, indicating the presence of a tendency to act even when the act is not being performed, and the potential activities of all organs, mind, ears, eyes, and the rest are present as abilities or predisposed "sentiments." The human *hsing*, in the thought of Hsün Tzu, also comprehended those constancies that make possible man's unique activity of participating in social organizations

* See the discussion of *wei* on p. 142.

—the mind's innate ability to know what to do (*i*), the mind's assumption of a ruling position, and the innate naturalness to the sentiments of being regulated. None of these points conflicts basically with the view of *hsing* in the *Mencius.* They introduce some new elements, such as the idea of participation in social organizations; they differ chiefly in Hsün Tzu's adopting an approach based more on actual human and social conditions and less on their ideal forms.

Conclusion

Our examination of the term *hsing* in early China has revealed that it referred to the regular behavior of a given thing, especially to actions unique to the species. Thus human nature (*jen-hsing*) included both the constancies shared with other animals and those unique to the human species—the second being manifested in social activities. Only man possessed an evaluating mind, whose functions were to discriminate the requirements of a situation, to direct the innate social tendencies unique to man into concrete manifestation accordingly, and to control the human drives so that those innate social tendencies could reveal themselves. This was the basic concept of *hsing* held by both Mencius and Hsün Tzu, two thinkers whose views on this subject have hitherto been considered almost irreconcilable.

It should be emphasized that my interpretation of *hsing* differs significantly from each of the two currently popular analyses. One of these, heavily influenced by Neo-Confucian thought, considers only the *hsin* or mind component of the character *hsing*, and defines the human *hsing* as "moral mind," a mind having some special metaphysical constitution. As has been shown, *hsing* perpetuates the sense of activity and responsiveness to things that is inherent in the term "life" ([a]*sheng*), from which it evolved.* Thus *hsing*

* Additional evidence to support this view can be seen in references in the *Mencius* to the *hsing* of water and of a mountain (*Mencius* vi.A.2.3 and vi.A.8.1). The former is indicated as "flowing downward," and the latter as growing vegetation. These examples of inanimate things are ignored by people who regard only the *hsin* (mind) element as significant in the graph *hsing.* When *hsing* came to denote, among other things, the attributes unique to a species, the social tendencies could be singled out as the behavior unique to the human species and included in the human *hsing.*

denotes not only mind, but also concrete behavior. The other current interpretation is that of the late Professor Fu Szu-nien, who stressed the *sheng* ("give birth," "to produce" [*ch'u-sheng*]) element in our present character *hsing*. He felt that the character now read as *hsing* in the *Analects*, *Mencius*, and other works was written as *sheng* until the Han, when it was changed to *hsing*; and that if any pre-Han *hsing* character existed, it was merely an alternative form of *sheng*, the "mind" radical being without meaning. Thus his conclusion was: first, that in Chou works *hsing* meant only "born with"; and second, that no additional sense of "mind" was present.[108] However, I have shown that *hsing* had the additional meaning of the specific regular behavior innate to a species. Furthermore, it has been demonstrated that "mind" (the essence of which is the moral sense [b]*i*) was becoming associated with the human *hsing* in the Warring States period. Because discussions of *hsing* usually focused on human nature, it was inevitable that the mind radical would be added to *sheng*. The link of mind to *hsing* was very definitely pre-Han.

There were two reasons for carrying out the analysis with which this chapter has been concerned. First, the preceding study has clarified the particularly Confucian variation on the theme of natural equality, namely, equality based on the fact that all men equally possess an evaluating mind. This was demonstrated through a study of the relationship between mind and the human *hsing*; when we examine the early Taoist conception of man, another basis on which to argue for human equality will be seen. Second, the analysis has served to explicate exactly what that evaluating mind was considered to be.

The major result of the idea of human equality, for Confucians, was that education was regarded as the key to the solution of urgent political and social problems. If men are without innate defects (all possessing the evaluating mind), whether or not they become good or evil depends on the environment in which they live, especially on the educational situation. And the cure for the appearance of human evil is improvement of educational procedures so that the evaluating mind can be developed and allowed to function fully. This reliance on education as a panacea was reinforced by one other factor. By treating the social tendencies as unique and the chief glory of man, the Confucians were concurrently downgrading the animal constancies. When Mencius said that "*Jen* [humanheartedness] is man," he omitted any mention of the animal constancies. The tendency to regard man's social behavior as his essence caused Confucians to overestimate the extent to which man (in effect, social man) is malleable through education. There was a corresponding inclination to disregard the limiting effect of more obvious biological features in his nature.

By adhering to the doctrine of the equally possessed evaluating mind, the early Confucians had the strongest possible argument to support their contention that merit rather than hereditary status should be the criterion for awarding political and economic privilege. In the next chapter it will be seen that they defined merit in terms of the utilization of the evaluating mind; theoretically, the path to privilege was open to all. By contrast, the Taoists derived a rejection of the very idea of privilege from their particular thesis on human equality. In the following chapter we will explore additional reasons why the Confucians could base a doctrine of natural equality on equal possession of the evaluating mind, and why they could still advocate a social hierarchy—even though, as Hsün Tzu said, "The superior man and the mean-minded man may be the same in ability, original nature, knowledge, and capacity."[109]

CHAPTER 4

THE PATH TO PRIVILEGE

THE SOCIAL hierarchy is natural, according to early Confucian writers. Thus we can now see how they used the idea of natural equality: when the idea of equality was combined with the belief in the necessity of social hierarchies, the result was the Confucian notion of an aristocracy of merit. If men equally possess an evaluating mind, then privilege should go to those who use it to guide their innate social tendencies into concrete manifestation. This chapter is concerned primarily with the path to privilege. In other words, it answers the obvious questions: How does one bring the evaluating mind into full operation? How does one achieve the merit that is theoretically open to all, according to the doctrine of natural equality? In the course of the analysis one other point will emerge that is directly relevant to the central theme of natural equality. The Confucians believed that people are naturally attracted to and seek to emulate only those who use their evaluating minds to direct their conduct. These are virtuous models, and social stability depends on their existence. This fact explains why the other attributes that do objectively differ from man to man, such as strength or cleverness, are rejected as insignificant, and hence why a doctrine of natural equality can be based on belief in the evaluating mind as a common possession.

The Sources of Evil

In spite of the natural equality of men—all of whom are equally endowed with the attributes of the human *hsing*—both individual men who flout the natural order of things and the social chaos that they produce make regular appearances. Why? Is it "fate," a divine hand that predestines certain men to lead evil lives and certain societies to crumble into decadence? Not entirely: throughout

Confucian writings we find a belief in what could be called "limited fatalism." According to this view, although certain specific events, qualities, and things are caused by supernatural intervention in human and natural affairs, not all are. The actual number of predetermined events is relatively small. Therefore, man is usually able to use his evaluating mind and to act in accordance with its dictates; and when men in general act this way, there is usually nothing to prevent the formation of a well-ordered society. There is no consistent feeling in Confucian thought that the goals for which men strive are beyond their power to secure. Although Confucius may speak of wealth and poverty as subject to the decrees of Heaven, the *Great Learning* assures us that "virtue is the root, wealth the branches."[1] One's first consideration should be doing what is right; but if one acts virtuously, wealth will come along. However, as we shall see below, doing right was considered to be its own justification, regardless of the consequences.

The term *ming*, which in the past has been translated as "fate," "mandate," "decree," and so on, is most directly relevant to this conception of limited fatalism. In the early part of the West Chou (1111–771 B.C.) *ming* had two basic senses as a verb and a parallel two as a noun. As a verb it meant "to command" or "to give," and as a noun "a command" or "that which is given." The term that later people consistently referred to as *ming* was derived from *ling* ("to command"), and was often written as *ling* on bronzes in the West Chou; indeed the sense of "command" was dominant in it throughout the West Chou.

Heaven intervened in the world through Its commands. For example, Heaven had commanded the Chou to destroy the Shang,[2] to rule the various regions,[3] and to be lenient in punishment.[4] The ruler had an obligation to know what the commands were, and if he neglected or despised them he would reap punishment.[5] Heaven commands (*ming*), and the ruler receives ([b]*shou*) the command. It was possible for men to disobey these commands, though not with impunity. Moreover, some commands could be "retained," or continued in effect, as in the case of the command to rule a certain region (in popular terminology the "mandate"). One did have some control over this retention, since in many cases virtuous conduct was a means of achieving it. Heaven also commanded certain disasters (plagues, destruction of cities) and bounties (a good harvest) for man. Prayers could sometimes affect these events; but it is clear that they were usually considered impossible to avoid or alter after they were commanded, partly because their occurrence was unpredictable by men.

From the time of K'ang Wang (1067–1041 B.C.) *ling* and *ming* had developed the additional sense of "to give."[6] The meanings "to command" and "to give" being close, the one is an easy extension from the other. For example, one can see this meaning in the phrase, "The king commands that you govern the royal domain and gives [*ming*] you a set of jade pendants and horse trappings."[7] The meaning of *ming* in the following sentence from the *Shu ching* (Book of Documents)* is similar: "So Heaven endows [*ming*] with wisdom, it endows with good or bad fortune, it endows with so-and-so many years."[8] *Ming* as a noun came to have the sense (in addition to "a command") of "that which is given" or "the given." Then, by extension, it took on the meaning of "life span," or that which is given by Heaven, as in the phrase "receive this *ming*" (*shou tzu ming*) from Heaven.[9] Generally, when *ming* was used to mean "that which is given," it differed from "a command," which was also received and possessed, in that it was unavoidable, impossible to reject, and beyond man's ordinary control. The only qualification to this would be suggested by the the existence of occasional prayers that one's allotted time be extended.†

In the West Chou then, two types of situation were outside human control; certain specific incidents were beyond human

* The *Shu ching* contains short speeches, warnings, and so forth by kings and ministers from the mythical period into the early Chou. Some parts are late forgeries, some are of the middle and late Chou. Certain sections dating from the early Chou are relatively reliable historically.

† *Ming* with the sense of "endowment" overlapped in meaning somewhat with [e]*hsing*. But the sense of Heavenly bestowal was dominant in *ming*, including the attributes bestowed to an individual thing (such as an individual's life-span). *Ming* did not have the meaning of the nature common to a species, as did *hsing*. However, the meanings of the two terms were close enough for them to be combined in the late Chou to form the compound *hsing-ming* (life). See Chapter 3, Notes 47 and 50.

power to avoid once they had been decreed by Heaven; and certain lasting aspects of the personal endowment from Heaven could not be altered. But the idea of *ming* was not necessarily associated with a belief in predestination, like that current in ancient Greece. In order to apply that term, three conditions would have had to be met: that an event was decreed by Heaven, that its content or occurrence was unpredictable by man, and that the event, *along with others,* had been planned in advance by Heaven (for example, Heaven might decree that one would be orphaned at the age of ten, occupy the throne at fifteen, cope with a rebellion at twenty, and so forth). The first two conditions were met in some cases by the attitude toward *ming* in the early Chou works; but the relative absence of the third condition sets the early Chinese conception off from the Greek view of fate as that which falls to one's lot (*heimarmene*), the inexorable destiny laid down for each individual.[10] In West Chou works the advance planning of a person's life is usually limited to length of life, and the advance planning of one event is hardly "destiny" in the Greek sense.*

The same holds true of the concept of *ming* in the Spring and Autumn period (770–481 B.C.). One does find a new occurrence, i.e., that the length of a life span is predetermined not just for an individual but also for a dynasty. For example, the *Tso chuan* for the year 605 B.C. states that the Chou dynasty was to last for 30 generations (over 700 years), after which the "command" to rule would change to another house.[11] But once again, these are isolated specific events that are predetermined; there is no reference to a continual series of events affecting the lives of the people all being foreseen by Heaven and laid out in advance.† A new consideration appears in discussions of "fatalism" in Chinese thought when one gets to the Ch'in-Han period. The commentaries

* When the *Analects* speaks of wealth and poverty being determined by *ming,* it means only that these things are decreed by Heaven, perhaps spontaneously. There is no reason to infer the advance planning of a person's lot in this case.

† The association of foreknowledge by a god with determinism has very early roots in the West. The Epicureans attacked Plato as a determinist because the demiurge in his *Timaeus* established the order in the universe and was viewed as having foreknowledge of what would occur in it.

to the hexagrams in the Book of Changes* imply that all possible changes that can occur in the universe are antecedently fixed and are encompassed by the 64 hexagrams. If one properly understands the meaning of the hexagrams and knows how to apply them, one can know what will happen. In some passages the implication is that all occurrences are determined by principles beyond human control.

The Classic Confucians of the Chou, however, adhered to the view that only certain specific occurrences were decreed by Heaven and could not be altered by man. These included the human life span, some natural calamities and social disasters, some human abilities, and perhaps the length of a dynasty. Sporadic and unpredictable interventions by Heaven in human affairs might occur: a teacher like Confucius, for instance, could say that Heaven had decreed that his doctrine would not be put into practice at a given time. But generally speaking, there was no predetermined blueprint that prevented a man from following the dictates of his evaluating mind; nor did any antecedent plan prevent action in accordance with the moral sense from aiding the establishment of an ordered society. The imputation of fatalism to the Confucians stems from Mo Tzu, who was strongly opposed to any belief of this kind because of its effect on people: no one will act virtuously if he believes that the rewards of virtuous men have been arbitrarily dictated on high and are not a consequence of their conduct. However, there is no doubt that the Confucians called for human effort—and it could succeed. The master said: "A man can enlarge his Way; but there is no Way that can enlarge man."[12]

Even though all men possess an evaluating mind and innate social constancies, some guide their conduct with these endowments, and others do not. We know now that this variation cannot be explained by "inexorable destiny." instead, the ultimate cause of evil conduct, for the Chinese, is the effect of external objects

* The *Book of Changes*, or *I ching*, contains an original body of divination material dating from the early Chou period plus a number of appendixes written by Confucians (whose ideas are saturated with Taoism) in the early Han dynasty.

on a man's senses. These objects can lead man to abandon his innate characteristics and the behavior unique to his species.

According to Mencius, things ([a]*wu*) have the power to establish contact with the senses and obscure them: "When external things contact the ear or eye, they lead them astray."[13] External things can create a physical disturbance in a person's *ch'i* ("ether or "matter"). The *ch'i*, in turn, influences the will, and the person responds to the external object; in a sense, he is manipulated by the object. By "nourishing the *ch'i*" (*yang ch'i*), however, one can achieve a state where externals are unable to distract one's *ch'i* from obeying the commands of will.[14] In the thought of Hsün Tzu, [a]*wu* are the objects toward which the responses of the sentiments ([b]*ch'ing*) are directed. As in the *Mencius*, things have the power to control a person; if this happens, the person can be called "a servant of things" (*wu-i*).[15] "There is no one who externally prizes things [*wu*] who is not internally burdened with worries,"[16] said Hsün Tzu. "Things lead the mind astray; the mind's uprightness is externally changed, and its internal equilibrium is destroyed."[17] Moreover, things present themselves in multiplicity, and the human mind can only cope with one at a time.[18] One must "make the mind the ruler and carefully control it";[19] then he is "master of things" (*i-wu*), rather than "mastered by things" (*wu-i*).[20] A man who masters things not only regains his self-control but also benefits positively, since things are by nature valuable to man. For this reason, it is said that "the superior man is good at making use of things."[21]

Both Mencius and Hsün Tzu emphasized economic deprivation as a primary external cause of evil conduct. The position of Mencius is easily summed up: "If the people have a constant livelihood they will have a constant mind; without a constant livelihood they will not have a constant mind."[22] Hsün Tzu emphasized the fact that goods are not unlimited. He wanted to avoid exhausting the supply of things, and he wanted to avoid the frustration of any man's desires because of an insufficiency of things; to do this, desires and things had to be balanced. Therefore, Hsün Tzu wanted each man to control himself by observing the rules of proper conduct ([a]*li*) and the dictates of the moral sense([b]*i*), "in order that desires should not be frustrated by a shortage of things, and neither should things be exhausted due to the demand of desires; but these two should support each other and should continue to exist."[23] His entire political theory stems from his recognition of the mutual involvement of things (in short supply) and desires (in surfeit). This—and not the popularly quoted views on the evil nature of man— is the core of Hsün Tzu's thought.

We must conclude that environmental conditions, for the ancient Chinese, were the primary "source of evil." Thus the path to privilege was still open to all, because evil could not be traced to the inherent nature of any man. The social consequence of external interference, which prevents men from guiding their conduct according to the dictates of their evaluating minds, is that selfish interests (*szu*) prevail over the interests of society as a whole.[24] Men try to satisfy their own needs and interests, or those of their families, and care little about the plight of others. In the ordered society the needs and interests of all are satisfied, albeit in different ways.*

Cultivating the Self

In the Confucian view, each man was partly responsible for dealing with the environmental factors that prevented his Heavenly gifts from functioning, and for turning his capabilities into actual practice. This notion goes back to the West Chou idea that man, as an individual, first "makes bright his virtue" (*ming te*) and is then noticed by Heaven, which may appoint him to the throne or entrust him with various political obligations. The conscious attempt to improve oneself was part of the Confucian "cultivation of the self" (*hsiu shen*) or "cultivation of one's nature" (*yang hsing*). It was assumed that human beings could overcome the distractions of "things," through their own efforts and those of their fellows, and could utilize their innate minds to guide conduct. There was no belief in a Fate that inhibited self-cultivation, and only rarely did re-

* Selflessness was a common Taoist and Confucian ideal. See the discussion in Chapter 6 of this work.

liance on gods or spirits take the place of this human effort. Skepticism about the existence or power of spirits emerges in Chinese documents dating from the end of the tenth century B.C. It may be tied to the fact that treaties and oaths guaranteed by spirits were being broken with impunity, or to the fact that some noble families were falling, throwing doubt on the power of the deified ancestors who were supposed to protect them. In any case, the Master himself suggested that people keep spirits at a distance. Hsün Tzu admonished people to pay attention to "human portents"—unweeded fields, broken equipment, and whatever indicated laziness and irresponsibility—instead of looking for supernatural portents.

The Confucians spoke of self-cultivation, but they did not mean that an individual had to rely on his own efforts alone. Both self-help and the instruction of teachers were necessary. Mencius said: "Heaven's plan in the production of mankind is this: that they who are first informed should instruct those who are later in being informed, and they who first apprehend principles should instruct those who are slower to do so."[25] This explains the Confucian belief that man is naturally disposed to improve the condition of his fellows. Thus in the *Doctrine of the Mean* is the passage: "The possessor of sincerity does not merely accomplish the self-completion of himself. With this quality he completes other men and things [*wu*] also. . . . Both of these are virtues belonging to the nature [*hsing*], and this is the way by which a union is effected of the external and internal."[26] A related sentiment was expressed by Hsün Tzu: "How can seeking the way in which things [*wu*] come into existence be as important as concern with how [man can help] them get completed."[27] One "completes" a nonhuman thing by establishing the conditions, when possible, for its natural development (e.g., by weeding and watering plants). There was an obvious parallel between nourishing things physically and helping the natural development of man along moral lines.[28]

Teachers acted as guides and models, but each man had to exert his own effort, consistently emulating the attitude and behavior of the model. The twin requirements of outside help and self-effort differentiate the Confucian from the Taoists and the Legalists.

Taoists maintained that the individual, by himself, could improve his situation: aid from others was powerless to induce changes; if anything, it impeded natural development. The Legalists stated that those who could help themselves were so few that they did not merit a second thought. Han Fei-tzu remarked: "If arrows are to be made only from self-straightened bamboo, there will never be a single bamboo, there will never be a single arrow in a thousand years."[29] Eternal compulsion was required; reward and punishment were the only answers.

Cultivation activates the mind's innate ability to distinguish right from wrong and to discriminate the hierarchy (including the hierarchy of values) that exists in nature. A cultivated man should develop a certain attitude toward what the mind distinguishes, and realize that "right" takes precedence over every other consideration, especially those of personal wealth or honor. With this outlook, the mind that evaluates will also go on to guide the innate social tendencies into concrete manifestation in accordance with its dictates, and to control man's other drives so that this can occur. The *Analects* often expresses this idea:

> The mind of the superior man is conversant with righteousness [[b]*i*]; the mind of the mean man is conversant with gain.[30]

> A gentleman, in his plans, thinks of the Way; he does not think how he is going to make a living . . . . A gentleman's anxieties concern the progress of the Way; he has no anxiety concerning poverty.[31]

> Riches and honors acquired by unrighteousness are to me as a floating cloud.[32]

Confucius was known as the one who "knows it's no use, but keeps on doing it."[33] He "kept on doing it" because his mind had determined that his actions, aimed at improving men and society, were *right.* This attitude or state of mind should be present wheneven one acts in accordance with his evaluating mind. Because so much of human conduct is dictated by the *li,* behavior has a tendency to degenerate into formalism, mere habitual practice of the customary norms. Ideally, a dedication to the right will prevent that from happening.

In saying that the mind should be trained to discriminate right and wrong and the hierarchy revealed in nature, the Confucians were advocating adherence to a fixed, abstract standard; concurrently, they were opposing those who based their teaching on the expediency of material benefit ([b]*li*). The term [b]*li,* which meant both "profit" and "utility," was used by Mo Tzu, for example, primarily in the latter sense. "Utility" was a keystone of Mohist thought, and derived its ultimate sanction from the conviction that Heaven orders the universe so that everything is most beneficial or useful to man (i.e., so that there is no waste). Besides using *li* to justify a doctrine of universal love (on the ground that the practitioner of universal love will receive as he gives), the Mohists used it to oppose many ritualistic practices that would be sanctioned by the Confucian standard of abstract "right." Mencius set the dictates of the moral sense ([b]*i*) in opposition to [b]*li*; but he purposively used *li* in the sense of "personal profit," perhaps because of his opposition to Mohism.[34] (For the Mohists, *li* usually involved a tangible benefit for people in general, and in this sense it was the most important of the three Mohist criteria for determining right and wrong.*) For example, when King Hui consulted Mencius about the *li* of some state policies, he was less concerned with personal profit—as Mencius interpreted him—than with practical measures to protect his kingdom from the state of Ch'in, an expanding neighbor. One concrete political reason helps explain the Confucian opposition to the utility standard. They were looking for a savior of the age, who would permanently unify all of the warring states. Power, they believed, would be illegitimate in the hands of anyone who did this without acting in accordance with what is "right": such a person would not have Heavenly sanction, and thus his power would be impermanent.

The idea that men should cultivate the attitude of preferring "right" to material advantage continued to distinguish Confucianism from other schools of thought, and it subsequently had great

* The other two were: agreement with the general experience of the multitude; and a precedent from the past to indicate that an intended action was possible.

political influence. It furnished the ideological underpinning of a famous governmental institution, the Censorate, whose officers in theory, were allowed to criticize all officials including the emperor, whenever they strayed from the right. In the Han dynasty, the doctrine of righteousness produced arguments against government monopolies: if a ruler sought personal profit rather than doing what was right, every one of his subjects would do the same, and social disharmony would result. The Legalists, however, inherited the Mohist utility standard; defining [b]*li* in the narrow sense of immediate wealth and military strength, they regarded it as the Confucians regarded "right."

The Confucian rejection of material benefit did not coincide with an other-worldly asceticism, as it often has in the West. The man who has cultivated his evaluating mind is able to discriminate the hierarchy found in nature, and this includes a hierarchy of values. In the *Great Learning* it is said that "things have their root and branches," meaning that some things are primary, some are secondary, and some are prerequisites to others. An example already noted is that virtue is the root and wealth the branches, meaning that material benefit will come if one puts considerations of "right" in first place. Plato would have found an echo of his own convictions in this doctrine. He attacked oligarchies as rule by the "acquisitive" (those interested in increased wealth), and he believed that this would lead to great social disunity. He ended the *Apology* with Socrates saying to his judges:

> When my sons grow up, gentlemen, if you think that they are putting money or anything else before goodness, take your revenge by plaguing them as I plagued you; and if they fancy themselves for no reason, you must scold them just as I scolded you, for neglecting the important things and thinking that they are good for something when they are good for nothing. If you do this, I shall have had justice at your hands, both I myself and my children.[35]

However, we have already seen that Plato's ideal seeker of goodness, unlike a Confucian follower of the "right," was supposed to be unmindful of material wealth, even when it came as a gift.

The aim of cultivation, then, was to stimulate the mind's innate ability to distinguish right and wrong, and to develop the attitude of putting what is right before all other considerations. We must now examine the kinds of cultivation that the Confucians advocated in order to achieve this development.

Inner Cultivation

The actual process of cultivation had two sides, which can be identified as "inner" (*nei*) and "outer" (*wai*), respectively. The former was introspective self-examination, termed *nei sheng* ("to look within"). The latter was emulation of the attitude and behavior of models, i.e., individual persons who had already cultivated themselves successfully. The Chinese idea of introspection is relatively easy to understand; the process of emulation is more complex.

In Confucian thought introspective examination had three purposes First, it caused the individual to refrain from self-deception and to achieve "integrity of thought" (*ch'eng i*), which helped prevent people from deluding themselves into thinking that they possessed no faults. "In the presence of a bad man, turn your gaze within!" said Confucius.[36] Introspection made a person aware of the possible contradiction between his external behavior (which might be artificial show) and his real feelings.[37] Mental tranquility was one of the attributes of the good life, and self-examination was a step that preceded it. "When internal examination discovers nothing wrong, what is there to be anxious about, what is there to fear?"[38] The second purpose of self-examination was to help a person understand his real nature, to become aware of his evaluating mind and his innate social tendencies, whose nature may be obscured by environmental factors. This is also known as "knowing one's nature" (*chih hsing*). Third, all men are equal in that they share the same responses to the same situations, such as lack of food or lack of opportunity to fulfill their family obligations; and they respond the same way to certain kinds of treatment by others, such as deceit, consideration, honesty, and so on. In order to know how to treat other people, then, a person must look within and try to understand how he would feel in a similar situation. He can generalize from his own reactions to those of others and act accordingly. Thus internal examination lies at the base of "reciprocity" ([a]*shu*).

The Emulation of Models

The "outer" aspects of cultivation is the imitation of models with the desired attributes—namely, a functioning evaluating mind, a constant attitude that "right" takes precedence over all other considerations, and a regular practice of certain types of social behavior commanded by the mind. The key to virtue lies in developing the constant attitude that "right" takes precedence, since this provides the link between making evaluations and actually guiding behavior in accordance with their dictates. The models to be emulated are sometimes exemplary men from the past—deceased ancestors, or sages whose exploits are recorded in writing. "Those who are learning take the Sage-King as model," says the *Hsün-tzu.*[39] Cultivation requires the study (*hsüeh*) of works describing their deeds. Sometimes the model is a living person, such as a teacher, father, official, or ruler. The Master remarked, "When one sees a worthy, one should think of equaling him."[40]

The Chinese theory of learning assumes that people are innately capable of learning from models. This learning can occur unintentionally, through the unconscious imitation of those around one; thus it is important to choose one's neighbors well. Or it can occur intentionally, through the purposive attempt to duplicate the attitude and conduct of a teacher, scholar-official, or ancestor. Although the behavior of a negative model (such as an evil neighbor) may "rub off" on the individual, most people are definitely attracted to and consciously seek to emulate virtuous models.

For the Confucians, model emulation was not just one way of learning: it was by far the most efficient way, and one could inculate any virtuous behavior in people by presenting the right model. This assumption lies behind much of the political writing in early China, which often describes the responsibility of the cultivated person to serve as a model for others to emulate, and praises the efficacy of virtuous models in changing the behavior of large numbers of people. In other words, disorder will not last long when models of moral excellence are around. According to the *Analects*, if the person in power leads the people with rectitude, no one will dare to be/act otherwise. Confucius said, "When those who are in high stations perform well all their duties to their relations, the people are aroused to virtue."[41] *The Great Learning* states: "When the ruler, as a father, a son, and a brother, is a model, then the people imitate him. This is what is meant by saying, 'The government of his kingdom depends on his regulation of the family.' "[42] And throughout China's history models were presented to the people for emulation, from the exalted men of the past, such as Kuan Yü (model of loyalty) and Shun (model of filial piety), to living and nearby models.

Previous scholarly discussions of the early Chinese argument over the best principles of social control have stressed the dispute between the respective proponents of [a]*li* (rites) and [d]*hsing* (penal law). This does not go far enough. *Li* and *hsing* both refer to the prescriptions for action. The *li* were customary norms, which were generally inexplicit and thus allowed for a certain flexibility in application; they were perpetuated by those associated with the ruling families, and covered a very wide range of interpersonal behavior, religious activity, and ordinary taboos. The *hsing* were explicit (inscribed at first on bamboo strips and bronze tripods), and they covered a narrower range of conduct. Although many members of the upper strata felt that the penal laws should apply only to the commoners, some officials sought to eliminate aristocratic privilege by having them apply equally to all people. The major issue in the dispute between *li* and *hsing*, however, has been overlooked: How does one induce compliance with the body of prescriptions one wishes to enforce? Should a ruler control the people through fear of punishment for transgressing a penal law, or should he urge them to develop the right habits through the emulation of models who embody the *li* in their own behavior?

The final element in the model theory is the belief that the object of man's behavior should not be to acquire wealth, but to be a model man, namely, one whose innate evaluating mind and social tendencies are operative. "Superior man" (*chün-tzu*) and "sagely man" (*sheng jen*) are the terms for these models: official position is to go to them, and they are expected to serve as examples for others. In concrete terms, this meant that Confucians acted as though respected position was the legitimate and natural aspiration of men, even though honor was, to Confucius, no more important than "a floating cloud."* But men in these positions were respected because they were treated as models for emulation; and ideally, this chance to influence others, not material advantage, was the goal of a man who sought official position. At a later time, those who actually were unmindful of personal gain while holding high office came to be known as "pure officials" (*ch'ing-kuan*).

As one might expect, model emulation was not an exclusively Confucian principle. The Mohist idea of "identification with the superior" was a technique for insuring absolute obedience from the lowest citizen up to the ruler himself, who "identified" with Heaven. The superior was the model for the subordinate, and the will of the subordinate should always agree with that of the superior. In Taoist thought, the sage takes Tao as his model, and the people model themselves on the sage. In each case, the non-striving, or *wu wei,* of the model is imitated. But the theory and practice of model emulation were developed more fully in Confucian thought than in that of any other school. As a result, there was a continual output of literary works that set forth the lives of worthy models for the edification of the young, and various examples of chastity, loyalty, and filial piety were revered almost to the point of deification.

Model emulation has been an important part of Confucian moral cultivation since the time of the Master himself. Even Mencius advocated it, in spite of the fact that his doctrines emphasized the introspective side of self-cultivation more than those of some other Confucians. He has always been associated in Chinese minds with an awareness of the importance of picking one's neighbors well, lest the wrong examples be imitated.[43] But the idea of model emu-

* Because man's aspiration was for respect, humiliation or disrespect was the punishment most to be feared, in some cases more than death itself.

lation is far older than the doctrines of Confucius and Mencius, and by studying its origin we can clarify exactly what this "outer" aspect of the cultivation process involved.

Emulating Virtue

In West Chou bronze inscriptions two terms meant "to emulate": [d]*hsing* and *shuai*.* These appear most frequently in conjunction with the term [a]*te*, usually translated as "virtue." The statements refer to one person emulating the *te* of another. For example, one inscription reads, "I now earnestly imitate [*hsing*] Wen Wang's political *te*."[44] Another reads, "I do not dare not to emulate [*shuai*] the *te* reverently held by my refined ancestors and august father."[45] Because the idea of model emulation often centered around the concept of *te*, we can best clarify the "outer" phase of the cultivation process by analyzing the meaning of *te* and the process involved in the emulation of a person's *te*. Model emulation in early China was not restricted to trying to match the model's *te*; but since *te* played a consistently major role in this connection, it can be selected for a case study.

The term [a]*te* does not appear in any inscriptions from the Shang. Its first known appearance on an artifact is on a West Chou bronze from the time of Ch'eng Wang (reigned 1104–1067 B.C.).[46] It appears frequently in some chapters of the *Shu ching* that date from the early West Chou. Nonetheless one can not say conclusively that it did not exist earlier, especially since it is already a fairly complex concept with a wide range of meanings when it does appear. Moreover, there is considerable time between its first appearance in the West Chou and the dates of most extant late Shang inscriptions. At the least, *te* may have had an antecedent in the Shang (see Appendix).

* Other terms used in classical texts to mean "to emulate" were *fa* and *fa hsiao*. Today the Chinese prefer the expression *kuan mo*. Whereas in traditional China models were identified as *sheng-hsien* (sages), *chün-tzu* (superior man), and so forth, today a specific term is often used to denote a "model": *tien hsing*. This term also means "typical" in the sense of the "typical character" that socialist realism requires writers to depict. There are also other more descriptive terms in current use, such as "advanced producer" (*hsien-chin sheng-ch'an che*).

In the West Chou a general term for the norms that governed ideal conduct was [a]*i*.[47] *Te* can be defined as a consistent attitude toward the norms, which displays itself in regularly appearing action in accordance with or in opposition to them (see Appendix). When the term is used, the reader should sometimes understand "attitude toward the norms," and sometimes "regularly appearing conduct"; but the idea of conduct (into which the attitude is translated) is necessarily bound up with its meaning. A further distinction is also necessary. Sometimes the term *te* in itself refers to an attitude and regular behavior definitely in accordance with the norms (i.e., to a "virtuous" disposition and conduct). *Te* in this sense can be called "ideal *te*"; an example would be the phrase "keep near to those who have virtue [*te*]."[48] Ideal *te* can itself be viewed as a standard, as conduct that accords with the Heavenly norms [a]*i*. In Confucian texts these Heavenly norms are subsumed under the *li* (rites). When the norms are embodied in the actions of an ancestor or any other person, that person's actions themselves serve as a norm against which good and evil can be measured. There was frequent use of the expressions "to make *te* the standard" (*ching te*) and "the standard of *te*" (*te ching*);[49] and an ode from the late West Chou says that the people observe the norms "because they love that beautiful virtue [*te*]."[50]

At other times the term *te* by itself carries no connotation of being a standard. It simply means an unspecified consistent attitude toward the norms, as displayed by conduct, and it is used in the neutral sense of "disposition." This is the usage in the phrases "could not change his *te*"[51] and "If the *te* is deflected and disorderly, the people will desert."[52] Critical modifiers like "bright" (*ming*), "excellent" ([b]*yüan*), and "evil" (*hsiung*) may reveal whether *te* is in accord with or in opposition to the norms. A further extension from the idea of "disposition" occurred in the late Chou, when *te* began to mean simply "regular activity," any connection with Heavenly norms having dropped out. A late passage in the *Chuang-tzu* states, "Weaving and clothing themselves, ploughing and eating, are the people's common *te*."[53]

Some people in the Chou period seem to have held a vague belief that an attitude toward the norms could be inherited. Occasionally a person's *te* is said to derive from his ancestors. In a passage in the *Kuo-yü* (Sayings of the States) discussing the effect of differing clans on fortuitous marriages there is the statement, "If they are of different clans, then their *te* is different."[54] Bronze inscriptions from the Warring States period refer to "inheriting the *te* of my father"[55] or "receiving perfect *te*" from an ancestor.[56] The social behavior denoted by *te* was believed to "run in a family," in the sense that members of some clans ([a]*hsing*) demonstrated political sagacity, having received it from their ancestors, while others were violent or unwise in their deeds. In some other cases the ultimate source of *te* was Heaven itself, which caused some men to behave in accordance with the Heavenly norms ("The Master said, 'Heaven produced the *te* in me!' ")[57] and others to oppose the norms (e.g., "Heaven . . . gave them a reckless disposition [*te*], but you raise them and give them power").[58] However, this belief in the innateness of *te* was never consistently held by the early Chinese. There are constant references to the obligation individuals felt to imitate the *te* of their ancestors, which would be unnecessary if it were innate. Also, people are continually exhorted to "change their *te*" or to "make *te* their standard."

I have said that *te* denoted an attitude toward the Heavenly norms that emerges as behavior.* One indication that it included the sense of actual conduct is the use of specific and purely behavioral modifiers to describe it. West Chou bronzes have inscriptions with the expression "political te" (*cheng te,* the political deeds of the ruler);[59] and the *Shu ching* has the phrase, "*te* of one drunk with wine."[60] In addition there are numerous phrases in the *Shu ching* in which only rendering *te* as "conduct" or "tendency" makes good sense. ("In both small and great *te*'s you, child, should be one-minded."[61] "It is not that I, the One Man, have disorderly *te*."[62])

The examples just cited date from the early West Chou, but passages from later texts prove that throughout the Chou period

* Although *te* also implied a consistent mental attitude toward the Heavenly norms, it never referred exclusively to a covert entity such as a "mind." There are examples in bronze inscriptions and in the *Shu ching* where *hsin* (mind) and *te* exist in the same sentence and are clearly differentiated (see Vessel 10; also Karlgren, *Documents*, K'ang kao 14, p. 42).

te continued to refer to a consistent attitude displaying itself in regular conduct—at least in Confucian writings. There are numerous standard expressions that clearly denote conduct, such as "*te* conduct" (*te hsing*), "practice *te*" (*wei te*),[63] and "to be erratic in your *te*" (*erh san ch'i te*).[64] Also, there are more passages where only rendering *te* as "conduct" makes good sense: "Tzu-hsia said, 'when a person does not transgress the boundary line in the great virtues [*te*], he may pass and repass it in the small virtues [*te*].' "[65] Finally, there are actual statements that *te* entails overt action: "When we say that this man has virtue [*te*] we mean that he initiates the various works";[66] "If walking, speaking, looking, and hearing all are blameless, it can be taken as knowing *te*."[67]

The Mana Thesis

From the West Chou on, ideal *te* was one of the major attributes of a model to be emulated. However, Western scholars have failed to understand *te* in terms of model emulation, in part because several distinguished commentators, intoxicated with anthropology, have explained *te* as a *mana*-like inner power that any object can possess. In the words of one writer:

> It is believed by many scholars that the term *te* originated in the mythomagical period of Chinese speculation, when *te* was conceived as a kind of mana-like potency inherent in substances, things, and human beings, a potency which on the one hand made them true to their essence, and on the other, made possible their influencing of other entities.[68]

This interpretation has led many scholars to regard passages describing the reaction by some people to the *te* of another as references to the *mana*'s magical power of attraction. In fact, the passages should be explained in terms of the assumption that people are attracted to and seek to emulate virtuous models, i.e., they imitate the positive attitude of a model toward the Heavenly norms, as well as his behavior, which accords with the norms.*

* *Te* was not the only term denoting the attributes that are to be emulated, although it was one of the most frequently used. Two others were "human-heartedness" (*jen*) and "rectitude" (*cheng*). The early assumption, stated in its most general terms, was that people are especially drawn to the emulation of virtuous models and will imitate the *te, jen, cheng* of the example in question.

Passages in the *Analects* like the following are often quoted to demonstrate that *te* meant a *mana*-like power:

The Master said, Moral force [*te*] never dwells in solitude; it will always bring neighbors.[69]

The Master said, He who rules by moral force [*te*] is like the pole star, which remains in its place while all the lesser stars do homage to it.[70]

The problem with this kind of evidence is that descriptions of "magnetic attraction" are not restricted to *te*; they are abundant in the early texts whenever the topic is the reaction of people to virtue. For example:

The people turn to humanheartedness [*jen*] like water flowing downward and like wild animals dashing off to the wilderness.[71]

If there were one who did not find pleasure in killing men, all the people in the empire would look toward him with outstretched necks. Such being indeed the case, the people would flock to him, as water flows downward with a rush that no one can repress.[72]

There are those who are great men. They rectify themselves and others are rectified.[73]

If the proponents of the "*mana*" thesis were consistent, one would expect them to explain *jen* as another magical force.

According to the early Chinese assumptions about model emulation, two consequences automatically result from the presentation of a virtuous model to people: first, they seek to emulate his virtue; second, their loyalty and affection are focused on him. Neither of these attitudes is caused by any magical magnetic attraction. Instead, the effect of *te* or *jen* on others can be explained in part as a natural response to philanthropic activity and compassion. In the West Chou and later, *te* often referred to conduct that took the concrete form of a bestowal of bounties on the people to insure their well-being.[74] That is to say, one of the forms taken by conduct in accordance with the Heaven-decreed norms was the giving of gifts, showing of leniency and compassion, and so on. Such activities are summed up in the *Shu ching*: "Go, my uncle. Be gentle with the distant ones, . . . be kind to the near ones. Be kind to and tranquilize the small people, do not be in useless repose. Inspect and zealously attend to your city, and thus achieve your illustrious virtue [*te*]."[75]

Te often seems to mean nothing more complex than "showing kindness" in examples from the West Chou, such as:

Your greatly illustrious dead father Wen Wang was able to make bright the virtue [*te*] and to be careful about the punishments.[76]

Wen Wang would have had no virtue [*te*] to send down on the state's people.[77]

Now may the king by means of virtue [*te*] harmonize and gladden and . . . take care of the foolish people, and thus gladden the former kings who received the mandate.[78]

The same meaning carries over into examples from the later Chou:

Even though I have no bounty [*te*] to give you, we will have song and dance.[79]

Three years have we served you [speaking to rats who ate their grain], but you have not been willing to be good [*te*] to us.[80]

Then follow this up by stimulating them, and conferring benefits [*te*] on them.[81]

Although that family has not great virtue [*te*], it dispenses bounties to the people. [Meaning that although their economic resources are not great and what they have to present is not great, they still bestow generously.][82]

On this account the other States cherish its favors [*te*] and dread its punishments.[83]

The sense of a ruler's bestowal of kindness (kindness being one of the concrete forms in which conduct in accordance with the norms manifests itself) increasingly came to dominate the meaning of *te* when the term was used in the East Chou. The result was that *te* seemed to become a political method for controlling the people, often being paired with "legal sanctions" or "punishments" (*[d]hsing*) to form the twin methods of governmental control.[84] In sum, the philanthropic activity (*te*) was believed to arouse a perfectly understandable feeling of gratitude and willing obedience. This is the source of the "magnetic attraction."

Proponents of the *mana* thesis have said that *te*, besides attracting people, also "attracts" good fortune. It is certainly true to say that good fortune comes to the person who has *te* in the ideal sense.

There is no kindness [*te*] that is not requited.[85]

Success bestowed where there is no virtue [*te*] is the prelude to calamity.[86]

The arrival of glory or disgrace necessarily reflects a person's *te*.[87]

But these examples can be explained in ordinary religious terms. The person who acts in accordance with the norms established by Heaven thereby establishes some kind of communion between himself and the deity that secures the grace of the latter. *Te* was "religious" activity in this sense. The following examples demonstrate the role of *te* in eliciting a response from Heaven.

It was not so that frequent offerings made with virtue [*te*] ascended and were perceived by Heaven. . . . Therefore, when Heaven sent down destruction on Yin and had no . . . mercy for Yin, it was due to his excesses.[88]

It is not the millet which has the piercing fragrance; it is bright virtue [*te*].[89]

I tell my former kings that I can follow *te* in order to glorify yon august Heaven.[90]

When a person's *te* accords with the Heavenly norms, Heaven responds to it with benefits; otherwise the response is calamity, as the following inscriptions from West Chou bronzes testify:

In the end, by creating *te* he receives much protection [from Heaven].[91]

August Heaven is very satisfied with their *te*, and patronizes our Chou rulers.[92]

Heaven was awesomely angered and sent down calamities because the ruler's *te* could not be upright.[93]

In the early sections of the *Shu ching* the same conception appears:

Heaven will be eternally satisfied with your *te* and increase your longevity.[94]

May the king . . . by means of virtue [*te*] pray for Heaven's eternal mandate.[95]

Formerly the Lord-on-High repeatedly observed Wen Wang's *te*, and so it sent down the great mandate to his person.[96]

Heaven did not give him [king Chieh of Hsia] favor, because he did not make bright his virtue [*te*].[97]

The benefit most frequently mentioned as Heaven's reward was the rulership of a realm and its people by mandate, and calamity frequently "sent down by Heaven" was the ruin of a ruler's cities by his rebellious subjects. Hence, although *te* evoked a response from the deity, the visible response was often one by men. However, the people's reaction to *te* could be taken as Heaven's reaction, since there was a community of interest between Heaven and the people: "Oh, Heaven also had pity on the people of the four quarters. . . . May the king now urgently pay careful attention to his *te*."[98] The belief that the people in a sense act as agents of Heaven is indicated in the following statement, made at a later time but probably applicable to the beliefs of the early West Chou: "Heaven's hearing and seeing . . . work through our people's hearing and seeing. Heaven's discernment and . . . severity work through our people's discernment and severity. There is . . . correspondence between the upper and the lower worlds."[99]

In later works, following the West Chou, the belief that the deity responds to *te* is still present.

Heaven blesses intelligent virtue [*ming te*]; on that its favor rests.[100]

Heaven blesses those with *te*.[101]

I have heard it said that only those with substantial *te* can receive much good fortune.[102]

I have heard that the Spirits do not accept the persons of men, but that it is virtue [*te*] to which they cleave. . . . Thus if a ruler have not virtue, the people will not be attached to him, and the Spirits will not accept his offerings. What the Spirits will adhere to is a man's virtue. If Chin take Yü, and then cultivate bright virtue, and therewith present fragrant offerings, will the Spirits vomit them out?[103]

This last example makes it quite clear that the practice of *te* was still thought of as religious activity, without which ritualistic offerings were unacceptable to the spirits.

Some have been tempted to seek proof of the magnetic power of [a]*te* in its association with [b]*te,* "getting." But this association came about only gradually, rather late in the Chou. It probably occurred both because [a]*te* implied "to get" (i.e., to get a response of affection and obedience from the object of one's kindness, and to get benefits from Heaven), and because the archaic sounds of the two were identical. However, the two characters for *te* were originally quite distinct, though their sounds were the same. There are bronze inscriptions from the West Chou in which the two are used in the same sentence and are definitely not confused.[104] Moreover the forms of the two characters are distinct; [b]*te* had a distinct form as early as Shang times, when it already had the sense of "to get."* There are numerous passages in the *Lao-tzu* and *Hsün-tzu* in which some commentators feel that the [a]*te* should be replaced by [b]*te,* and the use of the two characters in association is frequent in subsequent materials. These passages, however, do not link [a]*te* with the magnetic "getting" of any special kind of thing. In some examples where the two terms are used in association, the sense is that [a]*te* means to "gain" ([b]*te*) the self—either preserving it from the dangers of over-involvement with externals or keeping it "good." Another example refers to "getting" the loyalty or devotion of the people, while still another speaks of "achieving" proper practices in government.[105]

For a number of reasons, then, one can reject any attempts to explain *te* as a *mana*-like power that refer to its "magnetic attraction." There are other equally convincing reasons for rejecting the interpretation. *Mana* could be possessed by any animate or inanimate thing. However, except for rare references on bronzes to the *te* of ancestors who increase the prosperity of their descendents, and in texts to the *te* of Heaven expressed in its benefits to man, only two applications of the term to nonhumans occur in sources prior to the very late Chou. In both of these cases *te* can be explained as having a meaning extended from its basic sense of a consistent attitude and conduct toward the Heavenly standards.

* The bronzes use 德 for [a]*te* and 得 for [b]*te*; the Shang character for [b]*te* was 㝵 .

One is a case of "bestowal of kindness" by rats,[106] and the other pertains to the "mild, well-behaved" conduct of a horse.[107]

One might argue, however, that *te* is a latent (but *mana*-like) power that only humans can acquire, achieved by observing ritual and avoiding self-indulgence. But this interpretation cannot account for the numerous phrases in which *te* is evil: e.g., "*te* of one drunk with wine," "violent *te*," and "evil *te*." These can be understood only if one defines *te* as a consistent attitude toward the Heavenly standard, which displays itself in regularly occurring conduct in accordance with or in violation of the standard. Some writers have regarded *te* as a kind of "charisma" possessed exclusively by the royal family or by members of the nobility, which they receive from ancestors.[108] This magical charisma has the power of magnetic attraction on the masses. Such an interpretation is refuted by references in the earliest sources to the *te* of the common people.[109]

Finally, on the assumption that a *mana*-like power undergoes changes in potency, it has been inferred for two reasons that *te* is such a power: First, there are examples in which *te* is said to be capable of increase or decrease; second, *te* is supposedly linked in some way with "planting" or "plant growth," both of which are suggestive of "potency." It is true that *te* belongs to the same phonetic series as three words that are connected with planting or growth; but an analysis of all of the relevant terms reveals that "to plant," "to increase," and "to grow" are later extensions from more basic meanings of "straight," "upright," and "to set up." Furthermore, *te* is by no means the only human attribute described in terms of growth. For example, there are passages in which "learning" is described as a growth (ᵉ*chih*).[110] Speaking of "growth" was simply a colorful way of speaking about "improvement," and it had nothing to do with an actual quantitative increase of inner power.

Implications of the Analysis

Descriptions of the process of self-cultivation in early Chinese materials often speak of one person imitating the *te* of another. It is now clear that reference is not being made to some *mana*-like power, but to the emulation of the attitude of the other figure toward the Heaven-decreed norms, and also to emulation of his behavior, which accords with them. In Confucian writings *te* retained this sense; that is why the Master said: "Hold faithfulness and sincerity as first principles, and be moving continually to what is right [[b]*i*]; this is the way to exalt one's virtue [*te*]."[111]

Three factors were involved in the actual process of model emulation: "examination," "purification," and "grasping" of *te*. These aspects of the process can now be isolated, but they were never systematically delineated in the early works. "Examination" involved focusing one's attention on the conduct of a model and comparing this conduct with one's own behavior and attitude toward the norms. The *Shu ching* says: "Grandly take as pattern the active *te* [of the ancients]. Thereby make steady your heart, look at your own *te*, make far reaching your plans and intentions; then you will make the people tranquil, and I will not remove you or cut you off."[112] This first step was followed by a determination to alter one's conduct if necessary. Changing one's previous attitude and conduct was called "purifying *te*" (*che te*).[113] Unswerving persistence in the emulation of the model's *te*, which followed, was called "grasping" (*ping*, [d]*chih*, or *ts'ao*) *te*.

There is no need to explain *te* as a *mana*-like potency, since its power of "magnetic attraction," which is usually cited to support the *mana* thesis, can be explained in other terms. However, the fact that people are attracted to *te* is still enormously important, even when explained in nonmagical terms. Ideal *te* refers to an individual's consistent attitude that "right" (as determined by the Heavenly norms) takes precedence over all other considerations and to the behavior that follows from this attitude. In other words, *te* characterizes a person who is utilizing his evaluating mind. The fact that people are attracted to *te* explains why all other human attributes, which do objectively differentiate some men from others, were considered secondary in importance to the commonly shared evaluating mind, and why these other attributes were not regarded as grounds for speaking of men as naturally unequal. People are only attracted to those who use their evaluating mind to guide their conduct; that is, they are attracted to virtuous models. They are not necessarily drawn to the physically strong, the articulate, or the mechanically clever.

The Argument for Model Emulation

The idea of model emulation was enormously important in early Chinese philosophical debate. It was one of two contending methods of social control, whose relative merits were heatedly discussed. On one side were the Confucians, who emphasized control by the presentation of virtuous models, whose attitudes and behavior would be emulated by the people and made habitual. On the other side were the statesmen who advocated universally applicable penal laws, which controlled people primarily by inducing fear of punishment for transgressions of the law.

As states were consolidating in the Spring and Autumn period, the problems of administrators grew more complex. Increasing agricultural productivity and commerce, movements of peoples, and the growth of urban centers all created situations requiring some standardization of duties and responsibilities among the people. Explicitly formulated penal laws emerged quite naturally in this context. The *Tso chuan* lists three instances of the issuing of penal laws: in 536 and 513 B.C., when they were inscribed on bronze tripods, and in 501 B.C., when they were inscribed on bamboo tablets.[114] This does not, of course, mean that penal codes did not exist previously.

The Confucian opposition to control by penal law can be explained on two levels. From our perspective now, we can explain it in terms of the threat to their own position. Laws could be applied to all people regardless of their status, and this would remove the privileged position of the aristocracy and those associated with their houses. Some of these people may not have objected to penal laws being applied to commoners. However, many in the privileged classes felt that their own behavior was already controlled by the customary rules of conduct ([a]*li*) perpetuated by the noble families; there was no need for them to be subjected to the same rules as the commoners.[115] Needless to say, the Confucians and their predecessors in the *shih* class were often associated with the aristocratic houses. More important, the introduction of penal law could remove the very *raison d'etre* of the Confucians. They regarded themselves as purveyors of the customary norms (*li*): In their teaching roles they taught the *li*, and they served as virtuous models whose own behavior embodied the *li*. They could lose their function in society if a new technique of control was introduced.

On the other hand, the Confucians had their own arguments (which may still be valid) against control by penal law. First, when laws are issued, "the people will . . . not care to honor men of rank. But when there is no distinction of noble and mean, how can a state continue to exist?"[116] In other words, distinctions of noble and mean in human society have a basis in nature; it is essential to maintain the distinctions or there will be social chaos, and universally applied laws would undercut the distinctions. Second, laws cannot cover all possible circumstances. It is better to have men (good officials) decide each case on its own merits, using customary norms as guidelines, than to have impersonal law mechanically implemented, with no consideration of the unique circumstances of each case.[117] Third, and most important, law controls through fear of punishment; it does not change people's attitudes or habits. As a result, the people "come to have a contentious spirit, and make their appeal to the express words of the law, hoping peradventure to be successful in their argument."[118] That is to say, men will do everything they can to get around the wording of the law rather than submit to its spirit. Furthermore, since people's attitudes and habits are not changed, they will disobey the law whenever the policeman is not around.

For these reasons, Confucian thought prefers social control by the presentation of virtuous models. People will emulate them and develop a constant attitude toward the norms, which will insure proper conduct even when the policeman is not around—even when no one is around. The Master said:

> If the people be led by laws, and uniformity sought to be given them by punishments, they will try to avoid the punishment, but have no sense of shame. If they be led by virtue [*te*], and uniformity sought to be given them by the rules of propriety, they will have the sense of shame, and moreover will become good.[119]

And Mencius said:

> When one by force subdues men, they do not submit to him in heart. They submit, because their strength is not adequate to resist. When one subdues men by virtue [*te*], in their hearts' core they are pleased and sincerely submit, as was the case with the seventy disciples in their submission to Confucius.[120]

Force is simply the military counterpart of "punishment." The presentation of models whose *te* can be imitated is considerably more effective: when people develop the right attitude toward the norms and the habit of obeying them, control is internalized rather than being applied from without.

It should be noted that Chou Confucians did not totally reject penal law and "punishments," but sometimes acknowledged their supplementary role as a control technique. By Han times, with a vast empire to govern and a complex governmental machinery to do the job, Confucian officials saw the need to regularize people's duties. Therefore law existed, although it was infused with a Confucian spirit. The *li* were used as a basis for the law, and penal law was used to enforce the *li*. But in the last analysis, the Confucians placed far more confidence in control by model emulation, and it always occupied first place.

Conclusion

The doctrine of natural equality, based on the thesis that all men equally possess an evaluating mind, furnished the Confucians with a strong argument that merit should be the sole criterion for receipt of privilege. It combined with a belief in the necessity of social hierarchies to produce the Confucian notion of the aristocracy of merit; and this is its primary function in Confucian thought. Merit could be defined in terms of using the evaluating mind to express man's innate social tendencies. By cultivation, which involved both introspective self-examination (the "inner" aspect) and model emulation (the "outer" aspect), a man could develop the attitude that "right" always takes precedence over all other considerations; and, since his evaluating mind would be able to judge the "rightness" of an action, he would effortlessly do the right thing in every situation, with no passions distracting him from the proper course. Cultivated men select the proper course of action as naturally as "we hate a bad smell and love what is beautiful."[121] To the Confucians, these men have the qualifications for receipt of political privilege and economic advantage.

Of course, the path to the actual privilege had its romantic and its more realistic descriptions. Romantic writers visualized the people themselves — acting as agents of Heaven — as elevating worthy men to high positions, including the highest, or they had faith that the existing ruler would notice these men and reward them with rank. Less visionary Confucians doubtless put more stock in the expectation that a virtuous local reputation would eventually cause observant officials to recommend worthy individuals to candidacy for a suitable position. From the Han period on, there were attempts to institutionalize this recruitment on a regular basis as the needs of the civil service grew.

In Confucian writings, terms often used in discussions of the merit qualifications were "[b]*hsien*" and "*hsien ts'ai*." The two were used interchangeably, and they conveyed the idea that candidates should be men of "worth," "excellence," "preeminence." The *chün-tzu* was also a prime example of a person qualified for office. This term originally referred to hereditary noblemen; it may have denoted members of the hereditary aristocracy who had the qualifications to participate in the morning assembly of nobles in the various city-state governments of the early Spring and Autumn period (770–481 B.C.).[122] In the *Book of Songs** it retains almost the sense of "nobleman," "son of a ruler," or "gentleman." In works of the late Spring and Autumn and Warring States periods (480–222 B.C.) one continues to find this sense of social rank. In the *Tso chuan* references are made to *chün-tzu* who are simply governmental officers.[123] We learn that "the *chün-tzu* toils with his mind, the common fellow with his strength."[124]

Beginning with Confucius, however, one can see a change in the meaning of the term. Passages occur in which it refers to a

* A collection of folk songs, dynastic hymns, and religious pieces; some are early Chou, and the latest are from the eighth and seventh centures B.C.

person who is morally preeminent, and this new meaning takes its place alongside examples of the earlier meaning.* The *chün-tzu* in Confucian works was defined not in terms of his rank but in terms of his virtue. As the *Analects* states, "If a superior man [*chün-tzu*] abandon virtue, how can he fulfill the requirements of the name?"[125] Of course, there continued to be some residue of the earlier meaning in the later one. An example is the periodic admonition to the *chün-tzu* to maintain a "grave demeanor," presumably to gain the confidence of underlings. But the important new attribute of the *chün-tzu,* which was stressed in Confucian writings, is guiding his conduct in accordance with the dictates of a moral sense that discriminates right from wrong; he thereby realizes the particular virtues included in the comprehensive "Virtue Itself," [b]*jen* or *ch'eng*. This kind of person was the most qualified to occupy official position, according to Confucian writers, because the people respond to virtue and seek to emulate it; his presence is the antidote to troubled times. "The principle which the superior man [*chün-tzu*] holds is that of personal cultivation, but the kingdom is thereby tranquilized," said Mencius.[126] The point here is that *chün-tzu* referred to superior status. The original criterion for achieving that status was hereditary position; the subsequent Confucian criterion was moral excellence. One can be talented without being virtuous, and such a person is not fit for office.[127] However, the virtuous *chün-tzu* is also talented. Talent can be acquired by training, as can virtue.[128] Thus hereditary privilege is rejected.

Sage-kings (*sheng-wang*) were at the pinnacle of moral excellence, the most perfectly cultivated of men. From earliest times the term "sage" ([e]*sheng*) denoted primarily a personal (non-political) quality, the highest development of individual perfection.[129] "King" ([a]*wang*) gradually changed from meaning "noble" in Shang times to indicating a legitimate sovereign over all the known regions and peoples in the Chou.[130] Hsün Tzu spoke of the difference between them as follows: "The sage fulfills the duties

* This phenomenon is not unusual. In ancient Greece a similar transition occurred in the meaning of the term *kaloi kagathoi* ("the noble and the good").

of the natural relationships; the king fulfills the ideal of government." The early Confucian thinkers viewed the one as a logical extension of the other. "Hence unless he is a sage, he will not be able to rule as lawful king," said Hsün Tzu.[131] Anyone who reached the exalted status of sage should be selected as king. A phrase that first appears in the relatively late "T'ien hsia" chapter of the *Chuang-tzu* has come to symbolize the twin ideals "sage" and "king" for Chinese to this day: "Sage within; king without" (*nei sheng wai wang*). A man's personal goal should be to cultivate himself and become a sage; afterward, being recognized as "king" timber, he will assume the throne and enable all other people in the realm to cultivate themselves as he has done. One cannot be a "king without" unless one is first a "sage within." The sage loves his kin and behaves properly toward them; the king extends that conduct to others. ("Treating my elders as elders should be treated, I extend that conduct to the elders of others.") The sage serves as a model whose *te* is emulated by those near him; the king's *te* is emulated by all the citizens.

For the Confucians, the sage-king was a lofty ideal, whose status was rarely reached. The term was restricted to someone of the stature of the first Chou kings. Ranks more within the grasp of most men were the "superior man" (*chün-tzu*) and the "knight" or "gentleman" (*shih*). All of these Confucian terms for sainthood, although they suggest primarily moral excellence, still retain a sense of high social position. *Chün-tzu*, as mentioned before, was originally a hierarchical term, probably referring to one in the hereditary aristocratic class. The *shih* was originally a low-ranking member of the ruling group. The Confucian aristocracy held its position by merit rather than heredity, but a hierarchy was still present. Therefore, Confucian terms for the ethically advanced also carry a connotation of social rank. This is quite different from what one finds in Taoist thought. The ideal figures of personal cultivation who appear in Taoist writings are the "Heavenly man" (*t'ien-jen*), the "Spiritual man" (*shen-jen*), and the "true man" (*chen-jen*)—terms with no implication of social status.

To sum up, the Confucian path to privilege is one of self-cultivation, which chiefly depends on the emulation of virtuous models. It is open to all men, since all men possess an evaluating mind with the same capabilities. When self-cultivation makes a man morally worthy, he is entitled to a privileged place in the social order, where he can serve as a model for the emulation of others. Strength, cleverness, or noble birth will not qualify him for the same high position, for people are not attracted to these qualities and will not try to emulate them.

The whole Confucian system, however, implicitly recognizes the necessity for a social hierarchy, that is, a social order with varying degrees of privilege. In this chapter we have concerned ourselves with a process of self-cultivation that is directed toward finding oneself a place in the hierarchy. The next two chapters will examine Taoist ideas of human nature, which deny the inevitability of social hierarchy and set very different goals for self-cultivation.

CHAPTER 5

THE TAOIST CONCEPT OF MAN

ANYONE WHO tries to discuss the philosophy of the early Taoists encounters vagueness and uncertainty in most of the sources he must work with. The two great classics of Taoist thought, the *Tao-te ching* and the *Chuang-tzu,* show the work of many hands. The *Tao-te ching* contains material from the Warring States period, but it may not have been put into something even resembling its present form until the Han dynasty. The text also contains various pre-Han proverbs and maxims of uncertain authorship, some in prose, some in poetry. Most of the first part of the *Chuang-tzu* seems to reflect the thought of one man, but large parts of the second and third ("Outer" and "Miscellaneous") sections seem to be later products written by disciples of Chuang Tzu (who probably lived in the fourth century B.C.).[1] Both works are written in a style that ignores clarity. For instance, symbols play an important role: water suggests humility and self-effacement; the wheel indicates the relationship between Tao and phenomenal things; the eye stands for the life of involvement with material goods; and the belly stands for the inner-directed life. Moreover, the texts are replete with paradoxical statements aimed at shocking the reader into an awareness of the truth. We are told, for example, that good fortune depends on bad fortune, and that the person whose strides are longest does not walk the fastest. Confucian writings, in contrast, are generally prosaic, straightforward, and commonsensical.

Taoist writings, like those of the Confucians and others, have no systematic argument from premise to conclusion, which the reader of Western philosophy usually expects. Confucians often argue in one of three ways. They may use a "chain argument," in which the links between the statements are purely rhetorical rather than logical.[2] Another kind of demonstration is the argument from antiquity; for example, it is right for the ruler to turn over the throne to a virtuous individual and pass over his own son because the ancients would have acted in this way. Anyone familiar with the tendency of many people in the European Renaissance to justify an idea by appeal to the early Greeks and Romans knows that this form of argument is not exclusive with the Chinese. Finally, there was demonstration by analogy. In the *Mencius,* Kao Tzu, for example, compared human nature to the willow tree, and morality to a wooden cup fashioned from willow. Just as the wood has no natural tendency to be a cup before the carver goes to work, human nature is simply raw material with no predisposition to morality before educators go to work on it. Some of these same techniques of argument are employed by the Taoists. Chuang Tzu excels at the use of parables, allegories, and anecdotes that suggest an idea rather than explicitly stating it. There is an undercurrent of mysticism in all the Taoist texts, and one consequently finds numerous statements about the ineffability of the Absolute: it is said that no ordinary language can properly describe it.

It is not always clear to whom the Taoist works are addressed. In many passages, especially in the *Tao-te ching,* the message seems directed at rulers, indicating the kind of political attitude that can secure stability on the throne, together with peace and tranquility in the realm. Here, the sage is the ruler. But some of the same passages can also be read as advice to the ordinary citizen about adaptation to a hostile world.

The Taoist writings, then, are not easily susceptible to analysis; but the greatest stumbling block for the scholar is the fact that the two major works differ in their respective treatment of several important topics. One of these is the question of whether or not men should strive for specific ends. Relatively speaking, there are more passages in the *Tao-te ching* that refer approvingly to seeking certain goals than there are in the *Chuang-tzu.* One of these goals is personal survival and the avoidance of a violent death;[3] the other is defeating an enemy.[4] The key philosophical ideas in the *Chuang-tzu* rule out end-directed action, but it would be wrong to infer that the text is everywhere consistent. As I shall show in the next chapter, the consequence of our following the teaching of Chuang Tzu and not making distinctions between opposites like good and bad, life and death, and so on is that we are no longer distressed by situations that appear to other people as catastrophes. Thus tranquility is a goal for Chuang Tzu. There are also some passages in which the work praises the goal of long life.[5] Similarly, some passages in the *Tao-te ching* contradict the assertion that physical survival should be a goal.[6] Even in the *Tao-te ching* passages that idealize "taking over other states," however, the technique advocated is still "passivity." In the general emphasis on "passivity" there is no dispute with the *Chuang-tzu,* and goal-seeking through passivity is certainly different from what people usually have in mind when they speak of striving for something. Furthermore, the concept of *wu wei,* or "non-striving," is important in both works. Thus the difference between the *Tao-te ching* and the *Chuang-tzu* on the question of end-directed action is relative and not absolute.

A second difference between the two works concerns their treatment of the relationship between opposites. In the *Tao-te ching* there is more emphasis on the reversal of opposites:

> "To remain whole, be twisted!"
> To become straight, let yourself be bent.
> To become full, be hollow.
> Be tattered, that you may be renewed.
> Those that have little, may get more.[7]

Lao Tzu stresses not only the change from strength to weakness, but also the reverse.[8] ("Things are often increased by seeking to diminish them and diminished by seeking to increase them."[9]) But he does change the meaning of "strength," and the strength that follows weakness is different from the strength that leads to weakness. The former is desirable; the latter (physical might or military strength) is a humpty-dumpty sham. The former is defined in terms of ability to survive, which is usually, but falsely, attributed to possessors of physical or military might. In the *Chuang-tzu,* on the other hand, we find an emphasis on the identity of opposites. In Tao, life and death, good and bad, strength and weakness, beautiful and ugly are united. But once again the difference between the two Taoist texts is relative. There are a number of passages in the *Tao-te ching* that suggest the identity of opposites.[10]

A third topic on which there are major differences between the two works concerns the coming into being of "things" in the phenomenal world. In the *Tao-te ching* one of the functions of the term "Tao" is to answer the question, "Where did things come from?"—the question that a Christian would answer by saying, "God created everything out of nothing." Tao is the "empty vessel that never needs filling," the "mother," or the "ancestor"—in other words, it "produces" ([a]*sheng*) things. The *Chuang-tzu,* on the other hand, says that there is simply an endless changing of things, one "form" ([b]*hsing*) into another "form," and that Tao is the principle dictating the changes. In the *Chuang-tzu* "transformation" (*hua*) replaces "production" (*sheng*).[11] Chuang Tzu's symbol for Tao is the wheel, or more specifically, the pivot of the wheel. "Things" ([a]*wu*) exist on the rim of the wheel, which constantly changes. For him the pivot and the rim came into existence at the same time, rather than the former producing the latter; there was no actual production of things, as propounded in the *Tao-te ching.* Although there is a reference to the wheel in the *Tao-te ching,* just as there is reference to Tao as creator of things in the *Chuang-tzu,* the respective emphasis of the two works on the nature of things is different.[12] In the *Tao-te ching* they are viewed as products of a source, which must return to that source at death. The only "return" for Chuang Tzu is when a thing abandons one form and changes again, abiding with the cyclical changes of Tao.

The need for caution in discussing any aspect of early Taoist philosophy is now obvious. However, these problems have all too often been used as an excuse for presenting little more than an anecdotal summary of some Taoist ideas; and in spite of them, one can still discuss many ideas meaningfully. True, the Taoist thinkers themselves warn that ordinary language is insufficient to describe either Tao or the spiritual freedom of the person who understands its nature. But this did not stop them from writing at great length on both subjects, and there is nothing to prevent us from examining what they did say. One can still indicate some themes that overlap in the two works; the Han writers who first coined the term "Taoism" and applied it to the thought of both books did so because they saw a good deal of continuity. The *Shih chi* (Records of the Historian) of the Han scholar Ssu-ma Ch'ien states that Chuang Tzu based his major doctrines on the statements of Lao Tzu. The texts are composite, reflecting many hands, and they appeared in the formative period of philosophical thinking. Obviously, there are going to be many inconsistent statements in one and the same text. In the past, scholars have often gone to extreme lengths to reconcile these statements, or they have taken the inconsistencies as another reason for abandoning all but an anecdotal treatment. The best procedure, and one that will be adopted here, is to admit the existence of the inconsistencies and try to indicate the conclusions that follow from them.*

Common Themes and the Discussion of "Man"

Two general themes permeate all early Taoist writings. One of these is the attempt to make people cease treating man as if he were at the center of the universe. Where the Confucians read the human social order into nature, the Taoists tried to read nature into man. Taoist writers stressed the limited range of human knowledge and the incompleteness of human judgments. Men see only part of the truth; yet they affirm right and wrong, true and false as if they could leave their small corner of the cosmos to experience and understand all. There is a mystical quality in the Taoist denial that ordinary human language can convey the truth, and in Taoist insistence that the "light within" can be discovered only when man ceases to use human language and human senses.[13] Often their argument to prove the feebleness of human knowledge turns on the relativity of qualities men assign to objects with their

* In one of the best studies of the *Tao-te ching* to appear in some time D. C. Lau points out the inconsistency between Lao Tzu's doctrine of "submission" and the idea of the reversal of opposites, which is generally attributed to Lao Tzu (Lau, "*Lao Tzu Tao Te ching,*" pp. 26–29). However, his attempt to reconcile this inconsistency by tampering with the theory of the reversal of opposites may be just the kind of attempt at systematization that he decries elsewhere. It is best to accept the inconsistency and explore its implications.

language (e.g., "hot and cold," "heavy and light," "good and bad"). What seems hot to one man is cold to another, and so forth. How can we ever say that one of us is right and the other wrong? Do we not further entrap ourselves in our human condition by trying to make such judgments? There are certainly problems with the Taoist arguments, but they do succeed in bringing people to an awareness that men must take a much broader view of the world about them.

The second general theme in both the *Tao-te ching* and the *Chuang-tzu* is the idea of permanence amid change. Men live in a world of change—the birth and death of human beings, for example. However, undetected by the senses but existing nonetheless, there are things (or one thing) that are permanent and unchanging. The quest by men living in a world of flux for something unchanging characterizes early Greek thought as well. Parmenides (520–440 B.C.) sought to use the mind alone, without the senses, to discover "Being," or the "One," something indestructible, unchanging, immovable, indivisible, and uncreated. Plato, who learned from Parmenides, applied these same characteristics to the eternal Forms in which the many individual things participate. Platonic Forms are unitary, unchanging, and known by the mind alone; phenomenal things are many, changing, and known by the senses. The same thought dominates the fragments left by Heraclitus (530–470 B.C.). He is best known for maintaining that all is in a state of flux as a result of the strife of opposites found in all things: "In the same rivers we step and we do not step; we are and we are not." Heraclitus, too, sought for the eternal amid change, and he found it in the principle of change itself. Change occurs "according to fixed measure," he maintained; and, since "the eyes and ears are bad witnesses," the principle is learned through the mind alone.

In early Taoist thought, Tao is the permanent entity amid change. Although it supposedly cannot be described in words, we do learn that it is a unity, and (as far as the *Tao-te ching* is concerned) that it "existed before Heaven and earth." Tao is present in all things. It is best to treat Tao as the principle of change, for then the paths that things follow in their necessary transformations may be viewed as constant. In Western terms, the laws of change are constant. Moreover, there is no purpose in the universe. Things do not change for some end or goal; they just spontaneously occur in a regular fashion. The task for the sage is to understand Tao, so that he can live properly in a world of change. In other words, intertwined with the theme of permanency amid change are its implications for human life. Men should know the laws of change so as to adapt to them. Look beyond transitory phenomena, seek enlightenment about Tao, and submit to its dictates.

The Taoists lived in troubled times, as did the Confucians, and their instruction for men of the age was, "Submit." Two arguments tell people to "keep to the humble position." First, the laws of change cannot be altered, so one should submit to them. Second, Tao does not act for ends, so one should not contradict it by seeking to realize various goals. This warning is especially directed against those who seek power and glory that do not naturally fall to their lot. Taoism does not advocate a hermit-like withdrawal, however: Lao Tzu said that a person should "take part in the dirt of the world," and Chuang Tzu's ideal sage abides by the customs of his time. But a tranquil adaptation to whatever occurs is necessary.

A knowledge of the principles of change permits a man to live well regardless of the character of his age, and it can also guide political policies, for the ruler or anyone else concerned with government. It will teach the king, for example, that the most enduring government will be the one permitting the greatest freedom. This is not freedom in the sense of allowing individuals to control their own destinies, for this no one can do. It is freedom in the sense of absence of external compulsion or restraint; it is avoiding the establishment of institutions that prevent men from acting spontaneously, in accordance with their natures.

Now we can turn to the early Taoist concept of man, keeping in mind the broad themes just described, which link the *Tao-te ching* and the *Chuang-tzu*. The Taoist idea of human equality, to which we will turn immediately, should be understood in the context of belief in a permanent unitary entity that permeates the many changing phenomena; and the Taoist treatment of "mind" should be understood in the context of the attempt to dehumanize Nature and make men aware of their own limitations. In Chapter 1 we explored the religious and historical factors that lay behind the opposition to hereditary privilege, a sentiment shared by all philosophical schools in early China. We suggested that the doctrine of natural equality arose in part because of its great effectiveness in arguing against hereditary privilege. The Taoist writers accept this kind of equality; but they go much further than their Confucian opponents, and reject in addition the Confucian ideas of merit, natural rank, and social privilege. In other words, they adhere to a doctrine of equality not just among all men at birth but, in a certain sense, among all adults.

Natural Equality

The Taoists based their commitment to natural equality on the doctrine that each thing in the universe embodies an eternal metaphysical principle determining its nature—or, one could say, determining the changes that it will undergo.* With the characteristic logic of the mystics, the Taoists then declared that ultimately there is only one common principle (Tao) in diverse things: "The Universe and I came into existence together, and all things and I are one."[14]

What Lies Within: [a]Te

How is one to describe the eternal element equally present in all men and things, which puts king and beggar, Heaven and earth, or gold and garbage on the same plane? The internal principle in each person links him with Tao; alternatively, it can itself be viewed as Tao. It lasts on after his present human form is changed. The internal Tao can be known only through introspection, and not through any use of the senses or ordinary cognitive faculties; in other words, it is beyond bodily form (*ch'ao hsing*). Every single object—a grain of sand, a tree, a rock, or a man—contains this prin-

* The existence of this principle of change should in no way lead one to read one form of Western determinism into Taoism, i.e., the idea that the blueprint of the changes through which everything will go is worked out in advance.

ciple. The Taoists had several different terms for this principle, each referring to a different aspect of it.

One Taoist term for man's internal constant was [a]*te*. In the Taoist thought that began to flourish in the latter part of the Chou, *te* developed a new meaning that took a position alongside and was influenced by the traditional meaning already described in our discussion of Confucian thought. Indeed, even while using *te* in its new sense, the Taoists condemned *te* in the sense of "kindness," which had been extended from its early meaning. There were two aspects to the new meaning of *te*. First, it referred to the productive and nourishing qualities of Tao, as applied to the things (especially humans) in the world: "Tao gives birth to them [the myriad things], *te* rears them, the species shapes them, the environment completes them."[15] The sagely ruler did the same for the people in his realm: "[He] raises them, but not to control them. This is the mysterious *te*."[16] In both cases the process is impartial (directed to all kinds of beings) and disinterested (there is no aim of creating worshipful followers); it is not purposive activity.

Te also referred to something received by the individual from Tao through the operation of "nourishment," that is, to a life principle:

> When things got that by which they were born, it was called their *te*.[17]
>
> Life is the expression of *te*.[18]

As a life principle, *te* was a hypostatized entity, which allowed a person to come into existence and go on living. In the *Tao-te ching* the relationship between Tao and *te* (as it exists in individual things) is depicted by the analogy between an uncarved block of wood and that same wood cut into pieces.[19] *Te* in this sense is not only the nourishing activity of Tao but also a thing apportioned from Tao to the individual. It then explains everything about the individual himself, i.e., it explains how he is as he is. "*Te* is the dwelling place of Tao. It is through getting it that things live."[20] As each man's Tao, *te* is internal, and can be known only through introspection.[21]

Both aspects of the new meaning of *te* in Taoist thought had sources in earlier senses of the term. The first aspect, that of the productive and nourishing operation of Tao and the sagely ruler toward all things, may have had its source in the earlier meaning of *te* as the bestowal of something by one man to others (concrete action that accords with the Heavenly norms). Although the fundamental idea involved did exist from the earliest time (i.e., that the good ruler acts as a counterpart to Heaven—similar to the Tao of the Taoist school in benefiting the people), *te* was rarely used to refer to the kindnesses Heaven sent down; the term "blessing" (*hsiu*) was used instead. In the rare passages that speak of Heaven's *te*, the word is used with the extended sense of "kindness," extended from the notion of the bestowal of a bounty by a man. The Taoist thinkers, in like manner, may have taken this specifically human activity of *te* and made it primarily applicable to Tao. Tao's "bounty" was conceived of as the fostering of growth, or giving birth ([a]*sheng*): "The grand *te* of the Universe [*t'ien ti*] is giving life."[22] *Te* was originally a human function, however, and it continued to indicate a bestowal by a man to other men—in this case the "nourishing" of the people's lives by a sage who had perfect *te*. In Taoist passages that describe giving birth, rearing, or nourishing as *te*, both Tao and the sage ruler are often used interchangeably as the subject of phrases like these:

> Gives birth to/rears them and nourishes them;
> Gives birth to/rears them but does not make them a possession;
> Transforms them but not to lean on them;
> Raises them but not to control them.
> This is the mysterious *te*.[23]

The other aspect of the new meaning of *te* was the sense of an internal life principle that is received through the productive operation of Tao and links the individual with Tao. This developed from the association of [a]*te* with the word [b]*te*, "to get." We have seen in the previous chapter that [a]*te* had traditionally involved the expectation of "getting" some benefit, which was one reason for the later equation of the two terms. But a more basic sense of *te* was "bestowal," not "that which is received." The switch from "giving" (which was involved in the early sense of the term and was also implied in the sense of "giving life" or "giving nourishment" in the first aspect of the Taoist use of the term) to "that which is got" (the second aspect of the Taoist use of the term) was facilitated by the association of [a]*te* with [b]*te*, "to get." This can be illustrated by such phrases as:

> When things got [[b]*te*] that by which they were born,
> it was called their [a]*te*.[24]

> [a]*Te* is the dwelling place of Tao. It is through
> getting [[b]*te*] it that things live.[25]

Tao gives life (a process termed [a]*te*), and the thing received ([a]*te*) is obtained ([b]*te*) from Tao. This interpretation was facilitated by the two interconnected senses of [a]*sheng*: "to give birth to" (the act of giving) and "life" (that which is received). These two meanings often were not distinguished in the use of the character *sheng*. In the phrase "life (*sheng*) is the expression of *te*,"[26] *sheng* is a noun; but the sense that giving birth to things is the expression of *te* is also implied. Regarding the phrase "the grand *te* of the Universe is giving life," the commentator Ch'eng Hsüan-ying says: "Therefore, giving birth and fostering the myriad things is the expression of abundant *te*." Since giving life is [a]*te* as found in Tao (its bestowal), what man receives ([b]*te*) as his life principle is [a]*te* as well.

Te's new meaning of a life principle received from Tao may also have resulted, in part, from the religious nature of *te* in earlier times. Since at least the early West Chou *te* had been viewed as a source of communion between man and Heaven, and as a source of Heavenly benefits ("Heaven blesses intelligent virtue [*te*]"). In its new meaning among the Taoists, *te* continued to be a link between man and "deity"; but Tao had taken the place of the deity, and the nature of the relationship between the two had changed. *Te* was no longer viewed as simply the necessary precondition for contacting a higher power; instead, it was believed to be the actual vehicle for communion between man and Tao. In the earlier works *te* is said to elicit rewards from the deity, who is pleased because his commands (i.e., the Heavenly norms) are being obeyed. In the

Taoist writings "rewards" come to the person who takes care of his *te,* that is, he who obeys the dictates of his internal life principle.

Ephemeral Differences

In the *Chuang-tzu* the doctrine of the natural equality of all things is conveyed through symbolism. The unchanging aspect of Tao is compared to the center ([b]*shu*) of a wheel. It is hollow, and hence contains only nothingness ([b]*wu*); but its very hollowness allows the wheel to turn on a shaft and thus be effective. The characteristics that differentiate people from each other are "forms" ([b]*hsing*), temporary phenomena that are forever coming into existence and disappearing, one form replacing the next. This activity makes up the rim of the symbolic wheel, the realm of the ephemeral. As it rotates, the wheel has no beginning and no end; the text says, "One can't find a beginning."[27] As for an individual thing on the rim, one can say that birth is its beginning and end, and death its end and beginning. "Life" and "death" are human terms, and are meaningless from the standpoint of eternity.* "Under many diverse forms these things are ever being produced. Round and round, like a wheel, no part of which is more the starting point than any other. This is called the equilibrium of God [*t'ien*]."[28] The fact that every point on the rim of the wheel is equidistant from the center symbolizes the natural equality of things. Things can never leave their place on the wheel, whose turning represents the principle of change.

Taoists do not deny that men possess different characteristics and capabilities at birth, just as different species of things are different ("*yu so jan . . . yu so k'o*").[29] These differences, however, are ephemeral, and natural equality is based on the timeless principle equally possessed by all. In the case of Chuang Tzu, the distinc-

* A circular image of time is also found in early Western thought. The Greek dramatist Hermippus, in his comedy *The Birth of Athena,* describes the year in the following image: "He is round to look at, and he revolves in a circle, containing all things in himself; and as he runs round the whole earth, he brings us men to birth. His name is Eniautos; and being round, he has neither end nor beginning, and will never cease wheeling his body round all day and every day." (Cornford, *Plato's Cosmology*, p. 104.)

tion between the realm of bodily form and that which is "beyond form" is the rationale for denigrating the characteristics that do differentiate some men from others at birth. Obviously, men are not empirically the same as adults either: some obey the *li,* some do not; some are clever, some are not. There are differences between species of things, and between individuals within each species. Chuang Tzu granted the existence of these differences. Many commentators,[30] remarking on his chapter "On Making Things Equal" (*Ch'i wu lun*), have emphasized that he was not interested in considering all things as the same in all respects simply because they were "things"; each individual thing obviously had its own characteristics. However, the distinction between the ephemeral (the realm of bodily form) and the timeless still applied, and those characteristics that differentiated some men from others as adults could also be dismissed as ephemeral.

Why did Chuang Tzu acknowledge individual differences and still formulate a basis for universal equality? The answer probably lies in the fact that the Taoists shared the early ideal of most Chinese—a society in which men see each other as brothers, rather than mutual strangers. Moreover, they had a partly animistic, partly rationalized feeling of closeness to natural objects. The Confucians may have shared one or both of these viewpoints, but they were obsessed with seeing things in hierarchical terms, not only in human society but also in nature, where the model was the superiority of Heaven to earth; in addition they were prone to differentiate things qualitatively (e.g., virtuous and evil). To the Taoists, this concern with qualities that differentiated men led people to forget the principle that ties all men together. They stressed the presence of unifying factors without denying ephemeral differences; by focusing on the eternal principle of change present in all things, they were able to disregard the attributes that a thing possesses momentarily. Men were advised to direct their attention to the unity behind the many, and to avoid thinking about what differentiates any one thing from any other and any one species from any other.

In the *Tao-te ching* it is said that all things were produced by

Tao,[31] and this common source seems to be treated as another argument for overlooking the ways in which they differ.[32] The Taoist sage would never distinguish himself from other animals, but would easily consider himself now as a horse, now as an ox, and so forth.[33] The special qualities men have are temporal, and thus are insignificant. The whole intent is to end thought about man's uniqueness, to drive man from the center of the stage. In the words of Hou Wai-lu, Chuang Tzu "sends man from earth to Heaven, and thus denies even the actuality of man."[34] Chuang Tzu's symbol of this "non-man" is the sage who is also bodily deformed—a hunchback, for example, or a man suffering from tumors and other disfigurements.

An Inconsistency

The bulwark behind the Taoist tenet of natural equality is the assertion that Tao is unitary. Tao, therefore, cannot be less in one thing than in another; *te* is Tao as present in individual things. In one passage (*Chuang-tzu,* Tsa-p'ien) Chuang Tzu was asked where Tao is, and he replied that there is nowhere where it is not. Tao is no less present in the ordure than in the ant, or in the beggar than in the king. But the Taoist belief in natural equality presents an immediate inconsistency: there are statements about quantitative differences in the amount of *te* possessed by different people. Lao Tzu says, "When the sage substantially accumulates *te,* there is nothing he cannot overcome." Of course, this kind of passage refers to adults, so equality at birth is not disputed. But such statements contradict the doctrine that men are always differentiated only by the ephemeral. Further, they could be cited to show the theoretical possibility that *te* could also be different in each person at birth. Perhaps "accumulating *te*" should not be taken in a quantitative sense, but rather as a figurative way of praising those who abide by the dictates of the internal principle of change. It seems best, however, to face this apparent inconsistency with the egalitarian theme, examining its cause and implications.

The inconsistency arose because the Taoists were not able to solve a basic problem: how can a unitary thing be present in many lesser things without losing its unity? Natural equality is demonstrated by the fact that Tao is unitary and cannot be less in one thing than in another. Yet the moment a person starts speaking of Tao as present in the myriad things, it is no longer unitary, but "broken up"—and therefore it is divisible and subject to change. This problem also baffled Western thinkers; in the *Parmenides*, for example, Plato grappled unsuccessfully with the problem of how a unitary Form could be present in many particulars without losing its unity (e.g., how the Form of man could be present in all individual men).* Similarly, the Taoists were unable to prevent the inference that when Tao is present in all particular things, it loses its unity.

There was a long-range consequence of this inconsistency. Textual statements about "accumulating *te*" were used by religious Taoists at a later time to justify their magical pursuit of personal power and immortality, which they substituted for the impersonal immortality gained by identification with Tao. What had been in part a mystical quest degenerated into a crude search for power and eternal life through chemical formulas. But the idea of natural equality based on the unitary nature of Tao lingered on as well, and helped produce the Chinese Buddhist doctrine that all men were equal because they equally possessed the Buddha nature. Ultimate enlightenment revealed the Buddha nature to be unitary. This idea emerged in T'ien T'ai and Ch'an Buddhism, both distinctively Chinese sects.

Nature and the Human Mind

Our earlier discussion of the Confucian concept of man began with the Confucian tendency to read the human social order into nature. This led to the idea that men possess an "evaluating mind,"

* "How are we to conceive that each of them [i.e., each Form], being always one and the same and subject neither to generation nor destruction, nevertheless is, to begin with, most assuredly this single unity and yet subsequently comes to be in the infinite number of things that come into being—an identical unity being thus found simultaneously in unity and in plurality. Is it torn in pieces, or does the whole of it, and this would seem the extreme of impossibility, get apart from itself?" (*Philebus* 15b, in Hamilton and Cairns, p. 1091.)

which can detect nature's ethical signals. The possession and use of the evaluating mind was required in the Confucian doctrine because there could be no adjustment between man and nature if man was unable to grasp the qualities of noble and base or right and wrong, which are part of the nature of things. The Taoists, by contrast, repudiated belief in a natural basis for the social order, and, fully consistent with this position, they assigned the evaluating mind to the ephemeral (and thus nonessential) part of the human endowment. As a result, the Taoists, besides maintaining a doctrine of natural equality of men at birth and rejecting hereditary inequalities, rejected the Confucian categories for differentiating between adults. The ideas of "merit," natural social rank, and political privilege—in short, all the trappings of the aristocracy of merit—also disappeared.

The Taoist rejection of the Confucian natural order and social hierarchy is manifest in the description of Tao itself. "The Tao that can be told," of the *Tao-te ching*, refers to the Confucian set of social norms and virtues. In contrast, Lao Tzu and Chuang Tzu often used the term "Tao" to mean the unitary principle that dictates what changes will occur in the matter (*ch'i*) of which everything is composed.[35] It was most often described as "nothingness" ([b]*wu*): that is, Tao was without sensible qualities, and could not be characterized by such distinctions as good and bad or high and low. The absence of any natural basis for the distinctions that human beings make in their societies was proved by showing that Tao, the principle of natural order, was completely without the attributes "high" and "low." This contradicts the Confucian doctrine that the principle of order in the universe is [a]*li*, since an essential aspect of the *li* is differentiating the noble from the base. Furthermore, statements in the *Tao-te ching* such as "Heaven and Earth are not *jen* [benevolent]"[36] are meant to deny that nature exhibits any ethical qualities, opposing the claim of the *Mencius* that "integrity is the way of Heaven."

The Taoists also attempted to demonstrate the unnaturalness of ethical distinctions by showing that they are assigned by human beings, like all qualities that come in pairs of opposites, and are relative to the particular standard of comparison that a person has in mind. Since Tao is absolute and unitary, there is nothing beyond Tao that it can be compared to; therefore, no attributes can be assigned to it. Qualities like good/bad, noble/base, cold/hot, or wet/dry are completely relative to the point of view of the person who assigns them; they have no basis in nature.[37] As a consequence, these attributes, which are generally regarded as differentiating people, are ephemeral; the principle within, which is present in all, is timeless.

There are problems with Chuang Tzu's account of the relativity of qualities. One is that he made no distinction between qualities properly spoken of as relative (hot/cold, heavy/light, good/bad) and qualities subject to publicly observable confirmation with unvarying results, such as length, speed, and size. Another is that he completely ignored the conditions under which things are observed; even if sometimes the same thing will appear hot to one person and cold to another, heavy to one and light to another, under normal conditions normal people experience things as the same. Still another is that he ignored relationships between perceived objects. A teacup placed on the floor next to a table may look tiny to a man and like Mount T'ai to an ant, but to both the man and the ant the teacup will appear smaller than the table.

From the relativity of qualities (which seem to differentiate individuals) the Taoists inferred the existence of a unity underlying all things. Hui Shih (380–305 B.C.?), the "logician," developed this theme into a curious blend of Taoist and Confucian (or Mohist) ideas. Because of the relativity "Heaven and earth form one body," that is, all things are on an equal plane or are joined in a unity of some kind; and therefore one should love all things. As we shall see, the Taoists considered the behavioral implication of the "equality of things" to be treating all ideas, events, people, and things with toleration and adapting to them.

Dismissing the Evaluating Mind

Because the Taoists denied that there was any natural basis for human ethical norms, they denigrated the aspect of man's endowment that discriminates noble and base or right and wrong. Both the evaluations and the organ that evaluates, they felt, belonged to the ephemeral realm of "form" ([b]*hsing*). Taoist writings do not deny that man possesses an organ able to make discriminations. Men do have a "human mind" (*jen hsin*) which determines the qualities of things and evaluates; the Taoist portrait of it overlaps that of the Confucian's "evaluating mind," and in some passages the two are equivalent. It should be added that the discriminations made by the "human mind," in Taoist thought, are more extensive than right/wrong, good/bad, or noble/base. They also include all judgments involving one of a pair of opposites (e.g., hot or cold, light or heavy, sweet or sour). For example, the human mind says that wine X is sweet and tasty, more so than wine Y; or it says that end X is morally good, more so than end Y. Human "knowledge" is often of this kind, making discriminations and value judgments. The immediate result of these judgments is to elicit a desire for the object evaluated as "better" (e.g., wine X). A person then acts to secure what the mind has determined is good, to secure a private (*ssu*) end. Since the desires of different people are often incompatible, struggle frequently results. There is a natural progression: evaluating, desiring, purposive action ("striving") in order to secure the desired end, and finally struggle with others. Once again, symbols help to convey the message. The ruler who wants to return people to their natural state, in which their activity flows from the Tao within, will focus on the "belly" (standing for an inner-directed, desireless, knowledgeless life) and not on the "eye"[38] (which sees external things and receives their temptations).

In the *Chuang-tzu* we learn that the sage views knowledge of things as an obstacle, and that he does not judge things as right or wrong (*shih fei*).[39] Nor does he utilize his moral sense ([b]*i*). All these activities are associated with man's "prejudiced mind" (*ch'eng hsin*), which knows one fact and views it as the whole truth. "Each person follows his prejudiced mind as if it were his teacher"; hence men are blind to the other facts that must also be accounted for.[40] The knowledge available to the human mind is always partial, and no judgment should ever be made on the basis of it. In judging or knowing, the human mind deals with distinctions and pairs of opposites. In the *Chuang-tzu,* [b]*wu* ("nothing," "nothingness") should often be taken as a verb that denotes the act of denying distinctions and opposition.[41]

Since value judgments are at the root of desire, no external stimulus will be able to provoke desire in the individual who stops making them. To a Confucian thinker like Hsün Tzu, certain desires and the actions that they instigate are natural to man, constituting part of human nature. To the Taoist, these human characteristics belong to the ephemeral part of man's endowment, which should be forgotten. Chuang Tzu says of the man who acts naturally (i.e., in accordance with the eternal aspect of his endowment): "He has man's form but not man's sentiments."[42] The sage pays no attention to the things that his eyes and ears properly respond to and desire.[43]

Human Nature

Since right and wrong, noble and base, have no foundation in Nature, according to the Taoists, the evaluating mind can be dismissed as ephemeral. In addition, the behavioral constancies unique to man, which manifest themselves in social conduct guided by the evaluating mind, are ephemeral. Humane activity (*jen*) forms no part of the essential nature of Taoist man. The Confucians had fixed on the evaluating mind as man's unique possession, and had distinguished men from one another according to their respective use of this mind. What is left when a person "rejects" as unworthy of attention all of these characteristics, which by Taoist standards pertain only to the ephemeral part of his endowment? When a man ceases to evaluate and act on the basis of the evaluations, say the Taoists, when he ceases to concern himself with *jen*, he will discover the Tao within himself.[44] This is the aspect of his innate endowment that is timeless, and the only part he should consider important.

There are several ways of referring to Tao as existing in the individual, but all refer to different aspects of the same phenomenon. *Te,* as we have seen, implies a life principle within, which is necessary for a thing to come into existence, grow, and live. Another expression is "true ruler" (*chen tsai*),[45] which describes the role of the life principle in determining changes in the bodily form.[46] "Constant mind" (*ch'ang hsin*)[47] denotes concurrently that the life principle is the timeless aspect of one's endowment,[48] that it cannot be described in terms of those qualities discriminated by the human mind, and that both these aspects are related to a person's behavior. If we revert to the image of the wheel, constant mind is symbolized as the void hub of the wheel; it suggests that a state of mental emptiness is appropriate for viewing the particular things in the world, which exist on the rim of the wheel and undergo change.

In Confucian thought, the portrait of man emerged in discussions of man's nature (*ᵉhsing*). The character *ᵉhsing,* however, does not appear in the *Lao-tzu* or *Chuang-tzu* Nei-p'ien. In the early Taoist writings it is seen first in the Wai-p'ien and Tsa-p'ien of the *Chuang-tzu*; but there it differs from the concept that appears in the Confucian writings. To the Confucians *hsing* was a loaded term, suggesting something "worthy of attention," because the exercise of man's evaluating mind and the implementation of his innate social behavior—both aspects of *hsing*—secure a link between man and Heaven. Men must concern themselves with *hsing* in order to know how to establish the link. However, it should be remembered that an important element in the Confucian meaning of *hsing* was "that which is unique to the species" (cow, dog, man, etc.). Since man was most often the topic of conversation when the term *hsing* was used, the characteristics that Confucians most often found "worthy of attention" were those unique to the human species: the evaluating mind and the social tendencies. The Taoists, then, because they rejected concern with any factors that differentiated individuals or groups from each other, eliminated the evaluating mind and the social tendencies from that part of the human endowment that was "worthy of attention." According to the Taoists, there were two things wrong with these ephemeral aspects of the endowment, which are so important to the Confucians: first, the Confucians regarded them as unique possessions of man; second, their exercise was supposed to give some men a unique relationship with Heaven, a relationship not shared by other men and things. Therefore, when the disciples of Chuang

Tzu finally did introduce the concept of *hsing*, they gave it a meaning little different from that of the terms *te*, "true ruler," and "constant mind," which had been used in the early *Chuang-tzu* passages to refer to the part of man's endowment that was worthy of attention.

Among other things, [e]*hsing* had indicated behavioral constants in the Confucian texts, and numerous rather anecdotal passages in the *Chuang-tzu* retain this meaning. One learns that the *hsing*, or real nature, of a horse is to eat grass, drink water, and run, whereas the *hsing* of a tree is to stand in one place, grow leaves, and so on.[49] The text says of man: "The people have a constant *hsing*. Weaving and clothing themselves, ploughing and eating, are their common *te*."[50] However, in many of the more philosophical passages [e]*hsing* appears with a basically different meaning, which resembles most closely the "constant mind" of the *Chuang-tzu* Nei-p'ien. "Constant mind" was Tao as it existed in the individual, the principle received at birth that can be discovered only introspectively, after learning to ignore the ephemeral traits (desiring, evaluating, knowing). When the last two sections of the *Chuang-tzu* refer to "reverting to one's *hsing*" and "not abandoning one's *hsing*," they seem to be speaking of something very similar to the constant mind.[51]

The ephemeral human mind, which directs activity according to its evaluations, ceases to function when the Taoist acts in accordance with his timeless *hsing*. For this reason, the Taoists condemned their own times, in which men did not direct attention to the eternal principle within, as they had supposedly done in past golden ages. Instead, they were occupied with the discriminating and evaluating faculties of the ephemeral human mind.

> There is not one tiny creature that moves on earth or flies in air but becomes other than by nature [*hsing*] it should be. So overwhelming is the confusion that desire for knowledge has brought upon the world ever since the time of the Three Dynasties![52]

> Afterwards man rejected *hsing* and pursued mind.[53]

When evaluation ceases, desires for things are no longer elicited—and the Tao within can never be discovered when evaluation and desiring exist.

The five colors confuse the eyes, and the eyes fail to see clearly. The five sounds confuse the ear, and the ear fails to hear accurately. The five scents confuse the nose, and obstruct the sense of smell. The five tastes cloy the palate, and vitiate the sense of taste. Finally, likes and dislikes cloud the understanding, and cause dispersion of the original nature [*hsing*].[54]

From the Three Dynasties down there are no men who have not altered their *hsing* through things.[55]

Thus the writer soundly condemned the man "who buries himself in things, and loses his *hsing* in the mundane."[56] The end-directed activity rejected is not simply activity directed toward securing material objects; it is also moral activity, which is carried out in accordance with the mind's discrimination of right and wrong, and it often includes altruistic acts that bring about the desired goal of social harmony. The *Chuang-tzu* says, "Isn't it human kindness [*jen*] and the dictates of the moral sense [*i*] that alter *hsing*?"[57]

In sum, [e]*hsing* in particular Taoist passages is unlike *hsing* in the Confucian works, and even unlike the same word in other passages of the same Taoist text. The evaluating mind disappears. Also, *hsing* is not a description of actual behavioral constancies that are translated into concrete acts in connection with specific goals determined by the mind; it is inert and not characterized by differentiated responsiveness to external things. *Hsing* is the Tao in the individual. One author has suggested that *hsing* in the *Chuang-tzu* means simply "life" stripped of all qualifications;[58] this would be compatible with the presentation of its evolution given in Chapter 3. However, one should understand by "life" not the normal sense of the word but the principle of life that is Tao itself.

Each of the several terms that denoted the timeless aspect of man's endowment simply suggested a different attribute of it. The term *hsing* carried the sense of "innate endowment" (had from birth), and at times the idea that the eternal principle is embodied in matter: "When body enclosed spirit, each body having a definite principle [of growth and transformation], that was *hsing*."[59] It also seems that *hsing*, in the works of all Chinese philosophical schools, occasionally pointed to something physical.[60]

Conclusion

The idea of natural equality dominates both the Taoist and Confucian concepts of man. According to the Taoists, men are born naturally equal in that all possess a timeless principle within, which is responsible for the changes they undergo in life. This principle alone constitutes man's essential nature; it is Tao existing in the individual. The phenomena that do objectively differentiate some men from others belong to the realm of the ephemeral, and can therefore be dismissed. We have seen that this Taoist egalitarianism has one major inconsistency: because Tao is unitary and consequently cannot be more or less present in some things than in others, the equality of all things is assured; but because Tao *is* present in individual things, it is possible to talk of individual differences between things. The paradox of how the One can be in the many and yet retain its unity had long-range effects on religious Taoism and on Chinese Buddhism.

The conception of man's innate endowment in Taoist thought was very different from the Confucian idea, in spite of a shared belief in natural equality. In contrast to the Confucians, the Taoists rejected the idea that there is any natural basis for the human categories of noble and base and right and wrong. As a result they were not forced to treat the human mind, which "pretends" to read ethical signals in Nature, as part of man's essential endowment. For example, when the Taoists began to talk of the human *hsing* (nature) they referred simply to the eternal principle within.

The repudiation of the idea that the human social order has some basis in nature also led the Taoists beyond a doctrine of innate equality to a denial of any inequalities among men as adults. It enabled them to dispense with the notions of merit, social rank, and privilege—in short, to dispense with the trappings of the Confucian aristocracy of merit discussed in Chapter 4. The next chapter will examine the Taoist alternative to this aristocracy.

CHAPTER 6

THE PATH TO THE MIRROR

IN CHAPTER 1 we explored the religious and political reasons for the universal scholarly opposition to hereditary privilege in early China. Against the background of that sentiment, the idea of natural equality arose because it offered the strongest possible theoretical argument for the elimination of hereditary inequities; and both Confucian and Taoist writers shared it.

However, according to the Confucians, men are unequal when they mature, and should be treated unequally. Self-cultivation leads some people to moral excellence, and the morally preeminent are entitled to special privilege. Unequal receipt of power, reverence, and economic advantage is just, in spite of the natural equality of men. In contrast, the Taoists supported the idea of innate equality but rejected the reasons for the Confucian advocacy of unequal treatment of adults. They did this for three reasons. First, nature is not hierarchical; superior and inferior are human terms, and social ranks are unnatural. Second, the evaluating mind is ephemeral. In Confucian thought merit appears when the evaluating mind is used to guide behavior; but for the Taoists, merit is as ephemeral as the mind. Third, the wealth and office that are considered "privileges" by the Confucians are false gems. Ssu-ma Ch'ien reports that one King Wen sent an emissary to Chuang Tzu with many presents in order to entice him to the court to take a position. Chuang Tzu replied that a cow being led off to sacrifice is richly fed and covered with gorgeous brocades, but that it would give anything to trade places with a humble pig. He dismissed the emissary.* The Taoist who successfully cultivates himself achieves "understanding," not moral preeminence. Rather

* A similar episode is recounted in the "Autumn Floods" chapter of the *Chuang-tzu.*

than receive the special privileges accorded to moral excellence, he acts as a living model of the principle that equal treatment of all must replace unequal treatment for some. He treats the king and beggar the same, is tolerant of all men and ideas, and passively adapts to all situations. From the Confucian position follows the justification of privilege; from the Taoist one, its denial.

This chapter relates to the previous one as the discussion of the "Path to Privilege" did to the analysis of the Confucian concept of man. Both chapters are concerned with self-cultivation, but here we will see how men can learn to cease perpetuating the inequalities between people that are sanctioned by the Confucians. In Taoist thought, egalitarianism is carried to its ultimate extreme: men are equal in the descriptive sense of the term, since the Tao is equally found in all; and being also of equal worth (equality in the evaluative sense), they should be treated impartially. The ideal Taoist sage develops a "mirror-like" mind that permits him to respond to all people and to all goods and situations in the same way. Moreover, the more a person is able to "forget" the evaluating mind (on which the Confucians base their claim of natural equality), the more he will be able to discover the Tao within (on which the Taoists base their claim of natural equality).

Emulating Tao

In the Taoist counterpart of the cultivation process, model emulation is once again paramount. But in this case the model is not necessarily a teacher, ancestor, or sagely ruler. Instead, a person takes Tao (or [a]*te*, which is the Tao in the individual) as the model, and reproduces its qualities in his conduct.* Of course, the Taoists would repudiate anything as goal-oriented as a conscious attempt to remold oneself in the image of Tao, and would say that behavior will "spontaneously accord with Tao" when one discovers the *te* within. In actual fact, however, they do recommend techniques that amount to model emulation—although in their eyes the attributes of Tao that one seeks to imitate are ascribed only metaphori-

* As we learn from statements like those in *Tao-te ching* 28, the Taoist sage will serve as a model for people in the empire once he has cultivated himself.

cally or analogically to Tao, since Tao, being an unnameable unity, cannot be discussed in terms of several different qualities.

Two attributes of Tao imply conduct of a certain kind for man. The first, "non-striving" (*wu wei*), needs some explanation. Today the character *wei* has two pronunciations, one in the fourth tone, meaning "for the sake of," and one in the second tone, meaning "to act." In the classical period both senses were included in the single term *wei*, which meant "to act for the sake of something" or "to act purposively." The fact that *wei* refers to activity under the guidance of mind is stated quite precisely by Hsün Tzu: "By *wei* is meant the direction of one's sentiments as a result of the mind's reflections."[1] Thus the expression *wu wei* refers to the absence of purposive activity. The events that occur in the universe because of Tao are not consciously or purposively done, as could be said of the natural events decreed by an anthropomorphic deity; they simply unfold in accordance with the laws of change. Similarly, there should be no goal-directed conduct by men. Tao impartially "produces" all things, or determines all changes; it has no favorites. Moreover, in producing things Tao does not intend to create obedient servants (it "raises them but not to control them").[2] The man who models himself on Tao should also be disinterested and impartial.

The other attribute of Tao that implies action of a certain kind for man is "emptiness" (*hsü*) or "nothingness" ([b]*wu*). One meaning of these expressions is the absence in nature of "human" qualitative distinctions such as good/bad, beautiful/ugly, and so forth. The implication is that no man should respond to the people, ideas, or events that confront him by making such distinctions. Actually, the two attributes of Tao (emptiness and *wu wei*) are interrelated; and "emptiness" (the absence of evaluations made by an evaluating mind) is a necessary condition for *wu wei* (the absence of end-directed conduct).

The process of emulating the model Tao (or [a]*te*) has two aspects, one negative and the other positive. In the *Tao-te ching* the negative aspect is described as "returning." The person is to approximate in life the "return" to his source that occurs at death; he does this by fostering an "empty mind," which resembles the emptiness of Tao, static and without attributes. He returns from making the kind of qualitative distinctions or evaluations that characterize "human knowledge" to having no knowledge (*wu chih*),[3] from having desires to being without desires (*wu yü*),[4] from having private ends to having no private ends (*wu ssu*),[5] and consequently from contending with his fellows to not opposing them (*pu cheng*).[6] Moreover, the sage does not consciously implement acts for the sake of others, and thus lacks "humanheartedness" ([b]*jen*).[7] To Taoists, man's natural state is a blankness, like the condition of a child, with no end-directed responsiveness to things.[8] The point, then, is to eliminate the chain reaction: evaluating; desiring; purposive action to secure the desired; and finally, struggle with others. In the *Tao-te ching* there seems to be a parallel between the early period in the cosmos and the early period of human society: during the former, there were no individual things ([a]*wu*), but simply the undifferentiated One; during the latter, people were without purposive action to secure individual things and lived a simple life, accepting the conditions in which they found themselves.

Chuang Tzu once again uses the symbol of the wheel to convey his meaning. The hollowness of the pivot symbolizes the ideal attitude of seeing the apparent qualities of individual things as all relative to the particular viewpoint of the observer, having no other reality. A vertical pillar and a horizontal beam are the same from the standpoint of Tao. This attitude is a blankness of mind (Lao Tzu),[9] the counterpart to the hollowness of the pivot (Chuang Tzu). The sage who does develop this attitude is said to "rest in the natural sameness of things [the Heavenly pivot]."[10] In other words, one should stop seeing things in terms of the qualities that differentiate them from one another.

In spite of the theoretical differences between the Confucian and Taoist accounts of cultivation, there is one major point of de facto convergence. The Taoists disavow evaluation followed by purposive activity to secure the desirable; but they are guilty of precisely this process themselves. They treat two conditions that result from the emulation of *te* as desirable ends: tranquility, and a sense of union between self and something beyond the self. Clearly, the Taoist sage's decision to accept things passively may be called purposive activity directed toward these two ends. In the next chapter we will see that the ultimate purpose of self-cultivation for the Confucians was to achieve precisely the same goals. In the *Tao-te ching,* even "non-striving" occasionally seems to have a goal. The book suggests that a refusal to strive for ends is the way to achieve those ends. "Putting one's self in the background" is the key to success, especially in a situation of interstate conflict. The doctrine of the reversal of opposites, one of the laws of change, reinforces this idea, since any presently humble condition is sure to become one of strength. There is an apparent contradiction with the dominant theme of *wu wei* on this point.

The Taoist sage abandons his evaluating mind and no longer guides conduct by its dictates. He is left with the eternal principle within. Is he merely a vegetable? No: he does act in the world, but in a very special way. This is the positive side to the emulation of Tao, and the sage's activity can be described as toleration and accommodation. In order to tolerate all things it is necessary to understand Tao, which governs their changes. When one knows the changes, he understands the temporal nature of particular attributes undergoing change and rids himself of any attachment to them. Knowing all things are subject to the changes, he mystically blends with the changes and he can adapt to any thing or circumstance that presents itself; this is "letting the mind travel with Tao."[11] Chuang Tzu describes the man who achieves this state: "He can cause his mind to be placid and adapt to all things, and he will not lose his reality. He can cause his mind night and day to have no hiatus and change with things. This is to adapt to things and to produce the sense of time in the mind."[12]

Understanding the changes, the Taoist can "accord with the naturalness of things."[13] Whatever happens to him—i.e., whatever change affects him—he regards as determined by Tao, and he accepts it with the same obedience as he did the commands of his parents. This may be difficult when he is faced with the final change, death; but even then, the proper course is clear. "When a parent tells a child to go somewhere, he can do no other than obey. The *yin* and *yang* are no different to a man than his parents. If I should disobey them when they wish me to die, then I would indeed be recalcitrant. What fault is there on their part?"[14] Able to accept death as commanded, the sage will certainly be able to accommodate himself to any point of view, object, or circumstance that comes his way; he will know that he cannot force things to be as he might momentarily like them.

Toleration and accommodation are the responses appropriate to what Chuang Tzu calls the constant mind (as opposed to the "human" evaluating mind). "The perfect man's use of his mind ["constant mind"] is like a mirror. It neither resists nor welcomes anything; it responds to things but does not keep them. Thus he is able to master things and not injure himself."[15] The mirror is a common Taoist symbol for the all-receptive "constant mind" of the sage. Lao Tzu asks the reader whether or not he can "polish" his "mysterious mirror."[16] By doing so the sage retains a real toleration for all men he encounters, no matter what attributes they possess as ephemeral individuals; and he adapts to any environmental circumstance, no matter how distressing it appears. Apparent conformity with custom is no proof of inner partiality to the custom: "The men of old externally conformed but internally did not."[17] This total toleration is closely related to the Taoist refusal to make qualitative statements about things or to think in terms of their differences. Together, the two attitudes suggest what ultimately was meant by the expression "blankness of mind."

In theory, the Taoists distinguished *te* as an embodied "principle" from the physical substance *ch'i*,* which, by the union of its two opposing aspects (*yin* and *yang*) and the addition of form ([b]*hsing*), became the physical individual given birth.

The life of man results from convergence of the vital fluid [*ch'i*].[18]

[After a change occurred in the vast Chaos, producing *ch'i*,] the *ch'i* underwent change and there was form; the form underwent change and there was life.[19]

---

* See Chapter 5, Note 35.

Te determined the changes that affected the formed matter constituting the living thing. However, in spite of theory, the distinction between the principle of change and that which changes was hard to maintain. Sometimes *te* seems to be either confused with or closely linked to *ch'i* in its most refined state, the perfect blend of opposite materials received at birth. This blend was called a "harmony" (*ho*), as in Hsün Tzu's statement, "All things get their harmony in order to be born."[20] The following passages reflect the association of *ho* and *te*:

[The sage] lets his mind range in *te*'s harmony [*ho*].[21]

Te is succeeding in the cultivation of harmony [*ho*].[22]

He [the spiritual man] embraces *te* and nourishes harmony [*ho*] in order to accord with the world.[23]

The term "grand harmony" (*t'ai ho*), which appears frequently in texts from the Han period, refers to the blending of the opposing *ch'is* on a universal scale; the term "grand blend" (*t'ai ch'ung*)[24] found in the *Chuang-tzu Nei p'ien* had a similar meaning.

The qualities of this "harmonized" *ch'i* establish the model for overt behavior. The *Chuang-tzu* says that one should "not listen to external affairs with the mind, but with the *ch'i*."[25] The blend of two opposing *ch'is* is all-admissive of conflicting qualities. "The *ch'i* is empty and awaits things,"[26] says Chuang Tzu. Since the *ch'i* is thus empty and all-encompassing, *te* is similarly described. "Perfect *te* is like a valley,"[27] i.e., empty and all-admissive. Thus the behavior implied for the individual modeling himself on *te* is one of passive accommodation to all circumstances and ideas.

The idea of a "harmony" in the individual that is a counterpart of the harmony in the universe is also important in Platonic philosophy. According to Plato, man's task on earth is to reassert the harmony in his soul (and in the souls of others if he is a statesman), which should parallel the harmony of the universe; in the *Timaeus*, he says:

Now there is but one way of caring for anything, namely, to give it the nourishment and motions proper to it. The motions akin to the divine part in us are the thoughts and revolutions of the universe; these, therefore, every man should follow, and correcting those circuits in the head that were deranged at birth, by learning to know the harmonies and revolutions of the world, he should bring the intelligent part, according to its pristine nature, into the likeness of that which intelligence discerns, and thereby win the fulfillment of the best life set by the gods before mankind both for this present time and for the time to come.[28]

Comparison

In both Confucian and Taoist accounts of model emulation, *te* plays a role. Confucian thinkers would speak of imitating the *te* of a sage or ancestor, meaning his consistent attitude or conduct in accordance with the Heavenly norms. This was the "standard of *te*," which ideally would be embodied in a person's conduct to the extent that his own actions themselves came to serve as a standard. Taoists would also "emulate" *te*, but for them it had a totally different meaning, referring to the Tao in the individual. For the Confucians, the model was a compendium of "do's and don'ts"; for the Taoists it could be characterized only as "emptiness" ("*te* is like a valley"), which avoided any prescriptions for conduct. The Confucian model is external to the individual; the Taoist model can be found within, and the Taoist process of emulation combines the activities of introspection and model emulation.

In Confucian thought, self-cultivation necessarily involved a combination of self-help and the outside help of others. The teacher who served as a model for the person seeking moral improvement was an "outside aid," and cultivation was impossible without him. By contrast, the Taoists believed that men can only suffer from outside aid. Taoist thinkers stress the danger of man's being led away from natural action by external objects: "The five colors confuse the eye; the five sounds dull the ear; the five tastes spoil the palate."[29] In Taoist thought, men and things "recover their *hsing*" naturally when not interfered with.[30] Hence one should not feel the need for action on behalf of others; establishing conditions in which men can be "instructed" is merely interfering with their natures. Similarly, men should not evaluate circumstances with the intention of changing them; this is doomed to failure, for only when the human ego stays out of the picture do "things demonstrate by themselves what they are."[31] Left alone, men, like their fellow impermanent things ([a]*wu*), will undergo natural changes, finally changing so that the appearance they now present will be no more.

Using the language of moralists, one can say that the Taoist sage certainly "helps" other men;[32] but this means that he lets them develop naturally by not interfering with them. It is in the nature of "other people" and all creatures that, if allowed to so develop, they will flock to the person who is responsible for establishing the condition. The Taoist sage understands the changes that all things must go through and the impossibility of influencing those changes, so he lets things develop of themselves. A king, for example, does not govern paternally or demonstrate a purposive kindness (*jen*), which would inhibit the natural development of things.[33] The *Chuang-tzu* says: "Regarding the governing of the enlightened kings their merits covered the empire, but it was as if they did not take it as coming from themselves. Their influence reached to the myriad things, but the people do not rely on them. . . . They made things be joyful of themselves."[34] The human endowment has both ephemeral and eternal aspects, and the eternal principle within demands far more attention than the ephemeral biological tendencies. Since the principle is something internal and not knowable through the bodily senses, its discovery demands no external reference to the objective world. This inner search, which demands concern, causes man to withdraw his attention from other things. It is understandable, then, that the conception of this kind of innate endowment would be paired with a belief that other things actually do not need the attention of the first party in order to develop naturally.

For the Taoist, action modeled on Tao or *te* is natural activity. If Tao and *te* are defined as "emptiness," an attribute that in the emulator becomes "blankness of mind," the constancies that characterize human nature in Confucian thought lose their exclusive status as natural activity. Eating or not eating, drinking or not drinking, acting kindly or cruelly can be equally natural; and the sage can be tranquil in any course. The only unnatural acts are end-directed ones in pursuit or in avoidance of an object deemed desirable or undesirable by the "human mind." The sage "is able to dismiss mere things," says Chuang Tzu, and he even "dismisses his body."[35] A Confucian, who regards certain actions as natural to man and is always concerned about carrying them out, is tied to things; but the Taoist "does not have contact with things,"[36] and hence is unaffected by them.[37] The Taoist's acts do not stem from the tendencies or desires described by Hsün Tzu or Mencius in their discussions of *hsing*, but from "the realm of non-man."[38] True, men in their temporal form have the tendencies that the Confucians discuss; but these tendencies are only transitory, and to restrict one's actions to the practice of them is to tie oneself to the ephemeral, and hence to behave artificially.

There are two minor similarities in Confucian and Taoist prescriptions for "recovering the [e]*hsing*" (acting in accordance with the important aspects of one's innate endowment). From time to time, both schools talked of the process of cultivation as involving "returning" (*kuei*). For the Confucians, this meant a return from devious byways to the straight moral path, which in some cases was identical with the innate course of action. But for the Taoists, it meant either a return to the origin of birth (Tao) or return from a prejudiced adherence to one of two opposites to the middle point between them. Both schools also stressed the virtue of obedience. The Confucians advocated willing acceptance of the commands of father, emperor, and a moral Heaven, and valued virtues like filial piety (*hsiao*) and reverence ([a]*ching*). The Taoists stressed pliance (*jou*), humility, and willing obedience to the circumstances wrought by the changes of Tao; a person was supposed to regard these circumstances as a dutiful son regards the commands of his father. In spite of these similarities, the vast differences in the two prescriptions for "recovering the *hsing*" remain dominant. These stem from the different portraits of the human endowment in the two traditions.

Does the very suggestion that men should attempt to discover the *te* within and emulate its qualities carry an implicit repudiation of the Taoist refusal to differentiate between men? Surely the sheep who are successful in this quest will then be separated from the goats who are not. One Taoist reply might be that the equality remains, for the only difference between the two groups is that the sheep are aware of the equality whereas the goats are not. But in fact there are passages in both the *Tao-te ching* and the *Chuang-tzu* that speak of degrees in the perfection or quantity of *te*: "When one's *te* is abundant, one is comparable to a newborn child."[39] Obviously, this inconsistency is related to those discussed in Chapter 5. In common with other features of Taoist doctrine, the path to the mirror is not easy to describe in words.

CHAPTER 7

AT THE END OF THE PATH

OUR INQUIRIES into the concepts of man in Confucian and Taoist thought were followed in each case by a consideration of the cultivation process that must be undergone if a man is to realize the essential aspect of his endowment. In spite of the differing methods for "recovering the [e]*hsing*" advocated by masters of the two schools, the paths ultimately converged. Partisans of both philosophies shared a belief that the recovery produced a mental tranquility* and a kind of union between the self and something beyond the self. It is a common mistake for writers to regard tranquility and selflessness as distinctively Taoist ideals; the discussion below indicates the important place they occupy in the thought of both schools.

Tranquility

Both Taoists and Confucians agreed that the psychological state of a person who has "recovered his nature" is chiefly one of tranquility. One reason for the agreement here was probably a common belief that tranquility is the state of man at birth, before the aberrations from his nature occur. The *Li chi* states: "Man is born in a state of tranquility; this is his [e]*hsing* from Heaven."[1] The babe at birth is tranquil because he has not yet begun to involve himself with externals; and one source of tranquility in the adult is freedom from disturbance by external phenomena. For Mencius, human nature at birth is characterized by *jen* (humanheartedness), and *jen* is "man's tranquil abode" in life, as it is for Confucius. One of the occasional passages in the authentic *Chuang-tzu* chapters that reflect Confucian sentiments says: "The love of a child for his parents is decreed [*ming*]. It cannot be detached from his heart....

* In the history of Western philosophy tranquility continually reappears as an ideal. The quest for the ineffable tranquility, "the peace that passeth understanding," has occupied the lives of countless Christians.

Therefore, the perfection of filial piety is serving one's parents no matter what the place, and finding one's satisfaction [lit. "rest"] in so doing."[2] In Taoist thought, *te* and *hsing*, being names for the aspect of Tao in the individual, naturally share the undisturbed quality of the unity behind the many.

Confucian Tranquility

In Confucian thought, a tranquil state of mind can be attributed to two sources. The first is lack of the fear that others will harm one. This idea had very early origins in China, and the good ruler was described as being "tranquil in his position" (*an yü wei*) in the sense of being firmly on the throne, in no fear of being removed and in no conflict with his people. In the *Shu ching* is the statement, "Oh, if you have achievements, I, the One Man, will forever be tranquil in my high position."[3] The ruler may be concerned that "the people are not quiet, they have not yet settled their minds"; if he then proceeds to "tranquilize the people," he will be tranquil himself.[4] A passage in the *Analects* remarks that "the man having *jen* rests in *jen*." Because [b]*jen* (humanheartedness) and [a]*jen* (man) were cognates, this phrase is probably intended to convey two senses. First, the man having *jen* finds his contentment in human kindness ([a]*an jen*), that is, it is natural to him, and he has peace of mind in it (references to the fact that the man having *jen* has no enemies abound in Confucian writings). Second, he makes other men tranquil ([b]*an jen*).[5]

The second source of tranquility lay in eliminating the possibility that externals would lead one astray. A man should be in control of things, rather than allowing things to control him; this was especially true of objects that stimulate the senses, such as wealth or social position. We learn that "*Jen* is man's tranquil abode" and all men should "dwell in *jen*." Such expressions convey both the psychological sense of being mentally "at ease" (the sign of acting naturally) and the sense of something fixed, unmoving, committed (an abode, dwelling, stopping place), and hence incapable of distraction.

The *Mencius* discussion of achieving "an unmoved mind" (*pu-*

tung-hsin) centers on the interconnection between will (*chih*) and *ch'i*.[6] Mencius stressed training the ordinary bodily *ch'i* to obey the commands that the will, the active aspect of mind, passes on to it. The mind itself should be upright, and its uprightness is regained when one reduces the number of its desires by self-examination and learning.[7] The training is a matter of habitually practicing those acts determined by one's moral sense (*i*).[8] Once the *ch'i* is trained to obey the will, it undergoes a qualitative change, becoming "vast" *ch'i* (*hao-jen chih ch'i*); and vast *ch'i* is the *sine qua non* for having a naturally unmoved mind. When one has successfully carried through this process, external objects will be unable to move the bodily *ch'i*, causing it, in turn, to move the mind;[9] instead, the mind will be in control of the external objects and will stay on the straight path.[10] Only a naturally unmoved mind is a secure one. Kao Tzu (in the *Mencius*) had an unmoved mind, but his was forcibly so; it was not a natural outgrowth of vast *ch'i*. Kao Tzu had no vast *ch'i* because, "not seeking in the mind," he lacked the first essential for training the bodily *ch'i*, namely, a will that was the active manifestation of an upright mind.

Hsün Tzu discussed the technique for achieving what he called a "fixed" mind, also one that will not be deflected from the straight path by externals. First, a man needs practice in keeping the mind focused on one object that he seeks to know, without letting it stray to another object[11] (the virtue of "unity," [e]*i*) or go off into reveries (the virtue of "repose," [g]*ching*); nor must he allow an impression already stored to interfere with a new one (the virtue of "emptiness," *hsü*).[12] Second, after the mind learns which desires may be implemented in specific situations, the sentiments need training,[13] so that the person will be accustomed to desiring the right thing at the right time. This selective desiring contributes to achieving a balance between desires and the things available in the world.[14] Finally, a man needs to learn so that his mind can assume the ruling position, instead of letting external things govern him.[15] Hsün Tzu says: "When he has firmly grasped virtue, he will be able to fix his mind without distraction; when he has fixed his mind, he will be able to respond to the situation."[16]

Taoist Tranquility

Like the Confucian thinkers, the Taoists regarded tranquility as characteristic of one who acts naturally, in accordance with the essential part of his endowment. In the *Tao-te ching,* Tao, to which all things return, is unitary, empty, and quiet; to approximate Tao, one must "attain to extreme emptiness; hold on to tranquility."[17] Tranquility (*ching*) while one is alive is achieved, in part, by avoiding directed responses to particular things: "If men by absence of desires achieve tranquility, the empire will come to rest by itself," said Lao Tzu.[18] The tranquility of things in life parallels the unmoved state of all things after they die.

I have described how the sense of the "equality of things" and the knowledge of the changes things must undergo stressed by Chuang Tzu produces a toleration of all points of view and an accommodation to all circumstances. The Taoist sage "rests in the Heavenly pivot" and views everything as the same.[19] He is tranquil because he has developed the mental state of emptiness and does not make judgments or evaluative statements about things. Seeing some things as good and others as bad causes desires and aversions, and these lead to involvement with distracting externals. Stopping the judgments stops the chain reaction. The sage's ease also comes from the knowledge that he has no control over the presence or absence of any object or situation. He cannot fight against what is determined, so there is no need to bother; instead he "rests in the natural changes" (*an shih*), accepting whatever circumstance or object comes his way.[20] The sage is unlike most men, who "pursue their lives to the end, like a galloping horse, and can't stop."[21]

Comparison

How does the tranquility of the Confucian differ from that of the Taoist? The answer seems to lie in the condition that is viewed as tranquil. The Confucian sage evaluates, and guides his innate social tendencies accordingly. Ease, for him, is ease in guiding his behavior on the basis of the mind's determinations; he effortlessly makes the right choice and response in a given situation. In the

Great Learning, we find that a person with integrity (*ch'eng*) effortlessly and accurately responds in an approving or disapproving way to things. The response is as natural as the negative reaction to a bad smell or the positive reaction to something attractive to the eye.[22] Such ease in activity is also a joy in itself. By contrast, the Taoist sage is a receptive "mirror," who neither welcomes nor objects to anything. His ease is a calmness in the acceptance of all situations. It is the calmness of passive acquiescence in all matters rather than the effortlessness of action in connection with specific ones.

But when it comes to the ultimate tranquility of the sage, the division between Confucian and Taoist thinkers becomes very narrow. It almost seems as though the decision-making process fundamental to the evaluating mind ceases for the Confucian sage, so effortlessly or habitually does he select the right course of action. Hsün Tzu stated that when the regulation of the sentiments by *li* ("rites") is made habitual by training, then the sentiments always emerge as the right behavioral forms naturally and effortlessly. "The sage gives reign to his desires and satisfies his passions; nevertheless he is controlled by principle; so why need he be forced or repressed or anxious? For the acting out of the right Way (Tao) by the benevolent (*jen*) man is without effort."[23] And is it not the case that some "evaluating" has preceded the accommodating and tolerating conduct of the Taoists? Is not this conduct, in fact, a kind of purposive activity (*wei*), consciously chosen in order to attain peace of mind by avoiding the shock and sorrow of overattachment to precarious things?

Union of Self and Other

Another comparison can be made between Confucian and Taoist views of the life that is lived naturally, in accordance with the essential part of one's endowment. There seems to have been a common belief in both schools that acting naturally is concurrently a means for uniting the self with some greater or more comprehensive entity; in fact, the good life involved a conscious recognition of the need for this union. To the Chinese, this state of union is characterized by "unselfishness." There is an end to the domination of private or small-group interests over those of the larger group of people and other creatures.

There are significant differences about the final nature of the union between self and other in Confucian and Taoist thought. But it is highly probable that in both cases the belief stems from the early notion that certain men are able to act as "counterpart to Heaven" (*p'ei t'ien*). Roughly speaking, the belief that a few individual offspring of Heaven, after death, could assist their progenitor in the divine work developed into the belief that men can also take part in divine tasks during their lifetime through *te*; finally, it was considered that all men and things, being equal offspring of the Absolute, actually never lose their contact with Heaven or Tao. It is also likely that the practice of controlling conduct through the conscious imitation of models contributed to the doctrine of this "loss of self" through union with some other being. The more one models oneself on another, the more one loses one's own ego. The man who constantly acts as though he is a certain virtuous ancestor or seeks to imitate the qualities of Tao is able to overcome his own present fears, likes, and dislikes.

Confucian Union

There is a good deal of variation in the early Confucian descriptions of the union between self and other, which comes to the person who uses his innate evaluating mind to guide his innate social tendencies. In parts of the *Analects, Mencius,* and *Tso chuan* there is no metaphysical fusion of self and Heaven, but simply an establishment of rapport such that the Lord-on-High (a separate being) looks out for a man's interests as long as he is obedient, and promises that he will enter the kingdom above after death.

However, another view, which appears in the *Mencius* and the *Doctrine of the Mean,* is significantly different. It is a product of taking a particularly human virtue and reading it into the natural order. In Chapter 2 we have seen how "integrity" or "sincerity" (*ch'eng*) was transformed into a cosmic principle. Among other things, it came to refer to the principle by which all things act in accordance with their natures. In the *Doctrine of the Mean*, integrity is spoken of as "overspreading" and "containing" all things.[24] The person with integrity, then, was viewed as entering into a quasi-mystical union with this unitary principle. "Therefore, integrity is the way of Heaven. To think how to act with integrity is the way of man," says a passage in the *Mencius* that is repeated in the *Doctrine of the Mean*.[25] Again, in the *Doctrine of the Mean*,

> It is only he who is possessed of the most complete sincerity [integrity] that can exist under Heaven, who can give its full development to his nature. Able to give its full development to his own nature, he can do the same to the nature of other men. Able to give its full development to the nature of other men, he can give their full development to the natures of animals and things. Able to give their full development to the natures of creatures and things, he can assist the transforming and nourishing powers of Heaven and earth. Able to assist the transforming and nourishing powers of Heaven and earth, he may with Heaven and earth form a ternion.[26]

In later Confucian thought the concept of *jen* was taken over from the vocabulary of human ethics, read into the nature of the universe, and cited to explain how all men and things are part of the One. This is especially true in Neo-Confucian thought.

The notion of union of self and other is also important in Hsün Tzu's thought. For him, it is an achievement that comes to the person who can develop the innate attributes of his mind. In the *Hsün-tzu* the universe is presented as an ordered entity, each object having definite relationships to others. But the pattern cannot be grasped unless a person develops his mind: "No change is outside the Tao, though it embodies the constant, and a part cannot cover the whole of it. Those who have partial knowledge perceive one aspect of Tao, but they cannot know its totality."[27] The person who does train his mind, however, can gain complete knowledge. "He looks through all things and sees their nature. . . . He understands the whole of Heaven and Earth, causing all things to get their proper station and governs according to the great principle, and the universe is rectified."[28] It is obvious that this "union," for Hsün Tzu, is not mystical but intellectual; the sage sees how each thing is interrelated with certain other things to form an ordered whole. This intellectual process is termed "dwelling in unity" (*ch'u i*).[29]

Another form of union discussed in Confucian writings is equally important: the establishment of an emotional bond between the self and an ever-increasing number of other people. It is reflected in the repeated statements about the "humane man" (*jen che*) who extends the affection he feels for his kin from them to all people under Heaven. The ruler who carries out the humane government described by Mencius does this. "All men are brothers," and the virtuous individual will feel the emotional bond linking himself with mankind.

Taoist Union

Basic to most Taoist thought is the notion of a unity behind the many. For the sage who discovers his *te,* constant mind, or *hsing* and lives accordingly—i.e., with a blank mind—there is the reward of conscious union with the One. Exactly what this union was varied from passage to passage. In some cases, it was simply a conscious realization of a union that had existed all along; in others, it was the solidifying of a relationship that had become tenuous. In Taoist thought, this union generally had two aspects, intellectual and physical. In intellectual terms, achieving the union meant realizing that something ties all separate objects together. Depending on the passage, this could be the realization that all things derive their being from a common source, or that a single principle of change accounts for all the varying temporal changes in the universe. This principle is unitary and eternal, lasting on after the particular things are no more. It is the single "pivot." Describing intellectual union, Chuang Tzu said, "One takes the mass of confused things and unites it as one," and, "One places [his mind] in the One."[30]

There also seems to have been a belief in a physical union between man and the One (Tao). *Ch'i* is the physical substance of which the universe is composed, and Tao is a principle accounting for the changes that *ch'i* undergoes. Although the two concepts were supposedly separate, confusion was bound to develop between them. Sages seeking union with Tao sought by breath control to link the *ch'i* constituting themselves with the *ch'i* filling the rest of the universe. One had to "unite one's *ch'i* to the Vastness."[31] It is not at all clear what this involved. But it seems that the universal ether was viewed as a harmonious blend of *yin* and *yang* ethers. Each person was also composed of *yin* and *yang ch'i*, but the combination of the two ethers in an individual could become disorganized and unharmonious.[32] Breath control reestablished the harmony, and thus the link with the universal ethers. Finally, there seems to have been some vague link between this physical union with the universal *ch'i* and the psychological state of blankness, in which one's mind was like a mirror. Since the *ch'i* encompasses all things, the mind of the person unified with the primal *ch'i* is empty or blank, i.e., receptive to all things.

Conclusion

There are certainly similarities between the conceptions of union between self and other in Confucian and Taoist thought, especially in the Confucian discussions of "integrity" (*ch'eng*). Obviously, one can suspect Taoist influences in late Chou Confucian thought. But there is an essential difference as well. The Taoists would shudder at the thought of taking terms from the vocabulary of human ethics, which all reflect the partiality of human value judgments, and applying them to nature. This is seeing the universe in human terms; the Taoist wanted to eliminate the human point of view and see man in cosmic terms.

The portraits of man in Confucian and Taoist thought were generally irreconcilable, and so were the two descriptions of the paths to recovery of the essential part of the human endowment. But the two schools concurred in their statements about the life that is lived "naturally," in accordance with that essential part of the endowment. When such common ideals as tranquility and union between self and other could be maintained in spite of the different conceptions of man, this was a guarantee that the ideals would be firmly held in China for ages to come.

CHAPTER 8

THE CLASSICAL LEGACY

WHY DO certain assumptions, rather than others, seem to mold Chinese philosophical thought at a given time? The explanation often lies in the historical conditions of a particular time, and in the relative impact of various assumptions in the Chinese intellectual legacy. This study has examined some of the major assumptions in that legacy, in part as a guide to understanding many subsequent developments in Chinese intellectual history—for example the sinicization of alien doctrines like Buddhism and Communism. In any given period Chinese thought is usually a mixed bag of enduring assumptions and strikingly new ideas. Even the strongest themes often submerge, some to disappear, others to reappear in new forms. Many classical assumptions are still found in Chinese Communist thought today; but in order to illustrate the mixed character of the legacy at any given time, it will be useful to begin with an example of a Communist break with tradition. It is, after all, possible to overemphasize the continuity of ideas in Chinese philosophy, which is not at all a static thing.

Harmony and tranquility, as we have seen, were ideals in both classical Confucian and Taoist thought; and this agreement by two influential and otherwise divergent schools ensured that these ideals would be honored for ages to come. The Chinese Communists, however, are quick to condemn these elements in their intellectual legacy. Some present-day Chinese philosophers regard traditional Confucian virtues, such as "the love of mankind" (*jen*), loyalty, and altruism, as early attempts to harmonize relations between rich and poor, ruler and minister, and other conflicting classes; spokesmen for the feudal slave masters advocated these virtues in an attempt to blind the people to the actual contradictions that did exist in society. Similarly, the doctrine of the "mean" in early Confucianism was an attempt to justify compromises between mutually contradictory matters, such as belief in Heavenly *ming* combined with reliance on human effort; and Confucian discussions of "human nature" were actually meant to cover up class contradictions, since there is no class transcending nature. The Taoists are attacked for asserting, in their references to the dialectic, that opposites disappear in Tao. What happens to development and change, the Communists ask, if opposites "disappear" rather than exist eternally as the true nature of things? Chuang Tzu is said to have carried the denial of the "struggle of opposites" the furthest. He is said to recommend taking a middle position between opposites (e.g., good and bad, strength and weakness) as an expedient means for preserving life, or taking a "head in the sand" escape from conflict by transcending it with a flight into "absolute freedom."[1]

Mao Tse-tung glorifies the infinity of contradictions in society, and has replaced the ideal of harmony with that of "struggle." Philosophically, this requires an interpretation of dialectics that denounces the "reconciliation of opposites"; it also requires a repudiation of Chinese and European philosophical "humanism," which idealizes the fraternal harmony among all men.

> The modern revisionists have wantonly distorted and revised the Marxist-Leninist teachings on the laws of contradiction, and spread their views about the reconciliation of contradictions.[2]

> We are firmly opposed to substituting the theory of human nature in the abstract and the preaching of fraternity for the standpoint of class analysis and class struggle; we are against describing communism as humanism and against placing humanism above communism.[3]

Instead there is an emphasis on the struggle between contradictory classes of people. The classical legacy idealizing harmony is said to have created in the Chinese people a passivity and a tendency to avoid facing problems squarely. Humanism is a sham so long as actual barriers to the "fraternity of man" do exist—for example, the still extant gulf between "mental aristocrats" and "manual laborers." Humanism is merely an attempt to create the illusion that the barrier does not exist.

Traditional ideals (harmony and tranquility) have been rejected.[4] But the reason is probably Mao's feeling that they impede the realization of another ideal, which, as envisioned, has undeniable roots in the past: the transformation of the Age of Grand Unity (*ta-t'ung*), in which "all men are brothers," from Confucian slogan to Communist fact.*

Let us now consider the impact of the ideas considered in this study on subsequent periods of Chinese history, emphasizing ideas that still affect the lives of Chinese today. In dealing with this question, it is well to distinguish the conscious philosophical legacy from the unconscious one. The conscious legacy consists of ideas explicitly deemed worthy of perpetuating by later scholars. The Chinese Communists consider the following classical ideas worthy of "inheritance." First, a rudimentary materialism. It is said that Kuan Chung was the founder of the materialistic school, which was later stimulated by the Five Elements thought of the late West Chou and fully developed by Hsün Tzu. Second, atheism. Writers invoke Tzu Ch'an (sixth century B.C.) as an early atheist; they also point out that Confucius demonstrated a skepticism about spirits, and that Hsün Tzu and Han Fei-tzu denied the existence of "mandates" issued by an anthropomorphic Heaven. Third, an embryonic dialectical theory. Some find such a theory in certain Taoist writings, though they are quick to indicate the shortcomings of these writings in other respects, and others find it in the Later Mohists.

The unconscious historical legacy in Communist thought is made up of ideas about man or nature that were originally found in a philosophic setting but have, over the years, become unquestioned assumptions in the minds of educated Chinese. These assumptions were never held by everyone in China, but they affect the lives of

* The term *ta t'ung*, or "Grand Unity," is used in the *Book of Rites* (*Li chi*), which dates from the former Han dynasty (202 B.C.–A.D. 9). It describes a period in which everyone belonged to the same great family of men. The weak, the orphans, the widows, and others were all cared for, and so forth. K'ang Yu-wei revived the concept in the late nineteenth century, and spoke of it as the ideal toward which human societies were evolving. Mao Tse-tung has often used the same term to refer to the stage of Communism itself.

great numbers of people whenever they reemerge. The unconscious legacy in China is particularly strong in the area of assumptions about the control of man, i.e., about methods of getting people to act in a desired manner; and my remarks about the impact of the ideas developed in this study pertain primarily to enduring assumptions in this area.

One basic assumption in Chinese thought is that a change in educational techniques is a key to changing human behavior, and thus by implication a key to solving urgent political and social problems. It must be remembered that in China the concept of "education" contains the notion of "moral training." Three brief examples from different periods will show how a knowledge of this assumption can help us to understand various historical incidents in China: the reforms of the Sung dynasty; the policies of Republican China immediately after the revolution of 1911; and the policies of Mao Tse-tung during the years just before the Cultural Revolution of 1966.

During the Sung dynasty (A.D. 960–1279) the political and social problems stemmed from continual fighting with non-Chinese tribes (mainly Khitans and Tanguts) to the north and west. China faced a fiscal crisis because of barbarian demands for tribute and because of the costs of military defense. Furthermore, various administrative defects became apparent, such as the presence of cliques and corruption in the bureaucracy. A Westerner today is usually surprised to discover the nature of two of the major remedies proposed by the privy councilor and reformer Fan Chung-yen (989–1052). One (1044) was to establish a quasi-national school system. A school was to be set up in each department and district, and the local magistrate was responsible for staffing and administering it. The other policy was to change the content of the official examinations, which in turn would cause changes in the material studied by pupils preparing for the examinations. Fan advocated placing first priority on problems of history and politics and last priority on poetry composition, which often had been preeminent in the past. Another Sung reformer, Ch'eng Yi (1033–1107), in a famous memorial written when he was very young, took note of the many social and economic evils plaguing the land and decided that the first step toward remedying the situation was to change the civil-service examinations.[5] Such policy suggestions are not isolated instances. The same suggestions were made in the nineteenth century, when China was faced with the threats of Western encroachment and internal rebellions.[6]

Our second example pertains to the period from about 1916 through the early 1920's. After the 1911 revolution, in which the Manchus were overthrown, the Republican government failed to unify and stabilize the country. The seeds of warlordism sprouted. There was more international humiliation, this time in Japan's demands that she be allowed to take over Germany's former spheres of influence in North China. A knowledge of the "educational reform" panacea explains one significant response to these problems, that of Hu Shih (1891–1962) and his liberal colleagues. An analysis of Hu Shih's programs, however, should begin with a statement of current scholarly opinion on previous Chinese responses to the Western impact.

It is often held that after an initial intransigence (during which time some people spoke of controlling the barbarians through virtuous example, playing barbarians off against one another, and so forth) the Chinese made half-hearted attempts to adopt some Western ideas and techniques, while really trying to retain the Chinese cultural "essence." For example, many figures associated with the "Self-strengthening Movement," which developed in the 1860's, advocated preserving Confucian culture (the social virtues of sincerity and loyalty; the political system characterized by a social hierarchy and government by men of merit) while giving China Western technology (warships, firearms, railroads, and telegraph). The reformer K'ang Yu-wei (1858–1927) went a bit further, and maintained that the Chinese tradition, properly understood, included the sanction for adopting some Western political institutions, such as a constitution and parliament. But he still remained a Confucian, seeking justification for the reforms in the New Text version of the classics; and in the early twentieth century he advocated Confucianism as a state religion.

Hu Shih, educated at Cornell and Columbia and a student of John Dewey, is generally regarded as the first to make a clean break with the Confucian past. He advocated total Westernization as the solution to China's problems: "Overthrow Confucius and Sons" was the slogan. Hu demanded an end to the classical literary form in which Confucian ideas were spread, which was characterized by strict attention to word form and saturated with archaic terms; he wanted the vernacular language to replace it as the medium for writers. In addition, he repudiated Confucianism as living philosophy, holding that it promotes a feudal political structure in which the individual has no rights, and that it exalts compliance, yielding, and filial piety, all of which promote passiveness in the people. Hu Shih is viewed as the foremost anti-Confucian.

But, recalling the background assumption that education is a panacea, one can reinterpret the relation between Hu Shih and Confucianism. Hu Shih's mentor was John Dewey, who himself went to China in 1919 and stayed two years. In America, Dewey was the symbol of a revolutionary philosophy of education, and the author of a book entitled *Democracy and Education.* According to Dewey, political problems and educational solutions go hand in hand: "Democracy is a matter of beliefs, of outlook upon life, of habits of mind, and not merely a matter of forms of government."[7] Universal education will create the right beliefs in all people; and Hu Shih's cure for China's political and social problems was the creation of a vernacular language and literature suitable for universalizing education. "Save the country by education" became the slogan of Hu Shih and his colleagues.[8] Rather than dirtying their hands by political involvement other than the issuing of manifestos, many liberals followed them. Why was Dewey so popular? Why was his disciple Hu Shih initially so popular with Chinese intellectuals? One reason is that their proposals for China fit into the enduring Confucian assumption about the power of education.

The third example of the persistent assumption that educational reform is the key to solving urgent political and social problems concerns Mao Tse-tung in the period from 1964 until the Great Proletarian Cultural Revolution (which began to develop momentum between November 1965 and June 1966). Mao was faced with internal opposition to his economic and foreign policies at the highest party level, and with foot-dragging by officials charged with implementing them. There was the external threat of conflict with the United States, which was intensified by the Vietnam war; and there was the Sino-Soviet split. Mao's overall problem was the danger of "revisionism," which might well arise in China as it supposedly had in Yugoslavia and the Soviet Union. In addition, there was the threat that a "new class," composed especially of party officials and bureaucrats, would emerge in growing numbers. Soft, privileged, and aloof from the masses, they seemed to echo the evils in the officialdom of pre-modern China.

Mao began taking a number of specific measures to combat the problem of "revisionism" in spring 1964. Curiously enough, one of the most important of these steps was to reinvigorate the half-work, half-study schools.* In ordinary schools, Mao called for a reduction in the number of hours of academic work in order to make time for labor and political education. The aim of these educational reforms was to create a population with the "labor viewpoint," who would be immune to revisionism. There was a good deal of opposition to Mao's policies among teachers and administrators, and the policies do not seem to have fully succeeded. Thus when the Cultural Revolution began, having as its aim the prevention of revisionism and the creation of a classless society, one of Mao's first steps (June 1966) was to close the schools so that the educational system could be overhauled. His intention was to reform it along the lines outlined in early 1964 but imperfectly implemented then. The half-work, half-study schools were to serve as models for the entire educational system. Academic course content was to be reduced to allow time for more labor and political education, textbooks were to be revised, standard examination and

* Half-work, half-study schools are those in which students spend half of their time doing manual labor and half doing academic work; the division can be by alternate days, alternate weeks, or alternate seasons, depending on the needs of the factory or farm with which the school is associated.

grading procedures were to be altered, and new criteria (emphasizing class background and political awareness) were to be introduced in school admissions policies.

This, then, is the background assumption of Chinese social control theory: changing educational techniques and systems is a key to changing human behavior; and thus by implication it is the key to solving urgent political or social problems. Obviously, Chinese officials have relied on other methods as well. Fan Chung-yen tried to equalize official landholdings (to ensure an adequate income for regional officials and reduce corruption), to carry out land reclamation, and to institute administrative reforms aimed at wiping out nepotism. Dewey's disciples listened politely as he spoke of using the old Chinese guilds as a basis for building grass-roots democracy, and as he emphasized economic reforms to prevent a social revolution; but they seem to have ignored his words and the hard work they implied. Mao Tse-tung tries to carry out a sweeping party purge. Obviously, educational reform is not the only response to social problems. But over the years the Chinese have repeatedly shown a powerful faith in its ability to work wonders.

We can easily find other enduring assumptions by examining the nature of the education in which Chinese have such faith. The first of these other assumptions is the tripartite group of beliefs about model emulation discussed in Chapter 4: people learn through the emulation of models; the best way to inculcate any behavior in them is to introduce a model for them to emulate; and to be a model is the legitimate goal for men to seek (in other words, respect is preferable to material reward). These assumptions first come to light on bronzes that speak of "emulating the *te* of an ancestor." In classical Confucian thought, officials, including the emperor, are to serve as models for the people; this is the function of the *chün-tzu* or "superior man." Historical works in China had as a major aim the discovery of models for educating the youth. Traditional models were nationwide, such as Kuan Yü, who was a model of loyalty, or Shun, who was a model of filial piety. Often, models were local and contemporary: for example, a woman who did not remarry after her husband's death and was known for her virtue might be singled out as a model of chastity.

These same assumptions about model emulation dominate social control theory in Communist China today. As a general rule, Party members are to serve as models. In Mao's own words, "Members of the Communist Party cannot but consciously undertake the great responsibility of consolidating the whole nation and getting rid of backwardness. At this point, the function of the members of the Communist Party as heralds and models is extremely important."[9] In other words, the official in Communist China today, like the official in traditional China is to serve as an example.

Models in China can be differentiated as functionally diffuse and functionally specific. Nationwide models like the People's Liberation Army heroes Lei Feng and Wang Chieh are diffuse. They are models of selflessness, technical ability, hard work, how to study Mao's writings, and other generalized virtues. One example of a specific model would be a peasant-scientist who developed new hybrids. Thousands of other peasants might be brought to study the experimental method he followed in making his discoveries, and also to study his "attitude," which had been conducive to his developing that experimental method. Another example of a functionally specific model would be the case of certain Shanghai factories being designated as "models" in order to force the workers in them to reveal trade secrets that had been passed from one generation and guild to the next.

There are both individual human models and model organizations. For example, just as there may be a "five-good worker," there may be a "five-good factory." In the People's Liberation Army we find the "exemplary Red Ninth Company in the study of Chairman Mao's works," the "tough-bone Sixth Company," and so forth. Nevertheless, the selection of models seems to be one area in which the glorification of an individual rather than a group is tolerated (note the situation regarding Mao himself). A great deal of effort is frequently expended in trying to discover persons who would make suitable models. Those who do good deeds anonymously are often favored; they are tracked down in some way, and their anonymity disappears, to say the least. Each organization and each department within an organization often select their own models; these may be persons who excel at emulating the nationwide models. A certain store, for example, might have one worker who is best at emulating Lei Feng.

Two major purposes in setting up models are to induce people to conform with official norms and to produce more goods in the factory or farm. One Chinese writer comments: "There is a common saying, 'Without stimulation, the water will not leap, and the people will not exert themselves.' Once the young people come into contact with the typical models, a tremendous promoting power is rapidly generated. Truly, it is setting up one individual and motivating the entire group."[10] In accordance with the sentiment of this quotation, models have served as a primary incentive system in Chinese factories. There may be a selection by the individual workers in a "small work group" (*hsiao-tsu*, perhaps 25 men) every three months, and a major selection once a year. In theory, class background, political consciousness, and technical skill are all to be considered. The final decision is often made by the factory Party Committee on the basis of recommendations by the *hsiao-tsu*.

Various labels are assigned to such models, one of the most common being "advanced producer" (*hsien-chin sheng-ch'an che*). Everything is done to create an aura of reverence around them: they are given certificates for their homes; banners honoring them are set up in work units; they are made delegates to various congresses, and they tour their own factory or other factories, giving talks and acting as examples; they are even given shirts, tea mugs, and fountain pens with "advanced producer" written on them. All of this is the ideal incentive of "respect," but research shows that some material awards (bonuses, special consideration for housing or schooling, and promotions) do come in the back door.

A vast body of literature has developed to guide people in setting up models. It concerns such matters as how to cultivate a model to the point where he can assume that role (increase his responsibilities, visit his family, give him certain books to read, hold periodic educational talks with him) and how to spread a model's influence from a nucleus outward to a wider area (*ts'ung tien tao mien*). The qualities most important in selecting a model—and those that one should emulate—are proper attitudes toward officially sanctioned values or directives. For example, the model is chosen and imitated for his "spirit of collectivism," his "progressive thinking," or his "correct attitude toward productive labor." In traditional China literary works often presented models for the education of the people; and the same function is outlined today for all the arts. A Communist commentator stated, "The basic task of socialist literature and art is to work hard and create heroic models of workers, peasants, and soldiers."[11]

One element in the theory and practice of model emulation in China is acceptance of "respect" as a legitimate incentive, a respect that comes to the individual from being emulated by others. This being the case, it is not surprising to find that a common form of punishment is the converse of respect, namely humiliation. Maoists have often paraded an offender in a dunce cap through jeering throngs where others might have physically liquidated the victim. In his *Report on an Investigation of the Hunan Peasant Movement* (1927) Mao discussed the efficacy of this form of control.

Contemporary model theory differs from that of the past. Today, competition with the model is stressed, and the learner is encouraged to surpass him; this would have been considered pure *hubris* in Confucian China. But the main point is that we find a second assumption (or rather, a cluster of assumptions) from the early Confucian past still in force: people do learn through the emulation of models. This second asumption dictates in part the form that the "reform through education" panacea sometimes takes. Model emulation is not unique in China, but the degree to which it is used as a technique of social control is far greater in China than in any other land: the Chinese refuse to focus primarily on nationwide models, and instead insist on a widespread local selection process; model selection has been formally institutionalized; most important, there is a universal and unshakable faith in the efficacy of the system. Moreover, model emulation by the Chinese is not restricted to Mainland China. Ch'en Ju-i is the Senior Specialist of the Committee on Moral Education and Guidance in the Ministry of Education in Taiwan. His approach to moral education is reflected in the endless speeches he has given on the topic "*Fa ku-chin wan-jen*" (Emulate the Perfect Men of All Ages).[12]

A third assumption associated with the doctrines explored in the present study is that moral or political education should concentrate on changing people's attitudes toward the established norms. In other words, control is to be internalized. A corollary is that when people have the right attitudes or ideas, they will necessarily act in the right way. The actual behavior of those whose minds are "rectified" will invariably conform to the norms, and their every act will bear witness to the presence of the rectified mind. This conformity (the presence of the social virtues) will in itself assist the realization of the ultimate goal: a stable, strong, prosperous society. Early Confucian writings, as we have seen, constantly urge men to develop the attitude that right takes precedence over all other considerations: "The mind of the superior man is conversant with righteousness; the mind of the mean man is conversant with gain." The *Great Learning* describes the path from right thoughts ("making the thoughts sincere" and "rectifying the mind") to proper regulation of the family, to governing the state and bringing peace to the world.

This doctrine took its most extreme form in the philosophy of Wang Yang-ming (1472–1529). In his discussion of the "unity of knowledge and action," Wang stressed that true knowledge (moral knowledge) leads to desirable concrete results. The sole demonstration of the presence of "knowledge" or right ideas is that one's *actions* constantly conform to the norms; there is no knowledge that does not reveal itself in action. Neo-Confucian thinkers often wrote about the marvels that a "sincere mind" would create: "For in dealing with people, things, affairs, there is nothing that the moving power of sincerity [*ch'eng*] cannot affect. Cultivate the personality with sincerity, and the affairs will come out in good order. Approach people with sincerity, and people will be moved and influenced." Many Ch'ing dynasty (1644–1911) philosophers condemned Wang's doctrines for what they regarded as an excessive stress on moral intuition; some even tried to attribute the fall of the previous dynasty to the negative influence of his ideas (typically, a political event was traced to the effect of ideas on people). But they perpetuated his notion that knowledge divorced from action is nonsense, and rejected "pure speculation" in philosophy on the basis of this principle.

More modern theorists also agree on the need to remold thoughts and attitudes. Hu Shih's mentor, Dewey, decided: "China could not be changed without a social transformation based upon a transformation of ideas. The political revolution [of 1911] was a failure because it was external, formal, touching the mechanism of social action but not affecting conceptions of life, which really control society."[18] Hu Shih accepted that in order to build a democracy one must change people's ideas about political institutions, human "rights," and so forth through education. Mao Tse-tung, too, relies in part on the changing of people's attitudes for economic and military miracles. "Study sessions" (*hsüeh hsi*), prescribed for all Chinese, aim at producing the proper attitudes toward collectivism, toward the masses, toward manual labor, and so on.

The molding of ideas and attitudes can be directly related to what is often called "Chinese Communist voluntarism." "Voluntarism," in essence, generally refers to the doctrine that "willful," "purposive," or "conscious" men can bring about significant changes in their material and social environments; they are not at the mercy of deterministic natural or historical laws. The concept of voluntarism is very vague, and neither terms like "consciousness" nor the process by which consciousness supposedly effects concrete changes are adequately explained by those who speak of it. Any extensive treatment of the topic is beyond the scope of our present remarks on the impact of the Chinese classical philosophical legacy.* But some flesh and blood can be added

* Maurice Meisner has discussed the refusal of Li Ta-chao, a founder of the Chinese Communist Party, to link man's consciousness inseparably with the material conditions in which he finds himself; to do so would have denied the possibility of the development of a revolutionary socialist consciousness in backward China (Meisner, p. 147). Li Ta-chao's faith in the ability of purposive Chinese to remake their world is continued by Mao. Many non-Marxist

to one's understanding of Chinese Communist voluntarism by a knowledge of the traditional belief in the close relationship between "rectifying" minds and ensuring overt changes in conduct.

The Confucian thesis assumes that a correct mental transformation will reveal itself regularly in overt behavior. In other words, there will be continual manifestations of unselfishness, obedience to authority, respectfulness to elders, humane treatment of others, straightforward speech, and other virtues. To paraphrase the *Analects*, there will be no looking, listening, speaking, or moving in opposition to the norms. These behavioral changes are regarded as ends in themselves; moreover, they ensure the realization of a prosperous, stable society. Chinese Communist voluntarism, among its other characteristics, holds that people whose minds are properly "rectified" will continually give behavioral evidence of this change. Ideally, they will constantly act unselfishly, be obedient to official doctrines, and otherwise manifest the "Party Spirit" (*tang-hsing*). In actuality, continual writing, speaking, and campaigning on these themes is often regarded as almost equivalent to actively performing the deeds. Both forms of conduct (verbalizing about the deeds and performing them) pertain to what the Chinese Communists term "manifestation" (*piao-hsien*), and manifestation of the proper mental state is the traditional demonstration that the mind has been or is being rectified. Unselfishness and other socialist virtues, like the Confucian virtues, are ends in them-

---

Chinese in the first part of this century were attracted to other European voluntaristic philosophies, such as those of Schopenhauer or Bergson.

In its Marxist and Leninist context, voluntarism does not always refer merely to the belief that "where there is a will there is a way." There is often a definite cognitive element in it. This includes: first, a conscious awareness of a goal or set of goals; second, an understanding of the reason for selecting these goals; and third, the attitude that the goals are proper ones. The cognitive element is important in understanding Chinese voluntarism because for the Chinese it justifies long periods of political education. An added element in Chinese voluntarism is the belief that cognitive and attitudinal states will necessarily reveal themselves in behavioral manifestations. This is the only demonstration that these states are actually present. Hence, there is the expectation that people with the right socialist consciousness will always be writing, speaking, and acting in accordance with the norms. In other words, there is a tremendous emphasis on "manifestation"; and this "manifestation" of the rectified mind ensures ultimate achievement of the goals.

selves, and they are also the means whereby utopian goals can be achieved.* An industrialized China, characterized by a classless "grand unity" of all people, will develop from the continuing presence of the necessary manifestations. As was recognized in Chou times, the advantage of internalizing social control by creating the right ideas and attitudes is that this control is more stable than one based on fear of punishment; the desired behavior continues to appear even when the policeman is not around.† In any case, those who discuss political control in China today are fond of quoting an ancient proverb that stems from the classical philosophical doctrines we have encountered: "Through the use of force one causes men's mouths to submit; through reasoning one causes their minds to submit (*yi li fu jen k'ou, yi li fu jen hsin*)."[14]

The final strong assumption in classical Chinese education theory is that people are naturally attracted to virtuous models. In early Confucian works like the *Mencius* we learn that the weak but virtuous ruler has nothing to fear from a militarily powerful neighbor. The people are the most important consideration, and the ruler of even a very small kingdom can endeavor to "gain the people's hearts" (*te min hsin*) and sway their minds through his virtue ([a]*te*).[15] The people of the powerful neighboring state will be attracted to the weak but virtuous model king and come over to his side, weakening their former ruler.

This theme has been present in story and in philosophical writings since the Chou period; and it has merged with the Taoist doctrine of the reversal of opposites: in classical Taoist thought this often took the form, "in weakness is the seed of strength." In other words, the weak will necessarily become strong ("strong" in a special sense). In his pre-Marxist writings, Li Ta-chao expressed an optimism about China's immediate future, which he based on a dialectical view of change. He relied on the analogy of the alternation of opposites in nature, especially seasonal change. In the

* Benjamin Schwartz has made a similar point in "China and the West in the 'Thought of Mao Tse-tung.'"

† Perhaps it is not accidental that the most esteemed philosopher in Chiang Kai-shek's Taiwan is Wang Yang-ming at the same time that thought remolding is so heavily emphasized on the mainland.

death of a plant in winter is the seed of its rebirth in spring, and the same is true of nations. The decay of backward China contained the seed of a glorious future China.[16]

Some years later, just after the Second World War, Fung Yu-lan described the enduring influence of the idea of the reversal of opposites. "In the late war the concept [of reversal as the movement of Tao] provided the Chinese people with a sort of psychological weapon, so that even in its darkest period, most people lived on the hope which was expressed in the phrase: 'The dawn will soon come.' It was this 'will to live' that helped the Chinese people to go through the war."[17] In any case, the traditional Confucian-Taoist assumption was confirmed in Chinese Communist eyes by their experience with the objectively stronger Kuomintang forces during the 1940's. The American-equipped Kuomintang troops often defected to the materially weaker but "virtuous" Communist troops led by the virtuous model Mao Tse-tung, who had "won their hearts," and the Communists became strong. Similarly, there is a strong traditional element in the Maoist "paper-tiger" theory of imperialism.

The notion that virtuous weakness contains the seed of strength, combined with the assumption that successful actions follow when people have the right ideas or attitudes, produced the Maoist doctrine that "man is the primary factor,"* which denigrates objective difficulties in a situation. Although "in weakness lies strength" referred primarily to the military sphere, the idea that people (weak, "poor and blank" as Mao says, but having the right ideas and attitudes) rather than material conditions are of primary importance has been extended to the economic sector. For example:

How is this miracle [a sudden increase in grain and steel production] possible? Comrade Mao Tse-tung attributed it to the extraordinary high

* The specific phrase "man is the primary factor" was initiated by Defense Minister Lin Piao in the resolution of the Military Affairs Committee on the rectification campaign of 1960–61 ("The Resolution of the Enlarged Session of the Military Affairs Committee Concerning the Strengthening of Indoctrination Work in Troop Units," October 20, 1960). His reference was to the relationship between men and weapons (in his discussion of the famous "four firsts"). Subsequently, the phrase has often been used to refer to non-military situations—for example, to man's ability to conquer nature with a minimum of technical aids.

morale of the masses. This morale represents the communist labor spirit. . . . In the opinion of the Marx-Leninists, Communist labor is voluntary labor, which knows no limit, and the workers do not expect or care about pay. . . . It is upon this foundation that the grain and steel outputs were doubled. Having laid down this foundation, any task can be fulfilled and everything can be done well.[18]

Economic miracles can be achieved in the face of objectively difficult conditions in a backward country if people have the right attitudes.

Natural Equality and the Education Panacea

How is one to account for the lasting Chinese faith in the wonders that can be wrought by educational changes? The answer doubtless lies in the continuing strength of the fundamental idea that links early Confucian and Taoist conceptions of man: men are naturally equal. This idea did, in fact, remain strong in post-Chou China; it is beyond the scope of the present study to demonstrate this by exploring the next 2000 years of Chinese thought in any detail, but a few pertinent remarks can be made.

Certainly, it would be wrong to maintain that China produced no philosophers in whose writings one finds a belief in the natural inequality of men. Kuo Hsiang (d. A.D. 312) was a Neo-Taoist who held that all men spontaneously come into being with different allotments (*fen*) of talents, faculties, and capacities, which determine the kind of life they will be able to lead in this world. Acting naturally is acting within the limits of one's abilities. This doctrine helped pave the way for the Buddhist conception of karma, which was inherently alien to Chinese thought because of its attempt to explain natural inequality of men as the product of activities in previous existences. Han Yü (A.D. 768–824) reworked an idea that first emerged in the Han period, namely, that there are three kinds of people: the unalterably good, the unalterably bad, and those who can become either good or bad.

However, the classical belief that men are naturally equal remained dominant, even if apparently submerged. Its influence can be detected even where the casual observer might feel that he is in the presence of opposing ideas. For example, in Neo-Confucian works of the Sung (A.D. 960–1279) and Ming (A.D. 1368–1643) dynasties some writers ascribed inequalities to the relative purity or impurity of the *ch'i* (matter) with which men are born. However, even they tried to have their cake and eat it too by availing themselves of a substance-function (*t'i-yung*) theory. [c]*Li* (principle) is equally present in all men as their "substance" or essential nature; but differences between people's *ch'i* mean that in practice, or "function" (*yung*), men differ.* As a result, variations in social behavior and intelligence can be assigned to differences in physical endowment. These differences are correctable, however: *li* is equally present in all men; and a person's *ch'i* can be refined by education, making it easier for him to abide by this inborn principle. This Neo-Confucian idea probably owes as much to the classical Taoist doctrine that Tao is present in all things as it does to the early Confucian belief in an equally shared evaluating mind.†

The continuing Chinese belief in natural equality accounts for many other aspects of Chinese intellectual history. For example, it helps one understand why certain ideas from India flourished in China, whereas others died out. The Consciousness-Only (*wei*

* According to a study by Tai Chen (1723–77), [c]*li* (which should not be confused with [a]*li*, meaning "rites" or "rules of propriety") originally referred to the texture or grain of a material like jade. It pointed to the lines that it would be natural for a jade carver to follow. In Neo-Confucian thought, *li* had evolved into a term denoting the metaphysical principle in things that determined their natural paths of change or activity; for example, the *li* in an acorn determines all the changes that an acorn goes through in becoming an oak. According to Chu Hsi (1130–1200), the dominant figure in Neo-Confucian philosophy, *li* is immanent in all physical things rather than being transcendent. In man, it is present as his "good nature" (sometimes called his *li hsing*). The terms "substance" and "function" (which first achieved philosophical prominence in the work of Wang Pi, A.D. 226–49) have the respective connotations of latency-within-beginning-incorporeal, and actuality-without-ending-corporeal. Neo-Confucians contended that there was a direct link between substance, with which [c]*li* was identified, and function. In other words, a person's "good nature" (*li hsing*) would reveal itself in behavior if unobstructed by matter (*ch'i*).

† Egalitarianism is evident in the works of other Neo-Confucianists, who did not make use of the distinction of *li* and *ch'i*. For example, Chang Tsai (A.D. 1020–77) based his doctrine that all men are brothers on the existence of a common physical substance from which all are formed.

shih) or Idealistic school of Buddhism, deriving from Vasubandu (fifth century A.D.) was introduced to China by Hsüan Tsang (A.D. 594–664), but soon disappeared. This school had maintained that some men are born with many "impure seeds," which produce impure dharmas. These men can never escape the wheel of transmigration and achieve nirvana. Other men, born with more "pure seeds," can escape. This doctrine of natural inequality was not compatible with the dominant assumption in Chinese thought, the natural equality of man.* The schools of Buddhism that did flourish (and became distinctively Chinese) are those like the T'ien T'ai and Ch'an sects, which stress that all men are born with the "Buddha nature," so that the road to nirvana is open to all.

The idea that men are equal because they all possess an evaluating mind did not die easily, even in Chinese Marxism. However, the concept of the evaluating mind itself directly contradicted the Marxist principle that people's ethical ideas are determined by the specific economic conditions in which they live. One can see the tension between the two positions in the thought of Li Ta-chao (1888–1927), a founder of the Chinese Communist Party. Although he accepted the Marxist world-view, Li also stated:

> The natural sciences, law, politics, religion, and philosophy are all things one knows after studying them; they definitely do not possess any natural authority.... Because the ethics of men has been a powerful social ability since the most ancient period of human life, there has developed in the human heart a voice of authority that down to the present day still echoes in our hearts. It has a mysterious quality that is not due to the stimulus of the outside world, nor is it a matter of advantage or disadvantage; rather, it is a naturally produced authority. Its mysterious nature is similar to the mystery of sex, the mystery of mother love, and the mystery of sacrifice.[19]

Today, Mao Tse-tung would certainly reject the idea of any "natural authority in the heart." But even though the idea of equality

* In Japan, where hereditary elitism was pronounced, this same school of Buddhism flourished during the Nara period (A.D. 645–794), and is still in existence. When Chinese intellectuals sought to revive some of its doctrines in 1880, they were dependent on Japanese scholars for the texts. Of course, there are other reasons than the one cited for this sect's decline in China—notably the lack of mass appeal in a doctrine that was both elitist and very cerebral.

based on equal possession of an evaluating mind may now be taboo, the belief in man's plasticity and in the primary role of education in molding the individual that was implied by the old idea lingers on.*

Chinese and Western Equality

We have seen that the idea of natural equality was quite important in China and relatively unimportant in the West. Why, then, did the demand for government by consent and the concept of political democracy (which seem to rest on the assumption that men are created equal) arise in Europe, and not in China? One can only speculate. But certain facts are plain. The Chinese stressed equality in a descriptive sense, focusing on the human condition at birth, and on shared attributes that were, in theory, empirically or otherwise verifiable.† This approach implies that the state is obligated to maintain proper environmental conditions, permitting

* A good demonstration of this in recent times was the opposition encountered during the 1950's by educators who believed that students are born with different capacities and felt that "teaching should be geared to the students' abilities" (*yin ts'ai shih chiao*). Many of those who supported this position were Western-trained professional teachers. Their stand was attacked on the grounds that innate differences are of minor importance; and that all students in ordinary primary and middle schools should therefore study the same material in similar amounts.

† The fact that there is a basic distinction between the descriptive and evaluative senses of "equality" and "inequality" does not mean that the two senses never overlap. Sometimes evaluations are added to descriptive statements about human equality. Mencius, for example, regarded human nature (*jen hsing,* the behavioral traits and evaluating mind common to all men) as "good." Saint Augustine regarded some men as having more of the faculty of reason than some others, and hence as being "better." But the fundamental differences between the two kinds of usage still exist. In statements where a descriptive reference is present, the relative emphasis is on the equally or unequally shared attributes of the human endowment, and any evaluation is secondary. Moreover, the attribute "good" differs from the "worth" or "dignity" associated with purely evaluative statements about equality. For example, when Mencius called human nature "good," he was speaking about man's potentialities at birth (the sense of "when born" is strong in the term *ehsing*), not about a general characteristic of men as adults. The "good" refers to the fact that the future actions of men are likely to be desirable or in accordance with customary norms, given a proper environment. In purely evaluative references to equality, however, "worth" and "dignity" are qualities attributed by an external agent (e.g., Heaven) to men throughout their lives, and do not refer to any behavior that might be expected of men. Finally, statements that are basically descriptive do not necessarily imply that people

each man to develop morally; but it says nothing more about how people should be treated as adults. It is in no way inconsistent with a belief in the need for inequalities of social status, political power, rights, or privileges. These can be awarded to those who actually do achieve moral preeminence.

As we saw in Chapter 1, Western Christianity applied the idea of hierarchy to nature, society, and the human endowment (where it depended on differences in reasoning ability). This was the dominant strain in Christianity until the Reformation, and its roots lie in the hierarchical doctrines of Plato and Aristotle.[20] But an egalitarian strain was also present, especially in the early Church; Saint Paul is the apologist for this second body of ideas, which was submerged for so long. Early Christian egalitarianism, destined to reemerge under new political conditions, spoke of equality chiefly in the evaluative sense of the term. It emphasized not shared empirical characteristics but equal "rights" and equal "worth," with implications for how men should be treated.*

The Christian idea of equal rights was not unlike the Stoic ideal of a golden age in which there were no distinctions of rank and fortune, and no men were born with the right to rule others. This notion influenced Roman law. Justinian's *Institutes* begins, "By the law of nature, all men from the beginning are born free." In early Christianity, we find a variation of this idea: men were born free, but social and political equality disappeared with the fall from grace.[21] Egalitarian Christianity stressed that men were of equal worth, since God valued all souls equally. Thus it indicated pri-

---

should be treated in any particular way. Mencius's reference to the good nature with which men are born, for example, does not imply that all men should be treated impartially or justly, or given equal rights as adults. But in purely evaluative statements about equality, the primary stress is on the necessary implication: that all men should be treated justly and accorded equal rights throughout their lives.

* The idea of equality in the descriptive sense, as used in China, is not absent from European thought; but it was regarded as quite revolutionary when first put forward. Descartes, the father of modern Western philosophy, made the radical assertion that men are naturally equal because all men equally possess the light of reason. He accepted the older idea that the essence of man is rationality, but he rejected the notion that it can occur in varying degrees.

marily how adults should be treated, rather than saying something about natural attributes with which men are born.*

God gave no man the right to rule, and he regarded every man as equally valuable, regardless of his worldly accomplishments: the implication was that God did not recognize worldly hierarchical distinctions between men. These latent Christian ideas first made themselves felt in the English peasant revolts of 1381, when John Ball demanded a change in the social structure on the ground that men were originally free. Later, Nicholas of Cusa proposed a system of representative councils in church and state to embody the principle of government by consent. He was also reactivating the early Christian egalitarianism.[22] These men wanted egalitarian treatment now rather than on judgment day—when, according to orthodox church fathers, there would be an equal opportunity for salvation. The real flowering of the egalitarian idea occurred later, when conflict arose between the papacy in Rome and secular rulers who had their own ideas about the locus of political power.

The egalitarian revolt began in the church itself, and was directed against the church hierarchy. No better example can be found than the actions of Martin Luther, who rejected the attempts of the church in Rome to assign different rights, powers, and privileges to men depending on whether their status was clerical or lay and their occupation "spiritual" or "carnal." These distinctions, Luther felt, were not recognized by God, in whose eyes all souls are equally worthy. Further, he maintained that local congregations should have the right to ordain their own ministers and hold them "responsible unto themselves."[23] John Ball, Nicholas of Cusa, and Martin Luther were asserting that rulers should act in accordance with the early Christian idea that men are of similar worth and thus share certain common political rights. The very fact that their demands were making history shows that the egalitarian element in Christianity had been submerged. The story of the reemergence of this early Christian egalitarianism and of the changes

* Early Christian "equality" is also based on common descent from Adam and Eve.

it inspired, first in the church and then in the state, has been well told by Sanford A. Lakoff.[24]

John Locke, a "consent theorist" par excellence, maintained that men are unequal by most empirical standards (see his *Second Treatise of Government*, section 54). To say that "all men are created equal" (a maxim inspired by Locke and others) is not to say that all are born six feet tall, or with an evaluating mind, or with the capacity to feel pain. Instead, they are of equal worth in God's eyes; therefore, none have by birth the God-given right to lord it over others, and all should be treated fairly or justly. Men retain this equality of worth throughout their lives, and only by "consent" can some adults rule over others. To speak of men being equal in this sense is also to make a kind of procedural claim: if one does not treat men impartially or regard them as possessing equal rights, one should have to give some reason why certain men are treated differently from others (for example, that they have been convicted of crimes). In contrast, when "equality" is used in the descriptive sense, as it was in China, there is no implication that men are always of similar worth, that their "consent" must be sought if others are to rule them, or that they should always be treated impartially and regarded as having equal rights.

Whatever its differences from Western concepts, the Chinese idea of natural equality, by enduring for so long, has affected a large part of Chinese thought—especially theories of human behavior. "By nature men are nearly alike; by practice, they get to be wide apart"; "The sage and we are the same in kind"; and given the same "soil" and the same "nourishment afforded by the rains and dews," men will turn out the same—beliefs like these produced the conviction that people are without innate defects. Hence Chinese literati exaggerated the effects of environmental factors in their understanding of the human condition. The doctrine of natural equality, like Tao itself, breathed life over the years into endless variations on the theme that man is perfectible through education; and whatever its philosophical weaknesses, it helped to maintain some of the most lasting and effective forms of political control in human history.

APPENDIX

APPENDIX

THE ORIGIN OF THE CONCEPT OF *TE*

THE TERM *te* denoted a consistent attitude toward the Heaven-decreed norms, which, in the case of ideal *te,* displayed itself in regularly appearing action in accordance with the norms. This attitude served to establish communion between the individual and Heaven; hence *te* was religious in nature. Eventually, in the Chou period, *te* developed the extended sense of a bestowal of bounties by a ruler (or more simply, "kindness") because this activity was believed to accord with one of Heaven's major decrees. *Te* in this sense would automatically produce affection and loyalty in the hearts of the people, and would attract them to the person practicing it. By examining the antecedent of *te* in the Shang period, together with its definitions in the early etymological work *Shuo-wen chieh-tzu,* we can discover some of the reasons for these two meanings.

The Early Graphs

The most frequently encountered form of the character *te* in the West Chou is 德, composed of three elements. First, there is the element 彳, an abbreviation of the longer form 行, which is seen on oracle bones. It has been suggested that this was a picture of the paths between rice fields (i.e., [illegible]); its basic sense is "path," from which emerged the sense of "to go" and then the extended sense of "to act." It is possible that 彳, appearing as part of the antecedent of *te* in the oracle-bone inscriptions, initially had the sense of "to go," as will be shown. If its presence in *te* retained some sense of "to act," this assumption would certainly accord with the portrait of *te* put forth in Chapter 4. The second element is 心, "heart." This element in graphs often denotes mental activity, and in this case it most likely refers to "attitude" toward the antecedent Heavenly standard. The third element is [illegible] ; the line emerging from the oval appears either with a slight bulge in the middle ([illegible]) or with the bulge extended into a short line across the vertical line ([illegible]), both meaning the same. It is this third element that causes the trouble in interpretation.

To explain the third element, we must look first at four variations in the form of the character *te*. That these variations still represent *te* is indisputable; they usually occur in standard expressions that are rendered in the common form on other bronzes. One is [illegible] , a form encountered mostly in the East Chou (770–255 B.C.).[1] The lower right hand element [illegible] is the pictograph meaning "foot," and presents no problem because it often accompanies the left hand element 彳 without adding any new sense. The variant form [illegible] ,[2] in which the radical component, 彳 , is omitted appears on one bronze from the Warring States period and may have been used in the West Chou, too, though no examples from that period have yet been found; all examples from the early Chou have the 彳 component. Nevertheless, this character is not necessarily a fluke. It was not unusual for Chou writers to omit such a component. For example, the same element was sometimes omitted from *te* 得 ,[3] "to get" (bronze [illegible]), so that it was written [illegible] ; and *wen,* meaning "refined," was often written with a heart [illegible] , but sometimes not, as 文 . The third variation in form, [illegible] , which also omits the radical, appears on a bronze from a grave dated about 396 B.C. and probably did not exist in the West Chou.[4] It introduces the new element [illegible] , found on our present character *te* 德 and in our present character *chih* 直 : this element has not yet been adequately explained. The final variation is one in which the heart element [illegible] is omitted. All three examples of this date from the West Chou: [illegible] [5] and [illegible] [6] are probably from the reign of K'ang Wang (1067–1041 B.C.), and [illegible] [7] from that of Kung Wang (982–966 B.C.).

The concept of *te* first appeared in the West Chou (1111–771 B.C.). There is no firm evidence that it existed in the Shang. However, aware of the meaning and form discussed above, one can search the oracle-bone inscriptions for a possible antecedent graph, which might explain the element and the root meaning of the character as a whole. Three graphs present themselves for study: two, and , are similar in form to the element of the Chou graph; the other, (or), is practically identical with the three West Chou variations of *te* that omit the heart element. The third graph is the first clue to a possible Shang antecedent of the West Chou *te*.

Study of over 50 Shang bone inscriptions in which the first graph, , appears confirms that it had the sense "to look." For example:

Ask: Should the king not go look at the cows in ?[8]

The king goes to look at *ch'u* 出 .[9]

Frequently the word "to go toward" (*ᵇwang*) is not used before "look," although the sense of "to go" may still be implied by the context.

Should he not go to look at the hunting area?[10]

He goes to look at 盂 hunting area; will there be no disasters?[11]

Ask: if the king [goes to] look at 盂 hunting preserve will it not rain for a whole day?[12]

This sense of the bone character as "to look" is confirmed by the existence of an almost identical West Chou bronze graph, (present character 省 , seen in the earliest extant texts), which then clearly had the meaning "to look." Wen I-to holds that (and the other two graphs, and) meant "to travel around and inspect."[13] Because *ᵇwang* had to be added in the first examples, it is clear that the basic sense is not "to go look" but simply "to look" (or, by extension, "to inspect"). The explanation of Wen I-to that is the picture of an eye is generally accepted.[14] No adequate explanation of the upper part of the character ( ) can yet be made.

The other two graphs share the eye component and the sense of "to look." This is clearly demonstrated by their use in phrases almost identical to those in which was used:

Ask: On the day *keng shen*, should the king go look [[graph]] at *ch'u* 出.[15]

Should I not go look [[graph]] at the hunting preserve 盂?[16]

Should the king not go look [[graph]] at *ch'u* 出?[17]

The total absence of *ᵇwang*, "to go toward," in all examples indicates that for [graph] "to go inspect" may often be a more appropriate rendering, "to go" being derived from 彳.[18]

The two graphs [graph] and [graph] (or [graph]) are similar in having a single straight line rising out of the eye, unlike the [graph] of the graph [graph]. Kaizuka Shigeki[19] believes that this represents a line along which the eye sights, giving the sense of "to look directly," or possibly, "to look directly upward"; the explanation is tentative. The two also differ from [graph] in being associated with certain particular phrases and topics.[20]

The Antecedent of Te

The two graphs [graph] and [graph], besides their basic sense of "to look" or "to look directly," sometimes have a special religious meaning. This seems to have combined the ideas of consulting a divine being and making offerings to one. The consultation usually concerned what should be done to alleviate a present condition; and both consultation and offering may have occurred at the same time, as in the consultations at Delphi. Examples of this religious meaning follow:

(a) On the day *keng hsü*, divine; the king is cursed. Shall we consult/offer up to [[graph]] ancestor [Ta] I?
(b) On the day *keng hsü*, divine: The king is cursed. Shall we consult/offer up [[graph]] to ancestor Ta Chia?[21]

On the day ** *shen*, divine: Hsüan asks: Shall we pray to [the ancestral mother] Pi Kuei because the king is cursed?
** ; say, ** , consult/offer up [[graph]] owing to the curse.[22]

(a) Shall I not offer up [[graph] 㞢] to ancestor [Ta] I?
(b) Ask: Should I consult/offer up [[graph] 㞢] to ancestor [Ta] I?[23]

On the day *I szu*, divine: Hsüan asks: Should I not consult/offer up [[graph] 㞢] to Huang Yin?[24]

On the day ** *hai*, divine: the king himself asks: Po ** made a curse? I consult/offer up [𢓊]; will I receive help?[25]

The sense of "to look" remained, in that to consult is to focus attention directly on something.

Since the primary sense of the graphs in question was "to look," it is likely that a religious act involving looking was involved; perhaps the subject looked upward at the ancestor above. A rite of this kind did exist, and was deemed highly important in Chou times: a sacrifice to the mountains and streams that was termed *ᶜwang*, "to look from a distance"; it involved a ruler's looking from afar at the mountains and streams of his domain.[26] The oracle-bone antecedent of the present character *ᶜwang* is 望 , composed partly of an eye, like the graphs of concern to us. It often has the sense in those inscriptions of looking up at clouds and other heavenly phenomena for omens. Hence there is at least a precedent for a graph with a primary sense related to looking that refers to a religious ritual.

The Link

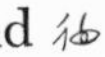

It may be possible to connect the oracle-bone graphs 直 and 𢓊 to the West Chou *te* in both form and meaning, beginning with form. The three West Chou examples of the character *te* that lack the *hsin* (心) element (𢓊 , 𢓊 , and 𢓊) are almost identical to the oracle-bone graph 𢓊 .[27] The only difference is the slight bulge in the middle of the line rising out of the eye in one of the Chou graphs, which could well be a product of time and style. The infrequently encountered oracle-bone graph has a probable descendant in the rare East Chou bronze graph for *te*, 悳 ; this includes the Chou addition of the heart and is the same character, 悳 , that appears in the early etymological work *Shuo-wen chieh-tzu*. In the Chou texts 悳 was probably used alternately (though less frequently) with the character having the radical, 德 .[28] Karlgren places *te* in a phonetic series whose root character is *chih* 直 .[29] Aware of the fact that the element ㄥ is a late Chou development, one can see the similarity of the Shang graphs 直 and 𢓊 (identical in meaning) to the later forms *chih* 直 and *te* 德 (德). There is also some evidence that 直 was used as a short form for 悳 in Chou texts.[30]

Let us now turn to the link in meaning. The Shang antecedent of *te* basically meant "to consult" (lit., "to look up at") a high-ranking tribal ancestor about what should be done, i.e., to ask what the divine being demands of man in a given situation. I would suggest that the Shang sense of "to consult" or "to focus attention on" a tribal ancestor to find out what is required gradually acquired the Chou sense of attention constantly focused on divinely decreed norms. In other words, *te* retained the meaning of "viewpoint." In the West Chou, *te* denoted a consistent attitude or viewpoint toward the Heaven-decreed norms, which, in the case of ideal *te*, revealed itself by regularly appearing conduct in accordance with them.*

In the West Chou, ancestors were frequently cited as models whose *te* must be emulated. The term *te* was applicable to ancestors because they too must abide by the Heavenly rules. Eventually, living men who embodied the norms also came to be regarded as models. Was there a gradual change from the earlier Shang notion of simply focusing attention (徝) on an ancestor to the Chou notion of focusing attention on a particular ancestor who embodied the norms? That is, is the Shang idea of "focusing attention on" or "looking up at" ancestors one source of the notion of model emulation in the Chou and later? Both the Shang and the Chou terms were essentially religious in nature. The Shang antecedent clearly involved establishing contact with deified ancestors through consultation and offerings. Likewise, maintaining the correct "viewpoint" (*te*) in the West Chou could establish communion between man and Heaven.

* This transition from the notion of eyesight to "mindsight" has a counterpart in early Greek philosophy. The Greek term that Plato used to denote "idea" (i.e., one of the Platonic "Forms" or "Ideas") was *eidos*, which is etymologically related to "eyesight." Apparently a transition occurred in the term's meaning—from "the common look" of all things of a given class (the common appearance of all men, trees, or white things, for example) to "that which it looks like" (all members of the class "look like" the "Ideas" of manness, treeness, or whiteness). Obviously *eidos* in the later sense could only be perceived by the mind. Thus, for Plato, the wise man focuses on the Ideas with the eye of his soul; that is, he has visions of the truth.

The Differences

Among the major differences between the Shang terms and *te* is that *te* involved explicit assumptions about the actions prescribed for men to carry out. One of these was acting so as to insure the well-being of the people; that is, bestowing bounties on the people. Another difference is that in the Chou there was a clear connection between *te* and receipt of the deity's blessings. But there is no necessary connection between the consultation/offering denoted by the Shang terms and any divine response.

During the Shang, the characters [illegible] and [illegible] were used as verbs, whereas *te* from the West Chou onward was usually used as a noun, with occasional exceptions in bronzes and texts.[31] Also, on the basis of the limited knowledge available, in the Shang ritual the sacrificing was done only to correct a concrete situation that already existed (e.g., to cease a specific illness).[32] In the Chou, action was carried on constantly to ensure getting the divine blessings. Moreover, in the Shang religious activity we have discussed the ancestors consulted and the recipients of the offerings were of the Shang clan, and the incidents with which the people were most often concerned were particularly relevant only to that clan. In the Chou, Heaven (or Shang Ti), which responded to *te*, was the deity of all clans;* and matters of most concern to the early West Chou people, as set forth in the materials we have, were frequently political and of immediate concern to all "under Heaven."

The Early Definitions of Te

Te's earlier religious content (stemming from the Shang) and its new political content are both reflected in the two pertinent

* The question of whether or not the Shang people had the concept of a universal deity has not been satisfactorily solved. It is known that *Ti* was originally the ancestral spirit of the clan; Kuo Mo-jo, *Hsien-ch'in,* pp. 11–12. A recent theory views the character [b]*t'ien* (Heaven) as a development of the form of [illegible], which meant "top" and was another name for Shang Ti in the Shang bone inscriptions; the Chou reference to Shang Ti as [b]*t'ien* was thus a continuance of a Shang appellation (Shima, pp. 218–19). There is some evidence for a smooth transition from the Shang to the Chou in the realm of religious beliefs.

entries in the *Shuo-wen chieh-tzu,* one under 德 (德) and one under 悳 (悳). Both forms appear on bronze inscriptions, but the meaning is the same; and retaining or omitting the 彳 was for a time a matter of style. Hence, although the dictionary gives two words, both are relevant to the one concept *te.* Each dictionary definition, however, emphasizes one of two elements in the meaning of *te.* One is the religious aspect stemming from the Shang ("to consult/to offer"). The other is the extended sense *te* took on in the Chou: bestowal of bounties on others, winning their hearts and loyalty. This extended sense (loosely, "kindness") developed because philanthropic activity was, in fact, one of the major forms of conduct required by the Heavenly norms.

The definition of *te* under 德 is "to rise up" (*ᶜsheng*),[33] and it has long puzzled Chinese commentators on the *Shuo wen.*[34] *Te* could be so defined because its meaning from the beginning, i.e., from the Shang period, included the sense of focusing attention upward to the deity (consulting). In the Chou, *te* retained the sense of focusing attention upward, this time focusing on Heaven's commands, which were often embodied in an ancestor who served as the model of *te.* In the Shang, the religious activity denoted by [illegible] and [illegible] involved some kind of offering to the deity. There are examples from the early West Chou in which *te* is spoken of as a kind of offering that rises up to Heaven: "It was not so that fragrant offerings made with virtue [*te*] ascended [*teng*] and were perceived by Heaven; . . . Therefore, when Heaven sent down destruction on Yin and had no mercy for Yin, it was due to (his) excesses."[35]

In the Chou, the connection of *te* with some kind of concrete process of "rising up" is found in references to the "fact" of the individual's *te* rising up to Heaven and becoming known to the Deity: "Because Wen Wang's *te* became known to the Lord-on-High above, he received the mandate of the Yin rulers."[36] This phenomenon came to be expressed with a standard phrase, "His *te* rose and was heard by Heaven" (*ch'i te sheng wen yü t'ien*). The idea is seen in a chapter from the *Shu ching* dating from about the eighth century B.C.: "The greatly illustrious Wen and Wu could be careful to make bright the virtue [*te*]; brilliantly it rose on high [ᶜ*sheng*], widely it was renowned here below. Then God on High placed his mandate on Wen Wang."[37] In all such cases, *te* is that which rises (*teng*, ᶜ*sheng*) to Heaven, linking man and deity and eliciting some benefit or reproach for man.

A new political content, possibly appearing first in the early West Chou, was added to the primarily religious meaning. This was the specific conduct dictated by the deity. Frequently required was some bestowal of goods on others, in order to harmonize and gladden them; additionally, it elicited a response of obedience or good will. This factor is reflected in the *Shuo wen* definition of 悳 ,[38] which is the other character used for *te*. The definition reads *wai te yü jen nei te yü chi.* Most commentators have followed Tuan Yü-ts'ai in giving a rather forced interpretation of this: "[The way] which one gets himself in mind and body [by self-cultivation]; the kindness [which he has as a result of the cultivation] he causes other men to get."[39] This reverses the actual phrases and renders them literally as: "Internally he gets it from the self, externally he causes others to get it." The explanation is compatible with the meaning of *te*; but a simpler interpretation, emphasizing the response to *te*, is possibly more accurate. One key component in the meaning of *te* was the eliciting of a response of loyalty or gratitude from the people. Thus the first part of this phrase should be interpreted as equivalent to *wai te jen hsin*, "externally achieving in man's hearts"—i.e., causing the people to respect and obey one at heart. The other part of the phrase, *nei te yü chi*, refers to "purifying" one's own *te* in accordance with the standard.

Notes to Appendix

1. It is on Vessel 23. Kuo Mo-jo, *Liang-chou*, B, p. 168b; expl. B, 160a.

2. On Vessel 8. Wu Ta-cheng, 9, 11b; ref. p. 603.

3. Yen I-p'ing, "Shih te" (Explaining *te*), in Tung, 1.6b.

4. On Vessel 9. Kuo Mo-jo, *Liang-chou*, A, 278b; expl. B, 239a. For the date of this, see Shirakawa, "Meimon koshaku," B, p. 42. This

bronze was made in the state of Chin; perhaps the element 𠃊 had appeared somewhat earlier in another state.

5. On Vessel 21. Kuo Mo-jo, *Liang-chou*, A, 20b; expl. A, 40b. Kuo dates it as K'ang Wang period. The bronze itself no longer exists. The rubbing is from *Hsi ch'ing ku-chien*, compiled by order of the Emperor Kao Tsung (1755), 8, 33ab; the work contains rubbings of bronzes in the royal family collection. In the opinion of Shirakawa Shizuka, although there are sometimes minor alterations in characters in the work, it is most likely that the *te* had no heart in this instance.

6. On Vessel 24; see Yü, *Shang-chou*, p. 22b, No. 89. The interpretation is in Yü, *Shuang-Chien-i*, B.1, p. 6b. The character is also listed in Jung, p. 86. Professor Kaizuka Shigeki of Kyoto University dates it as K'ang Wang period.

7. On Vessel 25; Fang, 4, 12b. Professor Kaizuka dates this as about Kung Wang period. Kuo Mo-jo, in *Chin-wen*, p. 21a, says that the *hsin* element is just indecipherable in this case. However, after consulting the original rubbing in Lo, 3, 45, I am assured that if there had been a *hsin*, the rubber would have found it. This opinion is shared by Professor Shirakawa.

8. Shang, A, 1b, No. 4; expl. A, 2b.

9. *Ibid.*, A, 41a, No. 382; expl. B, 54a.

10. *Ibid.*, A, 11b, No. 68; expl. B, 15b.

11. Kuo Mo-jo, *Yin-ch'i ts'ui-pien*, 2, 90, No. 966; expl. 4, 126.

12. *Ibid.*, 2, 86, No. 929; expl. 4, 121a.

13. Wen, p. 515.

14. Kuo Mo-jo has a peculiar theory regarding the element resembling an "eye" on bronzes. He holds that 省 is *hsiang* 相, the form of an eye and eyebrow; it meant "to look." 省, he says, is *sheng* 眚, the form of a seed sprouting, not an eye; it meant "to produce" or "to grow." Following the theory of Lo Chen-yü, he would connect the small seal characters *sheng* 省 and *hsiang* 相, and he views them as different from *sheng* 眚, "the original *sheng* 生 character." See Kuo Mo-jo, *Yin-chou*, pp. 31–32. The character *sheng* is defined in the *Shou-wen* as "an eye disease, growing a cataract." Tuan Yü-ts'ai says its extended sense is "fault." See Ting, IV, 1446. *Sheng* is defined as "to look at"; *ibid.*, III, 600. But in the early texts there are numerous examples in which *sheng* has the sense of "to look" and *hsiang* the sense of "fault." 省 is borrowed for *sheng* 生 "to produce" on several bronzes stating that on such and such a day "the moon brought forth (*sheng* 省) its bright section." The same expression occurs in Karlgren, *Documents*, K'ang kao 1, p. 39; but the character *sheng* 生 is used. This borrowing prompted Kuo's theory. Kuo ignores all 省 with the supposed "seed" shape that mean "to look," and the fact that in

texts from the earliest times 省 and 眚 were interchangeably used. His theory is generally rejected by Chinese and Japanese scholars. See Ogura, p. 154, n. 11.

15. Shang, A, 10a; expl. B, 13b.

16. *Ch'ien-shou-t'ang*, p. 11, No. 8; expl. in Wang Kuo-wei, p. 24b.

17. Chang Ping-ch'üan, Plate 21, No. 7; expl., p. 44.

18. The sense of "to inspect," which existed as one meaning in the bone characters 省, 直, and 徝, still exists in the West Chou bronze inscription character 省, which appears in the texts as 省. For example, "The king first inspected the territory that Wen and Wu had ruled with effort," on Vessel 26 (Kuo Mo-jo, *Liang-chou*, A, 25a; expl. A, 51a). The sense of "to go inspect" exists in the Chou bronze inscription character 𢓊. The earlier 省 or 省 usually has the more basic sense in bronzes and texts of "to look." See Vessel 27 (*ibid.*, A, 31b; expl. A, 59b). Wen I-to holds that the character *hsün* 循 evolved from the oracle bone character 徝; this bronze character seems close in meaning and form to 循 *hsün*. See Wen, p. 606.

19. He is associated with the Jinbun Kagaku Kenkyūjō (Institute for Humanistic Studies) of Kyoto University.

20. For example, in the 56 examples containing 省 that I have collected, there is no mention of the region (tribe) named *t'u-fang* (a frontier area inhabited by non-Shang peoples conquered by the Shang), or of "conquering" (*fa*); both terms are frequently mentioned when 徝 is used. The expression *mei jih* ("whole day") does not appear in phrases using 徝 or 直, but is frequently used in association with 省. If the graph 省 is just a variation of the other two, the difference between 省 and 直 (or 徝) could possibly be explained by examining the differing statements and looking for a time correlation between the appearance of one form or another and changes in political concerns and phrase usage.

21. Li Ya-nung, p. 3, No. 3; expl., p. 3b. Phrase (a) reads 庚戌卜王𠦪直祖已, and phrase (b) 庚戌卜王𠦪直大甲. Li says that 直 here is borrowed for *te* 德 with the sense of a sacrifice expressing gratitude for kindness. But this interpretation is inaccurate, being based on this one instance alone and lacking the identification of 夨. Comprehensive study of 省, 直, and 徝 would have revealed their interrelationship (denied by Li but important in understanding the meaning of 直 and 徝), as well as the fact that the character *te* did not exist at that time. Discovery of more examples of the religious usage, involving 徝 as well, plus a knowledge of the meaning of 𠦪, would have corrected the interpretation of 直 as an expression of gratitude. The identification of 𠦪 as "curse" has been made by Professor Itō Maruhachi of Kobe University (formerly assistant to Kaizuka Shigeki

at Kyoto University). 丰 was equal to 祟; it represented the spirit of an animal, but meant the curse of a spirit.

22. Kaizuka, *Kyōto jinbun kangaku kenkyūjō kokotsu moji*, No. 51; expl., p. 157. The apparent break in the tortoise shell evident in the rubbing was the result of its being dropped on the floor during preparation of the text and should cause no concern over reliability of joining the two pieces. The phrases read: 口申卜亘貞告于妣癸㛑王背口曰口祉祟. The term 告 written as 吿, meant "to pray." Regarding Pi Kuei as "ancestral mother," see Ch'en Meng-chia, p. 387.

23. Chang Ping-ch'üan, Plate 5.6; expl., p. 85. The phrases read: 勿𢦔㞢于祖乙貞𢦔㞢于祖乙. It is probable that both 𢦔 and 㞢 are verbs here; 眔 meaning "and" was never used between verbs, only between nouns. 㞢 had some reference to the act of sacrificing (see Kaizuka, p. 144), though the exact sense is not clear. I translate the two verbs with one term, although it is not absolutely certain that only one meaning was indicated.

24. Kaizuka, *Kyōto jinbun kangaku kenkyūjō kokotsu moji*, No. 738; expl., p. 288. The phrase reads: 乙巳卜亘貞勿𢦔㞢于黄尹. Huang Yin was probably a high official of one of the former kings.

25. Shang, A, 87a, No. 966; expl. B, 104a. The phrase reads: 口亥卜王伯𠬝迄[illegible]祉其受㞢祐. The characters 伯𠬝 refer to a deified person. In this case 㞢 and 祐 share the one sense of "help." Shirakawa Shizuka suggests that [illegible] possibly meant "curse"; cf. [illegible], Jung, p. 124, originally the representation of a dragon, meaning "fear" or "dread." A possible alternate translation of the last five characters would be: "If I consult/offer, will the ancestor accept my offering and help?"

26. Lu, p. 452.

27. On two occasions individual scholars have discovered an isolated example of the bronze character *te* minus the *hsin* component. Lo Chen-yü noted it on Vessel 28 and was challenged by Kuo Mo-jo (Kuo, *Chin wen*, p. 21a), who held that the *hsin* was just indecipherable. Ogura Yoshihiko noted it on Vessel 21 (Ogura, p. 143). In neither case were other instances brought forth that could offset an opinion that the *hsin* was indecipherable or that the character was a fluke. I cite three instances and have checked the original rubbings carefully in each case; my conclusion that these were the original forms of the characters as inscribed is supported by the Japanese specialist Shirakawa Shizuka. There is another example that I could cite but about which I am not completely sure, and there may be more.

28. Karlgren, though agreeing that 悳 is the same as 德, holds that the former is the earlier form; Karlgren, "Contributions," p. 221. However, although the bone graph 直 probably antedates 徝, it seems that

if anything, 悳 would be the later usage, not 德. Possibly they were interchangeably used from the beginning.

29. Karlgren, "Grammata Serica Recensa," p. 242.

30. Karlgren, "Glosses on the Book of Documents," p. 120.

31. E.g., "conferring benefits on them" (*te chih*); Legge, *Mencius*, iii.A.IV.8, p. 252. On Vessel 29 is the phrase "by making this vessel I sacrifice to my ancestor and demonstrate my *te*." See Kuo Mo-jo, *Liang-chou*, B, 267b; expl. B, 229a.

32. Itō, *passim*.

33. Ting, VIII, 4655a.

34. Previous attempts by Chinese scholars to explain this have been rather strained, usually based on the following "chain": *te* 德 equals *te* 得 equals [b]*teng* equals [c]*sheng*. The equation of *teng* and *te* 得 they base on archaic sound similarity and on one instance in the *Kung yang chuan* in which the two characters *teng lai* are supposedly equivalent to *te lai* (meaning "want to get" in the language of the people of the state of Ch'i). See *ibid.*, III, 809a.

35. Karlgren, *Documents*, Chiu kao 11, p. 43.

36. Ch'ü, *Shang shu*, Chün shih, p. 113 (K.14, p. 61).

37. Karlgren, *Documents*, Wen hou chih ming 1, p. 78. On the date of this chapter see Ch'ü, p. 145. For another instance of this usage of *sheng* see *K'ung tzu chia yü* (Sayings of the Confucian School), Chih pen 25 (SPTK 6, 4b–5a). The same expression occurs in the *Ta-tai li-chi*.

38. Ting, VIII, 4655a.

39. *Ibid.*, p. 4655b. He follows the Southern T'ang (A.D. 923–36) commentator Hsü K'ai in reversing the order of the two problems.

CHINESE CHARACTERS

[a] an jen 安仁
[b] an jen 安人
an shih 安時
an yü wei 安於位
ch'ang 常
ch'ang hsin 常心
ch'ao-hsing 超形
che te 悊德
chen chün 眞君
chen jen 眞人
chen tsai 眞宰
ch'en 臣
cheng chih 徵知
cheng ming 正命
cheng te 正〔政〕德
ch'eng 誠
ch'eng hsin 成心
ch'eng i 誠意
ch'i 氣
ch'i te sheng wen yü t'ien 其德升聞於天
chiao 郊
[a] chih 直
[b] chih 知
[c] chih 質
[d] chih 執
[e] chih (archaic d͡i̯ək) 殖
[f] chih (d͡i̯ək) 植
[g] chih (ti̯ək) 稙
[h] chih 置
[i] chih 志
chih hsing 知性
chih sheng 知生
chih tung fang yeh ch'un yeh chih erh wei yu wen yeh 直東方也春也質而未有文也
Chin-wen-chia 今文家
Ch'in 秦
[a] ching 敬
[b] ching 井
[c] ching 菁
[d] ching 經
[e] ching 徑
[f] ching 精
[g] ching 静
ching te 巠德
[a] ch'ing 卿
[b] ch'ing 情
[c] ch'ing 青
ch'ing-kuan 清官
ch'ing yung 情用
ch'u 矗
ch'u-i 處一
ch'u-sheng 出生
ch'üan te 全德
[a] chung 衆
[b] chung 忠
chung-jen 衆人
ch'ung 祟
chün 郡
chün-tzu 君子
erh-mu chih kuan 耳目之官

erh san ch'i te 二三其德
[a] fa 法
[b] fa 伐
fa-hsiao 法傚
fan pen 反本
fan wan wu i tse mo pu hsiang wei pi 凡萬物異則莫不相為蔽
fen 分
[a] fu 覆
[b] fu 復
hao-jen chih ch'i 浩然之氣
ho 和
hou 候
Hou Chi 合稷
hsiang 相
hsiang-chin 相近
hsiao 孝
hsiao-jen 小人
hsiao-tsu 小組
Hsieh 契
[a] hsien 縣
[b] hsien 賢
hsien-chin sheng-ch'an-che 先进生产者
hsien-ts'ai 賢才
hsin 心
hsin chih kuan 心之官
hsin chih so k'o 心之所可
hsin shih ch'i yüeh ch'iang 心使氣日強
[a] hsing 姓
[b] hsing 形
[c] hsing 行
[d] hsing 刑 (bronze 井刂)
[e] hsing 性
hsing chih (seishitsu) 性質
hsing chih ho so sheng 性之和所生
hsing-ming 性命
hsing o 性惡
hsing shan 性善
hsing-wei 行為
hsing wu ching 行吾敬
hsiu 休
hsiu shen 修身
hsiung 凶
hsü 虛
hsüan niao 玄鳥
hsüeh-hsi 學習
hua 化
Huang-** 黄[illegible]
Huang Yin 黄尹
hun 魂
[a] i 彝
[b] i 義
[c] i 異
[d] i 夷
[e] i 壹
[f] i 敦
i t'iao 馴調
i wu 役物
i li fu jen-k'ou, i li fu jen-hsin 以力服人口以理服人心
[a] jen 人
[b] jen 仁
jen-che 仁者
jen-che jen yeh 仁者人也
jen-chüeh 人爵
jen-hsin 人心
jen-hsing 人性
jen-i 仁義
jou 柔
ko-hsing 個性
ko wu 格物
k'o 可
k'o-neng 可能
kuan mo 观摩
kuei 歸

[a] kung 公
[b] kung 功
kuo 過
[a] li 禮
[b] li 利
[c] li 理
li-hsing 理性
li-i 禮義
ling 令
ling ming nan lau 靈命難老
lou 陋
mei jih 湄日
mei-shou yung-ming; wan-nien yung-ming 眉壽永命萬年永命
mi erh hsing 彌而性
mi erh sheng 彌而生
min 民
ming 命
ming te 明德
[a] nieh 孽
[b] nieh 櫱
[a] nu 奴
[b] nu 女
nei 內
nei sheng 內省
nei sheng wai wang 內聖外王
nei te yü chi 內得於己
nung-chia 農家
p'an 畔
pang po 邦伯
p'ei ming 配命
p'ei t'ien 配天
pen-chih 本質
pen-t'i 本体
pi 鄙
piao-hsien 表現
ping 秉
p'ing-tan chih ch'i 平旦之氣
po-hsing 百姓
po kuan 百官
p'o 魄
pu cheng 不爭
pu ts'ai 不材
pu-tung-hsin 不動心
seishitsu (hsing chih) 性質
shang 上
Shang Chia 上甲
shang te 上德
Shao Hao 少皡
shen 神
shen-jen 神人
shen te 甚德
[a] sheng 生
[b] sheng 盛
[c] sheng 升
[d] sheng 眚
[e] sheng 聖
sheng-hsien 聖賢
sheng-jen 聖人
sheng-lai 生來
sheng-wang 聖王
[a] shih 氏
[b] shih 士
[c] shih 事
[d] shih 勢
shih fei 是非
shih-fei-chih-hsin 是非之心
[a] shou 壽
[b] shou 受
shou tzu ming 受茲命
[a] shu 恕
[b] shu 樞
shu-jen 庶人
shu-yüan 書院
shuai 帥
shuai te 衰德
shun 純

shun hou 淳厚
so i ch'eng 所以成
ssu 私
ssu-fang 四方
ta-sheng chih ch'ing-che 達生之情者
ta-t'ung 大同
tai-fu 大夫
t'ai-ch'ung 太冲
t'ai-ho 太和
tan 丹
tang-hsing 黨性
[a] te 德
[b] te 得
te ching 德巠
te hsing 德行
te lai 得來
te min hsin 得民心
te yeh che te yü shen yeh 德也者得於身也
[a] teng 等
[b] teng 登
teng-lai 登來
Ti 帝
Ti K'u 帝嚳
t'i-yung 体用
tien 典
tien-hsing 典型
[a] t'ien 田
[b] t'ien 天
t'ien-ch'ing 天情
t'ien-chüeh 天爵
t'ien-chün 天君
t'ien-hsing 天性
t'ien-jen 天人
t'ien-ti 天地
[a] tsai 在
[b] tsai 哉
tsai ti tso-yu 在帝左右
[a] ts'ai 材
[b] ts'ai 才
ts'ai-p'o 材朴
tsao-hua-che 造化者
tsao-wu-che 造物者
ts'ao 操
ts'ung ch'i yü 縱其欲
ts'ung jen chih hsing 從〔縱〕人之性
ts'ung tien tao mien 從點到面
t'u-fang 土方
tuan 端
tun 敦
tung 動
t'ung 同
t'ung-hsing 同姓
t'ung hsing chih ch'ing 通性之情
t'ung-hsing pu-hun 同姓不婚
t'ung-hsüeh 同血
t'ung-lei 同類
t'ung-sheng 同生
tzu hua 自化
wai 外
wai te jen hsin 外得人心
wai te yü jen nei te yü chi 外得於人内得於己
[a] wang 王
[b] wang 往
[c] wang 望
Wang Hai 王亥
[a] wei 偽
[b] wei 偽 or 為
wei-shih 唯識
wei te 為德
wen-li 文理
[a] wu 物
[b] wu 無
wu chih 無知

[a] wu hsing 五行
[b] wu hsing 無形
wu-i 物役
wu kuan pu chih 五官不薄
wu ssu 無私
wu wei 無為
wu yü 無欲
[a] yang 煬
[b] yang 養
yang hsing 養性
yang sheng 養生
yu so jan...yu so k'o 有所然…有所可
yung 用
yung ming 永命
[a] yü 踰
[b] yü 欲
yü chu yung 寓諸庸
yü i jen 余一人
Yü Sheng 雨生
[a] yüan 嫄
[b] yüan 元

INSCRIBED BRONZE VESSELS CITED

1. Hsien i 獻彝
2. K'ang ting 康鼎
3. Po k'ang kuei 伯康毀
4. Ta k'o ting 大克鼎
5. Chung fang ting 中方鼎
6. Chou kung kuei 周公毀
7. Pan kuei 班毀
8. Ch'en hou yin tzu tun 陳侯因資敦
9. Szu tzu hu 嗣子壺
10. Shih wang ting 師望鼎
11. Ta yü ting 大盂鼎
12. Ching jen an chung 井人安鐘
13. Hsiang sheng kuei 香生毀
14. Kuo lü chung 虢旅鐘
15. Ta feng kuei 大豐毀
16. Yu chung 猶鐘
17. Yü ting 盂鼎
18. Mao kung ting 毛公鼎
19. K'o tsun 克尊
20. T'ien chün ting 天君鼎
21. Mo tsun 麥尊
22. Shih ** kuei 師訇毀
23. Wang sun i che chung 王孫遺者鐘
24. Hsin ting 辛鼎
25. Li ting 歷鼎
26. Chung yen 中甗
27. ** ting 竅鼎
28. Li ting 曆鼎
29. Chin chiang ting 晉姜鼎
30. Ch'i tzu chung chiang po 齊子仲姜鎛
31. Yeh kuei 也毀
32. Ch'i ta tsai p'an 齊大宰盤
33. Tsan ku kuei 絲姑毀
34. Ching jen chung 井仁鐘
35. Ta pao tun 大保敵
36. Wu tsun kai 吳尊盇

NOTES

Complete authors' names, titles of works, and publication data will be found in the Bibliography, pp. 241–49. When reference is made to a Chinese edition of the *Shu ching* (Book of Documents), the location of the same passage in the translation by Bernhard Karlgren appears in parentheses immediately following the Chinese citation: "K.21, p. 2," for example, means "Karlgren, line 21, page 2." If the name of a Western translator is indicated in the citation, that person's translation is the one used; otherwise, the translation is mine, and the standard Harvard-Yenching numbering is used to give the location of the passage. Page references to some of the works used are followed, in parentheses, by a reference to the same passage in the *Ssu-pu ts'ung-k'an* (abbreviated SPTK). Inscribed bronze vessels cited are numbered in accordance with the list on p. 203. Romanized Chinese terms will be found in the Chinese Characters section, pp. 198–202.

Chapter 1

1. Creel, *Confucius*, p. 119.

2. *Mencius* iv.B.32. The discussion in *Mencius* i.B.7 seems inconsistent with the sentiment of this passage about Yao and Shun. Actually, that chapter does not rule out talent. Mencius is opposing the haphazard offering of high position to mendicant sophists without consideration of their actual merit. He says that the ruler of Ch'i should look to the people for confirmation of a man's real merit. In the absence of confirmation, it is best to appoint men from the tried and trusted families that have proven themselves over the years. In fact, the chapter reveals the dynamic tension between the old hereditary standard and the new consideration of merit.

3. Wang Hsien-ch'ien, *Hsün-tzu*, Wang chih, pp. 94–95 (SPTK 5.1a). Translation is from Dubs, *Hsuntze*, p. 121.

4. Watson, p. 20.

5. Liao, I, 45.

6. Li Tsung-t'ung, I, 45.

7. Katō, p. 15.

8. Cheng Te-k'un, II, 217.

9. *Ibid.*
10. Li Tsung-t'ung, I, 48–49.
11. Cheng Te-k'un, III, xxvii–xxviii.
12. Katō, pp. 16, 26.
13. *Ibid.*, pp. 27–30.
14. *Ibid.*, p. 17.
15. Masubuti, p. 213.
16. Katō, p. 33; Hou, pp. 138, 383.
17. Hsü Cho-yün, p. 3. I summarize considerably from Hsü's study on this matter.
18. *Ibid.*, p. 7.
19. *Ibid.*, p. 86.
20. *Ibid.*, p. 31.
21. This disappearance of the hereditary noble families is discussed at length in *ibid.*, pp. 24–52.
22. Kuo, *Nu-li chih*, p. 10. An article reaffirming all of the arguments Kuo has advanced and condemning opposition to the slave society thesis has appeared, signed by one Ch'i Ta (a pseudonym of Kuo's?). See Ch'i Ta, p. 18.
23. Kuo, *Nu-li chih*, p. 10; Ch'en Meng-chia, p. 640.
24. They dispute the interpretation of characters like the ones mentioned as standing for slave. For example, Tung holds that *chung* represents three men standing below a certain place, not three toiling under the sun; and Hu and Shima say that *ch'en* stood for an official. All three feel that the *chung* and *chung jen* were free men who engaged in agriculture or were recruited for battle. Though denying that agriculture was in the hands of slaves, they do not altogether deny that there were slaves during the Shang period; Hu feels that slaves were the sacrificial victims in tombs. Shima, however, maintains that those buried with an important figure were not slaves but loyal retainers. See Shima, pp. 11, 482–86, 490; and Hu Hou-hsüan, Chia-ku-hsüeh, pp. 1a–4b.
25. Hsü Cho-yün, p. 76.
26. Cheng Te-k'un, III, 299.
27. Hsü Cho-yün, pp. 109, 111.
28. Li Tsung-t'ung, II, 246.
29. Kuo, *Nu-li chih*, p. 21.
30. Cheng Te-k'un, III, xxx.
31. *Ibid.*
32. Hsü Cho-yün, p. 95.
33. Liang Ch'i-ch'ao, p. 77.
34. Shih Ming, p. 163.
35. Legge, II, 406.
36. *Ibid.*, pp. 404–5.

37. Wang Hsien-ch'ien, *Hsün-tzu*, jung ju, pp. 39–40 (SPTK 2.10b). Translation is from Dubs, *Hsuntze*, pp. 60–61.

38. *Analects* xvii.2.

39. *Analects* xv.23, vi.28.

40. For example, see *Analects* xvii.3.

41. *Republic*, iii.415a, in Hamilton and Cairns, p. 659.

42. *Phaedo* 91c–95a, in *ibid.*, pp. 73–77.

43. *Timaeus* 41e.

44. Cicero, *On the Laws*, M., quoted in Abernethy, p. 53.

45. Cf. Lakoff, p. 16.

46. Galatians 3:28.

47. Lakoff, "Christianity and Equality," in Pennock and Chapman, pp. 116–17.

48. *Ibid.*, p. 119.

49. St. Augustine, *City of God* 11:22, quoted in Lakoff, p. 18. Lakoff points out the ambivalence of Augustine's position in Pennock and Chapman, p. 126.

50. There is an excellent discussion of this whole matter in John Wilson's *Equality*.

51. Lakoff, in Pennock and Chapman, p. 118.

Chapter 2

1. *Analects* xii.11.

2. Plato, *Republic* 397e, in Hamilton and Cairns, p. 642. See also *Timaeus* 24e.

3. Waley, *Analects* vi.16, p. 119.

4. *Analects* viii.2.

5. Waley, *Analects* xii.1, p. 162.

6. *Analects* xii.22.

7. *Ibid.* i.2.

8. See, for example, *ibid.*, xiii.19 and xvii.6.

9. See, for example, *Doctrine of the Mean* xx.8. The term *i* ("to be one") refers to *ch'eng*.

10. *Ibid.* xvi.5.

11. *Mencius* iv.A.12.1; *Doctrine of the Mean* xx.18.

12. Cornford, *Religion to Philosophy*, p. 16. Cornford's analysis has been very helpful to me.

13. Fung, II, 21.

14. From the *Su-wen*; quoted in Forke, *World Conception of the Chinese*, p. 252.

15. Legge, V, Chao kung 25, p. 708.

16. Wang Hsien-ch'ien, p. 236 (SPTK 13.4b–5a). Translation is from Dubs, *Hsuntze*, pp. 223–24.

17. *Mencius* iv.A.12.1, in Legge, II, 303.
18. *Doctrine of the Mean* xx.18, in Legge, I, 413.
19. Jaeger, p. 110.
20. Anaximander 9, quoted in *ibid.*, p. 159.
21. Plato, *Gorgias* 508a.
22. *Symposium* 186d.
23. Jaeger, p. 157.
24. *Ibid.*, p. 165.
25. See, for example, *Tso chuan*, Chou kung 25.
26. *Analects* xx.3.1, in Legge, I, 354.
27. *Mencius* i.B.16.3.
28. *Analects* vi.26.
29. Cheng Te-k'un, III, 303. Compare this with the account in Joseph Needham, *Science and Civilization in China*, I, 156, 161, and 226.
30. Cheng Te-k'un, III, 302.
31. *Ibid.*, p. 298.
32. Wang Hsien-ch'ien, p. 233 (SPTK 14.2b).
33. Forke, *Lun-Heng*, I, 104.
34. *Ibid.*, II, 156.
35. Plato, *Phaedo* 99c.
36. Lucretius iv.818–79, in Latham, p. 156.
37. See, for example, Plato, *Republic* 608d.
38. Aristotle, *De Anima* 1.2 (404b), in McKeon, pp. 151–52.
39. Plato, *Phaedo* 79d, in Hamilton and Cairns, pp. 62–63.
40. See, for example, John Wilson's *Equality*.

Chapter 3

1. The character that stands for "man in general" in many discussions of [e]*hsing* is [a]*jen*. Three arguments could be used against the thesis that *jen* referred to human beings in general. One is the view that in early China *jen* and *min* were distinguished (see the chapter "Shih 'jen' 'min'" [Explaining "*jen*" and "*min*"] in Chao Chi-pin. It is maintained, for example, that the *Analects* depict *min* as having no right to participate in political affairs, whereas the *jen* have this right; or it may be said that *jen* denoted members of the slave-master class, and *min* members of the slave class. Hou Wai-lu holds that *jen* was originally used only for *chün-tzu* ("superior man") (see Hou, p. 387). The second argument is that we may be misled about the sense of *jen* in the early works because of the T'ang dynasty (A.D. 618–906) change of all *min* ("people") characters in books to *jen*; this was due to a taboo against the indiscriminate use of the former character, which formed part of the name of the second T'ang emperor, Li Shih-min. Thirdly, it has been held that the term *jen* originally meant members of one's own

tribe, for whom one has feelings of closeness (see Waley, *The Way and Its Power*, pp. 147–48). This argument appeals to the fact that the cognate of *jen* meaning "man" is [b]*jen* meaning humanheartedness, which was defined in the *Shuo-wen chieh-tzu* etymological work (compiled c. A.D. 100) as "near" and included the sense of kinship feeling or affections (the sense with which Kao Tzu uses the term in the *Mencius*).

In replying to these arguments it is best to draw on oracle bone and Chou bronze usages of the term *jen*; no T'ang dynasty hands altered those phrases. These examples indicate two things. First, although *jen* at times may have indicated "clansmen," it did so only because it meant "man." More important, even if one grants that at times *jen* was used in contradistinction to *min*—and a good deal more evidence would be needed to make that convincing—it clearly was also used to mean human beings in general. On oracle bones there are references to "men of the king's clan" (*wang jen*, see Ch'en Meng-chia, p. 610), but most often the term was used to refer to common agricultural workers. Chou bronze examples use *jen* in referring to serfs as well as to members of the slave-master class. For instance, there are inscriptions such as "I will give you serfs [*jen*] of the X, Y, and Z districts" on Vessel 4 (Kuo Mo-jo, *Liang-chou chin-wen*, A, 110a, expl. A., p. 121a). Similar usages are found on Vessels 5 and 6. So there is evidence that *jen* was used to refer to human beings in general, not simply to those who could participate in politics.

2. For details on the Platonic doctrine that the body and mind or soul are different substances, see Plato's *Timaeus* and *Phaedo*.

3. According to *Mencius* vi.A.15a.

4. The three terms that today are translated as soul (*p'o*, "sentient soul"; *hun*, "spiritual soul"; *shen*, "soul") are late in appearing. The first two do not appear until the *Tso chuan*, and the last is not made applicable to living man until the Warring States period. The common element of the graphs *p'o* and *hun* originally depicted a person wearing a mask; the "impersonator" at the ceremony wore the mask and the dead man's spirit took up residence in it (Ikeda, "Kijikō shina," pp. 240, 248). When *p'o* and *hun* first appear in extant literature (*Tso chuan*, Chao kung 7), *p'o* refers either to bodily form or the activity of the bodily parts, and *hun* either to all conscious activity of the body or to knowing activity. (This interpretation by an early commentator is accepted by Ch'ien Mu, "Kuei-shen-kuan," p. 2; see also Ikeda, "Konpaku ko," p. 12.) The constitution of man was bodily form and active *ch'i* ("ether"), and it was difficult to introduce any other concepts independently; they had to be related to those two. So *p'o* became related to bodily form, and *hun* to active *ch'i*. For example, in the *Li chi* is the statement, "The *hun* and *ch'i* return to Heaven [after death]; the body and *p'o* return to earth" (*Shih-san-ching chu-shu*, VI, Chiao t'e sheng,

p. 229). The notion of rising and falling reflects the belief that the *yang ch'i* rises and the *yin ch'i* falls. This notion in turn influenced the conception of [e]*hsing* ("human nature") popular in the Han dynasty; *hsing* was composed of *yang ch'i* (pure, light, and good), and was distinguished from sentiment ([b]*ch'ing*), which was composed of *yin ch'i* (dense, heavy, evil). This relation of *yang ch'i* to *hsing* and *yin ch'i* to *ch'ing* is seen in their respective definitions in the *Shuo-wen chieh-tzu*. In effect, any new content that the Chou concepts of *p'o* and *hun* introduce into the constitution of man concerns mainly the idea of rising to heaven and descending to earth, notions concerning the time after death and relevant to *yin-yang* cosmology.

There is some evidence that *shen* was understood as the activity of *ch'i* in its refined state; as such, it played a role in man's cognitive activities. According to the *Chuang-tzu* commentator Liu Hsien-hsin, "The 'soul' [*shen*] . . . is blended over the entire body, not belonging to one part" (quoted in Ch'ien Mu, *Chuang-tzu*, Ch'i wu lun, p. 11); it was pictured, like *ch'i*, as "filling the body." Hsün Tzu regarded *shen* as activity present in the body ([b]*hsing*), coming into existence when the body does; like *ch'i*, it was paired with bodily form. He said that after Heaven has done its work, "the body is completed and the spirit comes into existence." (Wang, *Hsun-tzu*, T'ien lun, p. 206 [SPTK 11.17a]). In the *Chuang-tzu*, with reference to the living, *shen* is used with the sense of mental activity. This is probably a kind of direct intuitive knowing carried out by the "constant mind," as in the phrase "His *shen* fixed, he causes things not to suffer disease and the harvest to be bountiful." (Ch'ien Mu, *Chuang-tzu*, Hsiao yao yu, p. 5 [SPTK 1.12b]).

5. Wang, *Hsün-tzu*, Chieh pi, p. 264 (SPTK 16.5a).

6. Plato, *Timaeus* 90a, in Cornford, *Plato's Cosmology*, p. 353.

7. Jaeger, I, 153–54.

8. Plato, *Republic* 526b, in Hamilton and Cairns, p. 758.

9. *Republic* 479a, *ibid.*, p. 719.

10. *Thaetetus* 152d, *ibid.*, p. 857.

11. *Republic* 476a, *ibid.*, p. 715.

12. *Republic* 511a–e.

13. Plato, *Meno* 81d, in Hamilton and Cairns, p. 364.

14. *Analects* viii.2.i, in Legge, I, 208.

15. Plato, *Meno* 88c, in Hamilton and Cairns, p. 373.

16. Ch'en Meng-chia, p. 573. Among the ancestors frequently in this position were Wang Hai, Huang Yin, and Huang ** ; see Hu Hou-hsüan, *Yin-tai feng-chien chih-tu*, p. 8b.

17. *Ibid.*, p. 9a.

18. *Ibid.*, p. 24b; and Ch'en Meng-chia, p. 580.

19. Cheng Te-k'un, II, 223.

20. This is the conclusion reached in Ku and Lo, p. 122.

21. On Vessel 15; see Shirakawa, "Kinbun tsushoku ichi," p. 21.

22. On Vessel 16; see Hsü Chung-shu, "Chin-wen ku-tz'u," p. 10.

23. Karlgren, *Odes*, Wen Wang 1, p. 185.

24. See Ch'ü, p. 111.

25. The translation "to be an assessor of Heaven" is presented in Dubs, "Archaic Jou Religion," p. 240.

26. Karlgren, *Documents*, Chun shih 11, p. 61.

27. Ch'en Meng-chia (p. 594) holds that Shang Ti became identified by the Ch'in people with their first ancestor, Shao Hao. Ti k'u is fifth in line, according to the "free text."

28. Kuo, *Hsien-Ch'in t'ien-tao-kuan*, p. 16.

29. Karlgren, *Odes*, Sheng min, p. 200. For more on this myth see Dubs, "Archaic Jou Religion."

30. On Vessel 14; see Kuo, *Liang-chou*, A, 118b, Expl. A, p. 127b.

31. At least from the time of Wu-ting through Ti-hsin (1398–1111 B.C.).

32. Karlgren, *Documents*, To shih 18 and 19, p. 54.

33. E.g., on Vessels 17 and 18, dating respectively from the times of K'ang Wang (reigned 1067–1041 B.C.) and Hsüan Wang (reigned 827–781 B.C.).

34. For example, it was used by Duke Ai of Lu; Hu Hou-hsüan, "Shih 'Yü i jen.' "

35. Li Tu, p. 32; T'ang, "T'ien-ming-kuan," p. 8. It is interesting to note the extent to which Han dynasty writers broadened the application of previously restricted attributes. The New Text school maintained that the sages, and not just Prince Millet, had had no earthly fathers; Heaven had caused their mothers to give birth. See Lu, p. 456.

36. *Mencius* vi.A.16 and ii.A.7.

37. Wang, *Hsün-tzu*, T'ien lun, p. 206 (SPTK 11.17b).

38. Shima, p. 216. Among other places, it occurs on Vessels 19 and 20.

39. Ch'ien Mu, *Chuang-tzu*, Ch'i wu lun, p. 11 (SPTK 1.23a and 1.24a).

40. Chiang, p. 226.

41. T'ang, "T'ien-ming-kuan," pp. 13–14.

42. Richards, p. 79. A key difference between Mencius and Kao-tzu lies in this matter of the mind being its own law-giver, i.e., it centers around [b]*i*. Kao-tzu seems to acknowledge the innateness of [b]*jen*, albeit *jen* in a limited sense. He says, "*Jen* is internal not external; *i* is external not internal" (*Mencius* vi.A.4.1). This seems to contradict another statement: "The fashioning of benevolence [*jen*] and righteousness [*i*] out of man's nature is like making cups and bowls from the *ch'i*-willow"

(*ibid.*, vi.A.1.1). One scholar suggests that the *jen* in this latter passage should be eliminated, after which it would jibe with the view that *jen* is internal and *i* external; see Li Hsiang-yin, p. 10. Another explanation is simply to regard *jen* and *i* in the latter passage as used loosely, together approximating "moral sense"; D. C. Lau would take this position.

43. *Timaeus* 90a–c, in Cornford, *Plato's Cosmology*, pp. 353–54.

44. A question may arise: why focus on [e]*hsing*, since a number of other terms (e.g., [b]*ch'ing*, [c]*chih*, and [a]*ts'ai*) also seem to convey the sense of "natural endowment?" The answer is that Confucian discussions of human nature generally focused on the term *hsing*; moreover, in spite of some overlap in meaning, *hsing* differed from these other concepts in several important ways. *Ch'ing*, used to mean "reality" or "real nature," often seems close in meaning to *hsing*. For example, in the *Mencius* appear the phrases, "Can this be the *hsing* of the mountain?" and "Can this be the *ch'ing* of man?" (*Mencius* vi.A.8.1 and vi.A.8.2). In the *Hsün-tzu* is the phrase, "Therefore, if a person neglects what men can do and seeks for what Heaven does, he fails to understand the nature [*ch'ing*] of things" (Dubs, *Hsuntze*, p. 183). The *Chuang-tzu* says: "Life and death are by decree . . . men cannot do anything about them. Without exception is this the *ch'ing* of things" (Ch'ien Mu, *Chuang-tzu*, Ta tsung shih, p. 50 [SPTK 3.7b]). *Ch'ing*, like *hsing*, may derive meaning from both *hsin* and *sheng*. No Chou bronze graph [b]*ch'ing* exists, but there are examples of the phonetic it was derived from. [c]*Ch'ing* was written ; the top element is a [a]*sheng*, the bottom possibly a [b]*ching* ("well") or a *tan* ("red"). On Vessel 36; Wu Tacheng, XIII, 8a. It was also written and . At this time [c]*ch'ing* meant the color blue-green. In the *Shih ching* it is extended to mean luxuriant plant growth (sometimes with the addition of a grass radical), and is explained in one work as the color of a growing plant; another says "*Ch'ing* means *sheng*" (in the *Wen yüan*, quoted in Ting, IV, 2155b). "It describes the color of things when they are born" (see under [c]*ch'ing* in *Ching-chi chuan-ku* II, 353). The exact functions of [a]*sheng* or the complete element [c]*ch'ing* in the character [b]*ch'ing* are not known. I would speculate a close connection between the senses "just sprouted/born," "green," "light," "bright," and "pure" (the child, in Confucian and Taoist thought, is more authentic or pure than the adult)—meanings involved in various words of the same phonetic series as [b]*ch'ing*. In spite of these similarities, the emphasis of *ch'ing* was more on the sense of "what it is really like" or "the way it is." It was more abstract and does not seem to have denoted as clearly the concrete sense of responsiveness to environment, i.e., the specific behavioral constancies, although these would be included in any detailed attempt to de-

scribe the "reality" of a thing. Because *ch'ing* meant "the way it actually is," one could say that for objects of the same species to be different in quality was a matter of *ch'ing* (see *Mencius* iii.A.4.18). One probably would not use *hsing*, which indicated constants of the entire species. At times *ch'ing* had the sense simply of "true," with no relation to "sentiments" (e.g., "He has a temporary abode but no true [*ch'ing*] death"; Ch'ien Mu, *Chuang-tzu*, Ta tsung shih, p. 58 [SPTK 3.23a]). However, there are instances where one can see it as involving not only the sense of "true" but also that of "sentiments," of something relevant to the constitution of man. For example, in the *Analects* one finds, "If the superior loves trustworthiness, the people won't dare to hide their true feelings" (*ch'ing*) (*Analects* xiii.4.3).

Another term occasionally equated with *hsing* is "plain stuff" ([c]*chih*), which is close to *hsing* in containing the sense of "authentic," "without sham or artificiality." *Chih* was defined in the *Shuo wen* as "to exchange things for other things" (barter), and in some early works it connoted "hostage"; it also seems to have meant something like "tally" or "to be a true equivalent for," hence the meaning "truthfulness" or "trustworthiness" (Ting, V, 2764b), as in "The viscount of the Man tribe was not trustworthy (*chih*)" (*Tso chuan*, Chao kung, 16). It also gradually developed the sense of "stuff," eventually ending up as a designation for what we would term "corporeal matter" (Fung, II, 97). Both of these senses are involved in an example where *chih* has a sense similar to *hsing*: "The Master said, When natural substance [*chih*] prevails over ornamentation, you get the boorishness of the rustic. When ornamentation prevails over natural substance, you get the pedantry of the scribe. Only when ornament and substance are duly blended do you get the true gentleman" (*Analects* vi.16; translation is from Waley, p. 119). In an example like this, *chih* has the sense of the authentic, that which exists before acquired refinement; it also indicates anything that is thus authentic, and in the context above means especially various innate tendencies. But *chih* differs from *hsing* in that it does not imply activity, potential or actual, and it does not indicate something unique to a given species.

Finally, [a]*ts'ai* and [b]*ts'ai* (often used interchangeably in the early texts), when they have the sense of "material," have been equated with *hsing*. For example, the *Mencius* says, "If men do what is not good, the blame cannot be imputed to their natural powers [*ts'ai*]" (Legge, II, p. 402). In the *Doctrine of the Mean* is the statement: "Thus Heaven, in fostering things, bestows in accordance with their [b]*ts'ai*. So it nourishes the flourishing and rights the bent." (*Chung Yung* xvii.3. I take *sheng* as "to let grow" rather than "to create," and [a]*fu* as [b]*fu* ["to restore"], which is more in harmony with the *Mencius* doctrine of not killing off evil things, but improving them). The original meaning of the etymon *ts'ai* is not clear. In the *Shuo wen* it is defined as "the beginning of plants"; the graph is broken down into 丨 , depicting what rises up through the ground and grows branches and leaves, and 一 , the ground (Ting, V, 2664a). Hsü K'ai held that the top line (才) was a new branch and the bottom one (才) the earth. However, the bronze graph of *ts'ai* generally has been considered 十 or 丄 (descended from the oracle bone graph 中 or 丄). These all had a meaning denoted by our present characters [a]*t'sai* and [b]*t'sai*. In the *Shuo wen*, [b]*ts'ai* is defined as "a log that is usefully straight" (Ting, V, 2485a). Tuan Yü-ts'ai comments that it means "usable," and it has this meaning in many examples—e.g., "This really is a useless (*pu ts'ai*) tree" (*ibid.*, 2485b; Ch'ien Mu, *Chuang-tzu*, Jen chien shih, p. 36 [SPTK 2.25a]). When [b]*ts'ai* means "ability," it refers to what something "can do" or "is good for." These meanings may come close to some early sense of the etymon for which we have no examples on the inscriptions. Perhaps the shared meaning of [a]*ts'ai* and [b]*ts'ai* is something like "usable material," material that is good for something. If so, the terms would not be as comprehensive as *hsing*, which would refer to all natural tendencies, not just to those deemed valuable or useful.

45. By comparing the phrases containing [e]*hsing* in those early textual materials with identical or nearly identical phrases on bronzes of the same period, and with later texts in which the character [a]*sheng* ("born with," "life") was used, the late Professor Fu Szu-nien demonstrated that the scribes or editors of a later time had changed the character *sheng* in those texts to *hsing*, adding the heart radical. For example, in the *Shih ching* (dating mainly from the early Chou) is the phrase *mi erh hsing* ("fulfill your life-span"), which on bronzes appears in standard prayers for long life as *mi erh sheng* (see Karlgren, *Odes*, Chüan a 2, p. 209). If we discount the appearances of *hsing* in the *Book of Odes*, the first appearance of the term in works extant today is the phrase "by *hsing* close together, by practice far apart" in the *Analects*. Homer H. Dubs, in "Mencius and Sun-dz on Human Nature" (p. 214), calls this a pronouncement that was added to the original text at a later time; if this is so, the earliest appearance of *hsing* would be in the *Mencius*. There is a reference in the *Lun heng* (Critical Essays) of Wang Ch'ung (A.D. 27–c. 100) to Shih Shih, a disciple of Confucius who lived before Mencius and wrote a work titled *Yang shu* (On Cultivation) in which he maintained that *hsing* is both good and bad.

46. Oracle-bone examples prove that as early as Shang times [a]*sheng* had the sense of "life." West Chou bronzes also use *sheng* in this sense. On oracle bones the character *sheng* had four meanings. One was associated with offerings made in seeking offspring. "On the day *hsin* and

chi, divine: in seeking an offspring [*sheng*] from ancestors Pi Keng and Pi Ping [offer] a cow, sheep, and white pig" (Chin Hsiang-heng, "Sheng"; in Tung, V, 3b). When success was achieved, there were inscriptions ending in "got a child" (*shou sheng*). Thus one meaning of *sheng* would seem to be "offspring," and it would definitely be called a noun today. It is not certain whether or not it was used as a verb in the Shang. If so, this kind of example would be the only Shang written evidence for an early sense of "to produce" as basic to *sheng*. The second usage is the sense of "living," as in the statement "caught a living [*sheng*] deer" (*ibid.*, 7b). Perhaps the form of the graph that resembles a plant growing out of the ground indicates the same thing. (The bone graph 㞢 is composed of 屮 , which has been identified as a plant growing and 一 , which indicates the ground. Tung Tso-pin informed me of the definite isolation and interpretation of the graph.) The graph possibly denoted, among other things, both the senses of "to grow" and "to live," the meanings being close. There is one phrase that Shima Kuniyo (p. 318) interprets as "pray for the king's long life"; however, this *sheng* could equally well mean "child," i.e., heir. Third, *sheng* had the sense of *[a]hsing* ("official"), as in the phrase "many officials [*sheng*] eating together" (Tung, V, 9a). There is a difference of opinion about the correct interpretation of *hsing* in such an example. Ch'en Meng-chia (p. 615) holds that *po-hsing* refers to those of the *po-kuan* ("many officers") who have received *hsing* rank. Shirakawa Shizuka holds that the connection of *po-kuan* and *po-hsing* occurred later; in this instance above, *hsing* would refer to a group of families related to descent from a common ancestor. Finally, *sheng* meant "next," as in the phrase, "Divine: there will be a heavy rain next [*sheng*] month."

On West Chou bronzes the sense of "to produce" appears. It is seen in examples stating that the moon "produces" (written 眚 , borrowed for 生) its bright section; and it is reflected in the use of *sheng* in men's names to indicate some phenomenon relevant to their birth (for example, if one were born in a rainstorm, he might be called Yü Sheng). There are numerous examples of *sheng* in the sense of "living," and the meaning "life" is clearly seen in inscriptions requesting a full "life-span." For example, "By making this bronze I seek a lasting endowment and to fulfill my life-span" (Vessel 30; Kuo Mo-jo, *Chin-wen*, p. 3b). Moreover, the sense of "clan" (*[a]hsing*) occurs in the expression "numerous clans" (*po-hsing*). Several other uses appear that do not concern this topic. In the early chapters of the *Shu ching* the character appears only four times, three times with the sense of "to produce" and once as part of a name. In the *Shih ching*, among other meanings, it twice has the sense of "life" (Karlgren, *Odes*, Chi ku 4, p. 19, and T'u yuan 2 and 3, p. 48).

47. The meaning of "activity" applies not only to the English term "life" but also to [a]*sheng* when it is translated as "life." Chu Hsi said, "Life [*sheng*] refers to that by which man and things perceive and move" (in his commentary on *Mencius* vi.A.3.1). Hence before the emergence of *hsing*, *sheng* often had a sense wider than merely "born with." It described the "vitality" something has had from birth.

In numerous examples in the Chou texts one can read the character *hsing* as *sheng* meaning "life." For example, there is the passage "feeling their life [*hsing*] is not worth preserving" (*Tso chuan*, Chao kung 8, in Legge, V, p. 622). Note also the *Hsün-tzu* passage: "Will one who, like this, seeks external things nourish his life [*yang sheng*]? . . . For he desires to nourish his *hsing* [*yang hsing*], yet endangers his body." (Liang Shu-jen, *Hsün-tzu*, II, Cheng ming 325 [SPTK 16.18a]. The commentator here, Liu Nien-ch'in, takes *hsing* as *sheng*. So does Kanaya Osamu; see his *Junshi*, B 184.) Another example is the phrase "so that the people rejoice in their life [*hsing*]" (*Tso chuan*, Chao kung 10, in Legge, V, p. 675. Conversely, in many cases *sheng* as life could well be read as *hsing*, e.g. where the expression "make upright their *sheng* (*cheng sheng*)" occurs, and occasionally where "nourish sheng" (*yang sheng*) occurs. See Ch'ien Mu, *Chuang-tzu*, Te ch'ung fu, p. 40 (SPTK 2.32b). In the same work (Ta sheng, p. 144 [SPTK 7.1a]) is the phrase *ta sheng chih ch'ing che*, which occurs in the *Huai-nan-tzu* as *t'ung hsing chih ch'ing*. Mori Mikisaburo gives various examples of the closeness in meaning of *sheng* and *hsing* in the *Chuang-tzu* chapters in his article "Sōshi ni okeru sei no shisō." The close relationship between *hsing-ming* and *sheng-ming* is also suggestive of the residual sense of "life" in *hsing*. *Hsing-ming* often seems to mean *hsing* as well as "life"; both senses are involved in it: "Decadence set in, men fell away from their original virtue, their natures [*hsing-ming*] became corrupt, and there was a general rush for knowledge" (Ch'ien Mu, *Chuang-tzu*, Tsai yu, p. 81; translation from Herbert Giles, p. 109). Ch'ien Mu holds that *hsing-ming* contains the meaning of "life" and also connotes the essence (*pen chih*) and capabilities (*k'o neng*) of life (Ch'ien Mu, "Hsing-ming"; see also Mori, pp. 5–6).

48. Ch'ien Mu, *Chuang-tzu*, Keng sang ch'u, p. 193 (SPTK 8.17a). A similar definition occurs in the *Lieh-tzu*.

49. Wang, *Hsün-tzu*, Cheng ming, p. 274 (SPTK 16.1b). The characters *hsing chih ho so sheng* have never been satisfactorily interpreted. However, the remaining characters clearly mean: "Whatever actions naturally arise when [our natures] are in responsive contact [with the environment] are called *hsing*."

50. In the earliest Chou sources there is no explicit reference to man's *sheng* being produced by Heaven through the agency of parents or ancestors, although the nature of the prayers in which the term appears

shows that ancestors clearly had control over length of life. However, the term *ming* in the early West Chou bronzes had the sense of "endowment from Heaven" and "life-span." Some rather extensive remarks about *ming* are in order here, to prove that *sheng*, like *ming*, was used to mean "Heavenly endowment" long before the emergence of *hsing*. Moreover, the discussion of "The Sources of Evil" in the next chapter will attempt to determine exactly what circumstances in a person's life are determined by forces beyond his control, and his life-span is one of these. The evidence follows.

It has not been widely known that *ming* meant "life-span" in the early Chou. Used in this sense, it appears in prayers to ancestors (occasionally in prayers directly to Heaven) for a "long life" (*yung ming*). Its earliest appearance with this sense is on a bronze (Vessel 31) from the time of Chao Wang (reigned 1041–1023 B.C.). In Lo Chen-yü's *San-tai chi-chin-wen-ts'un*, the expression appears with inordinate frequency on bronzes from the time of Li Wang (reigned 878–841 B.C.). This was probably due to the concern for self-preservation occasioned by unsuccessful attempts to repel the Huai I tribe, who were moving into the state of K'ou at this time. The king commanded his minister K'ou Chung to conquer them, but the effort failed (see Fan, p. 30). It is clear that *ming* in these examples meant "life-span": it appears in standard four-character phrases, which vary the two two-character expressions within but in which each two-character expression always means something close to "long life," e.g., *mei-shou yung-ming*; *wan-nien yung-ming*.

The act (*ming*) that granted life ("Life and death are determined by decree [*ming*]: wealth and honor are determined by Heaven." *Analects* xii.5.3) was a momentary one; the thing received (*ming* in the sense of "life-span") was long-lasting. Man would "receive this *ming*" (*shou tzu ming*, as on Vessel 3) from Heaven, through the agency of ancestors. Ultimately, however, the act that produced a life-span (*ming* as a verb) was that of Heaven. On bronzes from the latter part of the West Chou one finds the prayer that "my *ming*, by the kindness [of Heaven] will not become aged" (*ling ming nan lau*); see Kuo Mo-jo, *Liang-chou*, B, p. 201b. Certainly *ming* in the sense of "life-span" did not suggest the vitality and concreteness that *sheng* did. Basically, it meant only "the given" or "endowment," and in the examples cited it had the extended sense of an endowment lasting for a certain length of time. However, its meaning overlapped with *sheng* because it denoted both what one is born with ("endowment") and one's life-span (duration of existence of what one is born with). Hence, although there are no explicit references in the very early existing sources to *sheng* ("life") being a gift from Heaven or the Lord-on-High, its overlap in meaning with *ming*, which was such a gift, allows us to infer that *sheng* was considered so as well. On two early bronzes (Vessels 30 and 33) the two terms actually occur in adjoined phrases as the object sought—long life. This idea had explicit statement in later references, e.g., "Oh, my life [*sheng*], has it not been decreed in Heaven" (Karlgren, *Documents*, Hsi po k'an li 5, p. 27).

Because of their early overlap in meaning, *sheng* and *ming* remained intimately linked throughout the Chou period. Finally, they were combined to form the compound *sheng-ming* ("life"), which first appears in the *Kuo yü* (*Sayings of the States*, a collection of discussions on historical matters probably compiled in the very late Chou or early Han but covering almost the same period as the *Tso chuan*, i.e., 722–481 B.C.). *Sheng-ming* is closely related to the compound *hsing-ming*, which first appears in the *Chuang-tzu*, Wai-p'ien and Tsa-p'ien (probably late third and second centuries B.C.). Thus the roots of the ultimate link of *sheng* with Heaven and *ming*, and hence those of *hsing*, actually extend back to the early West Chou.

51. E.g., "What cannot be learned or acquired through effort but depends on Heaven is *hsing*"; in Wang, *Hsün-tzu*, Hsing o, p. 290 (SPTK 17.3a). The *jen* ("man") in this passage is a mistake for *t'ien* ("Heaven"). In another place reference is made to "losing the Heavenly *hsing*"; *ibid.*, Cheng lun, p. 226 (SPTK 12.17b). Also, the text says, "*Hsing* is what is brought forth by Heaven"; *ibid.*, Cheng ming, p. 284 (SPTK 16.14b). Cf. *Mencius* vii.A.1.1.

52. Wang, *Hsün-tzu*, Cheng ming, p. 274 (SPTK 16.1b).

53. *Analects* iv.5.1, in Legge, I, p. 166.

54. "Ease" should be taken as effortlessness, not as Taoistic quietude. Professor T'ang Chün-i has indicated the importance of these criteria with regard to the *hsing shan* ("good nature") of Mencius in "Meng, Mo, Chuang, Hsün, chih yen hsin shen-i," p. 36.

55. *Mencius* vi.A.7.8.

56. *Ibid.*, vi.A.16.1.

57. *Ibid.*, ii.A.7.2.

58. *Analects* vi.18.

59. *Ibid.*, vi.9.

60. *Ibid.*, iv.2.

61. *Ibid.*, xvii.21.

62. DeWitt, p. 220.

63. *Mencius* ii.A.6. Cf. Lau, "Human Nature," p. 549.

64. *Mencius* vi.A.7.5.

65. "According to the human *hsing*, the eye can see, and the ear can hear"; Wang, *Hsün-tzu*, Hsing o, p. 290 (SPTK 17.3a).

66. *Ibid.*, Jung ju, p. 29 (SPTK 2.17b); translation is from Dubs, *Hsuntze*, p. 60.

67. "Give a man a stimulus, and they come forth of their own accord" (*ibid.*, Hsing o, p. 291 [SPTK 17.5a]; translation from Dubs, *Hsuntze*, p. 305). "*Hsing* is what is brought forth by Heaven; the sentiments are the essence of *hsing*; the desires are the responses of the sentiments" (Wang, *Hsün-tzu*, Chang ming, p. 284 [SPTK 16.14b]). With reference to the *ch'ing* D. C. Lau says: "These are important only insofar as they manifest themselves as responses to outside things (become desires), as they lead to action" (Lau, p. 552).

68. Wang, *Hsün-tzu*, Chieh pi, p. 269 (SPTK 15.13b).

69. *Ibid.*, Hsing o, p. 289 (SPTK 17.1b).

70. *Ibid.*, Li lun, p. 249 (SPTK 13.24a). This interpretation is shared by Kanaya Osamu; see his *Junshi*, B., 115.

71. Tai, p. 10a.

72. *Mencius* vi.A.3.3.

73. *Ibid.*, vi.A.4.2.

74. *Analects* ii.7; see also *Mencius* iv.B.28.6.

75. *Mencius* vii.B.16.

76. The translation of *tuan* as "font" is borrowed from George William Kent, "Seven Terms of the Chou-Han Traditional Ethics." The term *tuan* is introduced in *Mencius* ii.A.6.6.

77. *Mencius* vi.A.5.2.

78. Richards, p. 69.

79. [b]*Jen* first appeared in the Spring and Autumn period, possibly in the middle of the seventh century B.C. (see Kuo Mo-jo, *Nu li*, p. 48, and Hou, p. 93). It appears as part of a name on Vessel 34. Its *Shuo wen* definition suggests that it referred to the affection felt between kin. In extant texts it also implies an extension of that feeling to those outside the kinship sphere. It is often defined in early texts as "that by which the ruler protects the people." This extended kinship sentiment could develop into the conception of a "perfect personality embracing all virtues" because it was concurrently viewed as uniquely human. In fulfilling the qualities of being human, a man would always possess *jen*.

80. DeWitt, p. 220.

81. *Ibid.*, p. 30.

82. Wang, *Hsün-tzu*, Wang chih, p. 104 (SPTK 5.13a).

83. *Ibid.* (SPTK 5.12b).

84. *Mencius* vi.B.15.2 in Legge, II, 447.

85. Quoted in Chan, "Evolution of *jen*," p. 298. The same idea has been expressed elsewhere; e.g., by Ch'en Ta-ch'i, p. 3.

86. *Analects* vii.29.

87. *Ibid.*, vii.33.

88. *Mencius* vii.B.16; *Chung yung* xx.

89. *Mencius* iv.B.28.6.

90. Plato, *Protagoras* 323c.

91. *Mencius* ii.A.6.4 and vi.A.6.7.

92. I have found the discussion in D. C. Lau's "Theories of Human Nature" very helpful, although the present analysis is my own.

93. Kanaya Osamu, " 'Junshi' no bunkengaku teki kenkyū," p. 31.

94. Wang, *Hsün-tzu*, Jung ju, p. 40 (SPTK 2.18b).

95. *Ibid.*, Li lun, p. 243 (SPTK 13.15b–16a).

96. *Ibid.*, Chieh pi, p. 264 (SPTK 15.8a).

97. Liang Shu-jen, p. 304 (SPTK 15.16a); the commentator takes *i* as *k'o*.

98. " 'How does man know Tao [i.e., [a]*li*]'? 'By the mind' "; Wang, *Hsün-tzu*, Chieh pi, p. 264 (SPTK 15.7b).

99. *Ibid.*, Cheng ming, p. 277 (SPTK 16.5a).

100. *Ibid.*, p. 278 (SPTK 16.5b).

101. "The heart is established in the central cavity to control the five senses—this is what is meant by the natural [*t'ien*] ruler"; *ibid.*, T'ien lun, p. 206 (SPTK 11.17b). Translation is from Dubs, *Hsuntze*, p. 176.

102. Wang, *Hsün-tzu*, Chieh pi, p. 265 (SPTK 15.9a–b).

103. *Ibid.*, Cheng ming, p. 284 (SPTK 16.14a). D. C. Lau clarifies the distinction between the possible and the permissible.

104. "By *wei* is meant the direction of one's sentiments as a result of the mind's reflection"; *ibid.*, Cheng ming, p. 274 (SPTK 16.2a).

105. Andrew Cheng, p. 49.

106. Wang, *Hsün-tzu*, Li lun, p. 237 (SPTK 13.8b).

107. *Ibid.*, Hsiu shen, p. 20 (SPTK 1.23a–b).

108. Fu Szu-nien, III, 69. Fu held that it did not abandon the basic meaning of [a]*sheng*, which he says was to "give birth," "to produce" (*ibid.*, pp. 77–78). That is, in some cases where our texts have [e]*hsing*, the meaning is verbal, meaning "when born," as in the *Analects* phrase "Men when born are close together, through practice far apart" (*ibid.*, p. 58). Generally, Fu felt, a grammatical change had occurred from the basic sense of *sheng*, "to give birth," to its status as a resultative noun (different tone) meaning "what one is born with" (*ibid.*, p. 122). He also felt that the phrases "good hsing" (*hsing shan*) and "bad hsing" (*hsing o*) meant only that when one is born (*sheng-lai*) he is either good or bad. He finds additional support for the enduring sense of *sheng* where we read *hsing* from the fact that on bronzes the cognate word [a]*hsing*, "clan," was also written as [a]*sheng*, without the female radical. This, too, was a grammatical variant of the basic sense of *sheng*, i.e., a change from a verb, "to give birth," to an ablative noun "the source to which a thing owes its birth" (hence the meaning "lineage

group," "clan," "family"); hence it is inferred that *hsing* ("[human] nature"), being similarly a variant, was also written as *sheng*. It is necessary to say "infer," for no character [e]*hsing* or usage with the sense of [e]*hsing*, even if written as *sheng*, has been found on Chou bronzes thus far.

109. Wang, *Hsün-tzu*, Jung ju, p. 38 (SPTK 2.15b); translation is from Dubs, *Hsuntze*, p. 58.

Chapter 4

1. *Great Learning* x.7.
2. Karlgren, *Documents*, K'ang kao 4, p. 38.
3. *Ibid.*, To fang 19, p. 63.
4. *Ibid.*, To fang 5, p. 63.
5. *Ibid.*, Ta Kao 1, p. 34.
6. On Vessel 1; see Kuo Mo-Jo, *Liang-chou*, A.45b.
7. On Vessel 2; *ibid.*, A.84b.
8. Karlgren, *Documents*, Shao kao 19, p. 51.
9. As on Vessel 3.

10. Misleading translations of early Chinese references to "destiny" have helped to create the false impression that the Chinese had this conception of events being antecedently laid out or foreknown. For example, compare the following two translations of the same passage, the second being more accurate:

> Lastly, Dr. Lu said: "Your illness is attributable neither to God, nor to man, nor to the agency of spirits. It was fore-ordained in the mind of Providence when you were endowed with this bodily form at birth. What possible good can herbs and drugs do you?" (Lionel Giles, *Taoist Teachings*, p. 100.)
>
> Mr. Lu said: "Your illness is not from Heaven, nor from man, nor from spirits. Ever since you were endowed with life and body, you have known what it is that governs them. What can medicine and the needle do for you?" (Graham, p. 129.)

11. *Tso chuan*, Hsüan kung 7.
12. Waley, *Analects* xv.28, p. 199.
13. *Mencius* vi.A.15.2.

14. Chu Hsi speaks of the *p'ing-tan chih ch'i* (mentioned in *Mencius* vi.A.8) as "the pure, clear *ch'i* at the time when one has not had contact with any external thing."

15. Wang, *Hsün-tzu*, Cheng ming, p. 287 (SPTK 16.18b).
16. *Ibid.*, p. 286 (SPTK 16.17b).
17. *Ibid.*, Chieh pi, p. 267 (SPTK 15.11b).
18. The Chieh pi section of the *Hsün-tzu* often uses the term [c]*i* to

stand for the mind's involvement with two objects, which become "mutually beclouding."

19. Wang, *Hsün-tzu*, Chieh pi, p. 260 (SPTK 15.3a).
20. *Ibid.*, Hsiu shen, p. 16 (SPTK 1.19b).
21. *Ibid.*, Ch'üan hsüeh, p. 3 (SPTK 1.8a).
22. *Mencius* iii.A.3.
23. Wang, *Hsün-tzu*, Li lun, p. 231 (SPTK 13.1a–b). See also Kanaya, "Yokubō no ari kata," p. 270.
24. See *Tso chuan*, Ch'eng kung 9.
25. *Mencius* v.A.7.5, in Legge, 363.
26. *Doctrine of the Mean* 25.3, in Legge, I, 418–19.
27. Wang, *Hsün-tzu*, T'ien lun, p. 212 (SPTK 11.23b).
28. *Doctrine of the Mean* 27.2.
29. *Han Fei-tzu* L, quoted in Hu Shih, p. 175.
30. *Analects* iv.16, in Legge, I, 170.
31. Waley, *Analects* xv.31, p. 199.
32. *Analects* vii.15, in Legge, I, 200.
33. *Analects* xiv.41.
34. *Mencius* i.A.1 and vi.B.4.
35. Plato, *Apology* 41e, in Hamilton and Cairns, p. 26.
36. Waley, *Analects* iv.17, p. 105.
37. *Mencius* iv.A.4.
38. *Analects* xii.4, in Legge, I, 252.
39. Wang, *Hsün-tzu*, Cheng lun, p. 228 (SPTK 12.12a).
40. *Analects* iv.17.
41. *Analects* viii.2.2, in Legge, I, 208.
42. *The Great Learning* ix.8.9, in *ibid.*, p. 372.
43. *Mencius* ii.A.7.2.
44. On Vessel 11; see Wu Shih-fen, 3.3.32b, expl. 907.
45. On Vessel 12; see Kuo Mo-jo, *Liang-chou*, A, expl. 150b.
46. It first appears on Vessel 7; see Kuo Mo-jo, *Chin-wen ts'ung-k'ao*, I, sect. 3, Tao-te ssu-hsiang (Ethical Thought), p. 21a.
47. The term [a]*i* in the broad sense was a general name for ritual vessels used in the ancestral temple, or for all prized food and drink vessels; in the narrow sense, it was the name for a vessel shaped like a chicken or bird. See Hsü Chung-shu, "Shuo tsun-i," p. 78. Thus there is good evidence that this concept of "constant rules" in the earliest time had a religious coloration. In *Mencius* vi.A.6.8 (quoting the *Shih ching*) the graph [d]*i* was used instead of [a]*i*. The concept of "constant rules" was occasionally expressed by the terms *tien* and *ch'ang* as well.
48. Karlgren, *Odes*, Min lao 3, p. 211.
49. For example, on Vessel 11 appears the phrase, "Revere and make harmonious the standard of *te*"; Wu Shih-fen, 3.3.32b. The phrase *ching te* also appears on bronzes. When *ching* is used as a verb in Karl-

gren's *Documents* (Chiu kao 9, p. 45), Karlgren would take [d]*ching* as a loan for [e]*ching* ("to walk," "to go"), which is equivalent to [c]*hsing*, meaning "to practice [*te*]"; see Karlgren, "Glosses on the Book of Documents," p. 302. However, I see no reason why it can not be taken with a sense close to its basic meaning of "norm" or "standard" when it is used as a verb in this instance, meaning "to make *te* the standard." Karlgren himself allows this sense of *ching* when it is used as a verb in *Odes*, Hsiao min 4, p. 142; see also Karlgren, "Glosses on the Book of Odes," p. 100. When used as a noun in the expression *te ching*, *ching* unquestionably has the sense of "standard."

50. Karlgren, *Odes*, Cheng min 1, p. 228. This ode probably dates from the time of Hsüan Wang (reigned 827–781 B.C.); see Kuo Mo-jo, *Hsien-ch'in*, p. 33.

51. *Mencius* iv.A.14.1.

52. *Tso chuan*, Chao kung 16.

53. Ch'ien Mu, *Chuang-tzu*, Ma t'i, p. 71 (SPTK 4.12b).

54. *Kuo-yü*, Chin yü 4, ch. 10, p. 259 (SPTK 10.10b).

55. Vessel 8; see Kuo Mo-jo, *Liang-chou*, A, 260b; expl. B, 219a–b. He inherits the *te* of his father, and through him the *te* of the Yellow Emperor.

56. Vessel 9; *ibid.*, A, 278b; expl. B, 239a. Regarding the fact that the receipt of *te* referred to on bronze inscriptions is receipt from ancestors, see Hsü, *Li-shih yü-yen yen-chiu-so chi-k'an*, VI, Nos. 1, 10, and 13.

57. *Analects* vii.22.

58. Karlgren, *Odes*, T'ang 2, pp. 214–15. This reference to Heaven as the source of evil *te* also occurs in the P'an keng chapter of the *Book of Documents* (see Karlgren, *Documents*, P'an keng 38, p. 24). Note also the *Chuang-tzu* phrase, "This is a man whose *te* is by nature shoddy" (Ch'ien Mu, *Chuang-tzu*, Jen chien shih, p. 34 [SPTK 2.20a]). In the latter example, t'ien (Heaven) has strong naturalistic overtones.

59. Wu Shih-fen, 3.3, p. 32b.

60. Ch'ü, *Shang-shu*, Wu yi, p. 109 (K. 13, p. 59). Professor Ch'ü Wan-li (of the Academia Sinica in Taiwan) often explains *te* as "conduct" (*hsing-wei*), as he does here. This chapter is not included among those that H. G. Creel considers early (Creel, "Shih t'ien," p. 65, n. 7); but the philologist Fu Ssu-nien considered it to be very early (Fu, p. 29).

61. Ch'ü, *Shang-shu*, p. 34.

62. *Ibid.*, p. 105 (K. 18, p. 56).

63. For an example of *te hsing*, see *Mencius* ii.A.2.18; for *wei te*, see Karlgren, *Odes*, Yi 8, p. 217.

64. The Chinese expression appears in Karlgren, *Odes*, Meng 4, p. 40; and also in *Tso chuan*, Ch'eng kung 13, in Legge, V, 380.

65. *Analects* xix.10, in Legge, I, 342.

66. Karlgren, *Documents,* Kao yao mo 3, p. 8. Ch'ü Wan-li dates this chapter as about the beginning of the Warring States period (Ch'ü, p. 18).

67. *Kuo-yü,* Chou yü B, ch. 3, p. 68 (SPTK 3.2a).

68. Boodberg, p. 324. This view has been put forth with variations by several people. It is alluded to in Granet, pp. 250–51; in Waley, *The Way and Its Power*, pp. 31–32; and in Li Tsung-t'ung, I, 39–40.

69. Waley, *Analects* iv.25, p. 106.

70. *Ibid.*, ii.i, p. 88.

71. *Mencius* iv.A.9.2.

72. *Mencius* i.A.6.6, in Legge, II, 137.

73. *Ibid.*, vii.A.19.4, p. 458.

74. Although in one place Kuo Mo-jo speaks of [a]*te* as "examining the mind" (*Chin-wen*, I, Sect. 3, Tao-te 22a), elsewhere he maintains that it also includes the functions of ruling the realm, activities that later people included in the "rites" (*li*); see Kuo, *Hsien-ch'in*, p. 26. See also Ogura, "Saken ni okeru ha to toku—toku gainen no keisei to tenkai" (Hegemony and Virtue in the *Tso chuan*—The Formation and Development of the Concept of *te*).

75. Karlgren, *Documents,* Wen hou chih ming 4, p. 80. Ch'ü Wan-li dates this chapter as from the time of P'ing Wang, eighth century B.C.

76. Karlgren, *Documents,* K'ang kao 3, p. 39. A similar pairing of *te* and "punishments" ([d]*hsing*) occurs in *ibid.*, p. 42. *Te* and *hsing* continued to be regarded as twin methods of control in texts from the Warring States period.

77. *Ibid.*, Chun shih 13, p. 61. Describing *te* as "sent down" by the ruler to the people was common.

78. *Ibid.*, Tai ts'ai 7, p. 48.

79. Karlgren, *Odes*, Chih hsia 3, p. 172.

80. *Ibid.*, Shih shu 2, p. 73.

81. *Mencius* iii.A.IV.8, in Legge II, 252.

82. *Tso chuan*, Chao kung 26, in Legge, V, 718.

83. *Tso chuan*, Ch'eng kung 8, *ibid.*, p. 366.

84. Masubuti Tatsuo has made an extensive study of the concept of *te* as it appears in early texts relevant to the Warring States period. He finds it frequently cited as a means for the maintenance of control by a lord over the retainers not related to him by clan ties (through the establishment of an emotional bond). *Te* referred to the expression of kindness in concrete behavior, such as a lord's granting food and lodging to low-ranking knights without ties, welcoming to his domain those in exile, etc.; see Masubuti, pp. 212–16. My own tabulation of the use of all examples of *te* in the *Tso chuan* would tend to support the conclusion that the sense of *te* as bestowal of concrete kindness engendering

a response of gratitude (in which case it appears as a method of political control) is dominant in the time covered by that text.

85. Karlgren, *Odes*, Yi 6, p. 218.

86. *Tso chuan*, Min king 2, in Legge, V, 128.

87. Wang, *Hsün-tzu*, Ch'üan hsüeh, p. 4 (SPTK 1. 9a).

88. Karlgren, *Documents*, Chiu kao 11, p. 45.

89. The *Tso chuan* quotes this phrase as from the *Chou shu*; see *Tso chuan*, Hsi kung 5, in Legge, V, 146. The phrase now appears in the forged Chün ch'en chapter of the *Shu ching*. See also Karlgren, *Documents*, Lu hsing 4, p. 72.

90. From Vessel 18; Wu Shih-fen, 3.3, 52b (ref. 910). Although Kuo Mo-jo takes this as dating from the time of Hsüan Wang, Tung Tso-pin, in a study made in 1952, places it much earlier, from the time of Ch'eng Wang (reigned 1104–1067 B.C.). Ogura Yoshihiko agrees with Tung's view; see Ogura, p. 156, n. 18.

91. From Vessel 21; Kuo Mo-jo, *Liang-chou* A, 20b; expl. A, 40b. One party interprets 㕛 as *yu* 友 ("friend"); see Yü Hsing-wu, A.2, p. 21. Kuo's analysis, retained in the recent revised edition of his classic work on bronzes cited in this study, seems to jibe with a belief that apparently became very common. Kuo dates this vessel as from the time of K'ang Wang (reigned 1067–1041 B.C.).

92. From Vessel 18.

93. From Vessel 22. Kuo Mo-jo, *Liang-chou*, A, 132a; expl. A, 139a. Kuo dates this as Hsüan Wang period.

94. Ch'ü, *Shang shu*, Lo kao, p. 100 (K. 27, p. 53). The commentator indicates the parallel between part of this passage and a phrase on Vessel 18.

95. Karlgren, *Documents*, Shao kao 20, p. 51.

96. Ch'ü, *Shang shu*, Chun shih, p. 113 (K. 11, p. 61).

97. Karlgren, *Documents*, To shih 11, p. 55.

98. Karlgren, *Documents*, Shao kao 10, p. 49.

99. *Ibid.*, Kao yao mo 7, p. 9.

100. *Tso chuan*, Hsüan kung 3, in Legge, V, 293.

101. *Kuo-yü* 12, Chin yü 4, p. 251 (SPTK 10.4a).

102. *Ibid.*, Chin yü 6, p. 303 (SPTK 12.5a).

103. *Tso chuan*, Hsi kung 5, in Legge, V, 146.

104. For example, on Vessel 14; Kuo Mo-jo, *Liang-chou*, A, 118b; expl. A, 127b. The early distinction between the two is emphasized in Hsü, VI, 29.

105. "[a]*Te* is internal; getting [b]*te* is external. 'Supreme *te* does not acquire' means that the spirit is not excessively drawn to external things. If the spirit is not excessively drawn to external things, the self is preserved. Preservation of self is called [a]*te*; [a]*te* is gaining [[b]*te*] one's self." (Wang, *Han Fei-tzu*, A. 6, Chieh lao 20, p. 217. I follow the Wang

interpretation of the original form of the last ten characters.) Also note the statement in the *Book of Rites*, "*Te* is gaining [*te*] one's self." (*Shih-san-ching*, VI: *Li chi cheng-i*, 61, Hsiang yin chiu i 45, p. 455.) It is permissible to cite the *Li chi* in this discussion of Chou thought, for the idea in question was certainly one present in the earlier period. Karlgren, in fact, regards the *Li chi* and the *Ta-tai li chi* (Book of Rites of Tai the Elder) as Chou texts, since their documents are Chou, formed into collections in the Han; see Karlgren, "Grammata Serica," p. 12.

One half of the *Shuo wen* definition of *te* 悳 (an alternative form of [a]*te*), which reads, "Internally get goodness in the self" (*te yeh che te yü shen yeh*), has the same meaning as the passage in the *Book of Rites*. On the other hand, the last part of the same definition refers to "getting" the loyalty or devotion of other people. (See Appendix.)

The first actual equation of the two characters occurs in the *Li chi*: "When the prince causes ritual and music both to achieve [[b]*te*] their proper roles, he is called a [a]*te* prince. [a]*Te* is getting [[b]*te*]." (*Shih-san-ching*, VI: *Li chi cheng-i* 37, Yüeh-chi 19, p. 300.) In this passage, what *te* achieves is "appropriateness."

106. Karlgren, *Odes*, Shih shu 2, p. 73.

107. *Analects* xiv.35. The commentator explains *te* as *t'iao liang*; see Liu Pao-nan, p. 321. This could be interpreted as *i t'iao* 馴 調 with the meaning "tame," "gentle," or "well-behaved" (the adjective *jou*, meaning "pliant" or "gentle," is used several times in the *Book of Odes* to describe a person's *te*).

108. Cho-yun Hsü, for example, takes this position in his *Ancient China in Transition*.

109. Karlgren, *Documents*, Chun shih 23, p. 62.

110. Supporters of the *mana* thesis about the original meaning of *te* have often referred to early statements that *te* is capable of increase from a small amount to an abundant amount; they have regarded these as references to the primitive belief that the inner power changes in quantity in different objects. Although in Taoist works references to "substantial" *te* may refer to quantity, in Confucian works the expression refers simply to degree of perfection of conduct (i.e., degree of accordance with the Heavenly norms, often manifested in the extent of one's largess to others).

The supposed connection between *te* and "planting" or "plant growth" has been cited in accounting for this quantitative "growth" of the mana (*te*). The etymon from which *te* was derived is [a]*chih* (archaic sound *d'i̯ək*). The antecedent of this character was probably the oracle-bone character [oracle-bone character], which seems to have meant "to look directly" or "to look directly upward," and also had a special religious sense. *Chih* itself never had a meaning connected with planting or growth during the

Chou. Such a meaning is first attributed to it by a Chin dynasty text permeated with *yin-yang* thought. (The phrase *chih tung fang yeh ch'un yeh chih erh wei yu wen yeh* ["*Chih* represents the east. It means the spring. Things have substance but no refinement."] appears in *T'ai hsüan ching*, T'ai hsüan wen [SPTK 12.9.1a]. Fan Wang, commenting on it, says: "[a]*Chih* means [e]*chih*; the myriad things open forth. When they start to grow there they do not yet have branches, so the substance is in its rough form with no fine adornment.") The character *ch'u*, which combines three *chihs*, is defined in the Sung dynasty text *Chi yün* (Collection of Rhymes) as "a plant flourishing." The character first appears in a Han *fu* in which it clearly has the sense of "flourishing" only by extension, the earlier sense of "upright" being more accurate. *Te* belongs to the same phonetic series as three words that do have some reference to planting or growth: [e]*chih* (archaic *d̑i̯ək*, "to plant," "to grow," "to flourish," "upright," "to set up," though defined in the *Shuo wen* as "rancid oil"); [f]*chih* (*d̑i̯ək*, "to plant," "to set up," "to grow," "upright," though defined in the *Shuo wen* as "a bolt for a door"); and [g]*chih* (*t̑i̯ək*, defined as "to plant grain early"). *Te* has sound and graphic similarities with these characters; however, the first two terms also mean "to set up" and "upright." These senses are similar to the meaning "straight" of [a]*chih*, and are probably late derivations from the oracle-bone meaning of "to look directly (upward?)." In no example known to me does the oracle-bone graph have the sense of "upright." "To plant," "to increase," and "to grow" are even later extensions from "upright" and "to set up." Tuan Yü-ts'ai, in commenting on the *Shuo wen* definition of [f]*chih*, says it means "an upright wooden bolt" (Ting, V, 2509b). [h]*Chih* was often interchangeably used for [e]*chih* in the early texts, and meant "to set up."

One might say that just as what is planted grows, so may the potency [*te*] grow, in the sense of increase. There are references to the "increase of *te*" in texts. However, this process of increase is not descriptive of *te* alone, but is used to describe other activities that have no possible etymological connection with "to plant" or "to increase inherent power," such as "learning" (*hsüeh*). (E.g., in *Tso chuan*, Chao kung 18, is the passage: "Learning is a steady growth. If people do not learn they will decline. The Yüan clan will perish.") One might point to the term [b]*sheng* ("abundant," "to flourish"), which is commonly used to describe both the flourishing of plants and the state of perfect *te*, as indicating a link in meaning between "increase of *te*" and the potency for growth of what is "planted." But the opposite of *sheng te* is "declining *te*" (*shuai te*), and *shuai* would be irrelevant to any discussion of what is planted. It is probable that *sheng* was used with the simple sense of "great" or "substantial." On bronzes the adjective used to describe perfect *te* is a graph now interpreted as *shun*, meaning "great" or "substantial." [b]*Sheng* is used to describe other ethical phenomena that could not possibly have any etymological relation to what is planted, and in such cases it seems to mean "great." In Wang, *Hsün-tzu*, Li lun, p. 250 (SPTK 13.24b–25a), is the remark "[Sacrifice] is the grandest state of rites and refined conduct." In the early texts a variety of expressions were used for perfect *te* in addition to those cited—*Chuan te, shen te,* etc.

111. *Analects* xiii.10.1, in Legge, I, 256. *Ch'ung* ("to exalt") was a term commonly used to convey the idea of venerating something. It was used not only with reference to *te*, but other virtues as well. This fact, plus the matters described in the preceding footnote, prevent one from translating it (the way Waley does) as "to pile up."

112. Slightly revised from Karlgren, *Documents*, K'ang kao 22, p 43.

113. 悊 is an early form of the character *che* 哲 ; it was written as 誓 on Vessel 13 (Kuo Mo-jo, *Liang-chou*, A, 130a; expl. A, 133a), and as 質 on Vessel 12 (*ibid.*, A, 140b; expl. A, 149b). 悊 itself appears on Vessel 4 (*ibid.*, A, 110a; expl. A, 121a). The earliest meaning of 悊 seems to have included both the senses of purifying the heart and swearing before Heaven, according to Professor Shirakawa Shizuka. An exhaustive study of the term "to make bright" (*ming*) in the phrase "to make bright one's *te*" reveals no such religious coloration to it. It seems to have been simply an honorific expression.

114. *Tso chuan*, Chao kung 6 and 29, Ting kung 9.

115. Cf. Balazs, pp. 6–9.

116. *Tso chuan*, Chao kung 29, in Legge, V, 732.

117. *Ibid.*, Chao kung 6, p. 609.

118. *Ibid.*

119. *Analects* ii.3, in Legge, I, 146.

120. *Mencius* ii.A.3.2, in Legge, II, 196–97.

121. *Great Learning* vi.1.

122. Kaizuka, "Rongo ni arawareta ningen tenkei toshite no kunshi," p. 8.

123. Hsü Cho-yun, p. 164.

124. *Tso chuan*, Hsiang kung 9.

125. *Analects* iv.5, in Legge, I, 166.

126. *Mencius* vii.B.32, in Legge, II, 495.

127. *Analects* viii.2.

128. *Mencius* iv.B.7.

129. In the *Shu ching*, [e]*sheng* is contrasted with *k'uang* ("mad," "foolish"), and clearly had the sense of "wise" (see Karlgren, *Documents*, To fang 17, p. 63). On Vessel 23 it is used as an adjective, one of several laudatory attributes of a person's personal demeanor, in the phrase "sedate, brilliant, wise [*sheng*], brave, can implement *te*." (See Kuo Mo-jo, Liang chou B, 168b; expl. B, 160b.)

130. According to a famous study by Wang Kuo-wei, quoted in Hou Hsien-ch'ien, pp. 76–77.

131. Wang, *Hsün-tzu*, Cheng lun, p. 216 (SPTK 12.3a).

Chapter 5

1. It will sometimes be necessary to refer to texts compiled or written in part or in whole in the Han dynasty. However, this is done only when the ideas selected for citation are those extant in the earlier period, simply receiving more explicit statement in the later work. In this connection, some word should be said about the primary sources, the *Tao-te ching* and *Chuang-tzu.* There seems little reason to doubt that the *Tao-te ching*, even if compiled in its present form relatively late, at least incorporates materials dating from the Warring States period. Most scholars regard it as a composite work showing several hands. The Lao-Chuang expert Wang Shu-min (of National Taiwan University) holds that much material certainly predates the *Chuang-tzu* (e.g., P'ien 1). In a new study, Kimura Eiichi holds that the *Tao-te ching* was edited in the early Han, using materials that had existed for some 300 years; and that half of the content of the work was different from what we have today (Kimura, pp. 231–34). Traditionally, the Nei section has been viewed as from the hand of Chuang Tzu, whereas the Wai and Tsa sections have been viewed as later works by his disciples. Wang Shu-min (pp. 1a–b) notes that the present arrangement into three sections was made by the Chin dynasty scholar Kuo Hsiang, that early texts refer to 52 chapters instead of the present 33, and that numerous passages now in one section formerly belonged in others. But in general, the content of the Nei section is authentic, he feels, though he would supplement it by the following authentic chapters in other sections: Keng sang ch'u, Wai wu, Yü yen; parts of Ta sheng, Shan mu, T'ien tzu fang, and Chih pei yu. Neither Wang nor Professor Wu K'ang of the same institution accepts the Ch'ien Mu thesis that the authentic *Chuang-tzu* predates the *Tao-te ching* (see Wu K'ang, p. 67). There are differing estimates of when Chuang Tzu lived. Hou Wai-lu accepts the chronology of Ma Hsü-lun, i.e., that he was a contemporary of Mencius during the fourth century B.C. (Hou, p. 310). Kanaya Osamu dates the work as a whole from the period just before the Ch'in dynasty to the beginning of the Han (third–second century B.C.), except for the T'ien hsia chapter, which he dates as about 200 B.C. (see Kanaya, "Sōshi tenka hen no imi," p. 41). Whether or not the time when a passage was written is relevant to the interpretation of terms included in it is a matter that must be examined in each particular case. In connection with *te* and ideas directly relevant to it, I find no difference in the conception in the earlier and later chapters.

2. Cf. Waley, *Analects*, p. 172, n. 1.

3. Chiang, *Lao-tzu* 42, pp. 278–84.

4. *Ibid.*, 61, pp. 372–77; and 68, pp. 413–15.

5. This is primarily true of the Wai and Tsa sections (see Mori, pp. 5–6).

6. Chiang, *Lao-tzu* 13, pp. 67–70.

7. Waley, *The Way and Its Power* 22, p. 171.

8. On this topic see Lau, "Treatment of Opposites," pp. 349–53. The importance of the idea of "submission" in the thought of Lao Tzu is confirmed by Hsün Tzu, who criticized him in these terms: "Lao Tzu understood about being bent, but not about being straight." In other words, he overstressed submission (bent means humble). See Wang, *Hsün-tzu*, T'ien lun, p. 213 (SPTK 11.25a).

9. Waley, *The Way and Its Power* 42, p. 195.

10. See the first few lines of Chiang, *Lao-tzu* 62, p. 378. In *ibid.*, 2, p. 12, we learn of the error of responding to something as excellent or bad: deciding that something is bad means that a person already has a prejudicial idea of what good is. Later we learn that the sage does not abandon anyone, i.e., reject the "bad" and only concern himself with the "good"; *ibid.*, 27, p. 183. Again, it is said, "Of the good man I approve, but of the bad I also approve"; *ibid.*, 49, p. 305 (translation is from Waley, *The Way and Its Power*, p. 202). See also Chiang, *Lao-tzu* 14, p. 79.

11. The evidence for this conclusion is scattered throughout the text. For example, see the discussion in Ch'ien Mu, *Chuang-tzu*, Ta tsung shih, p. 58 (SPTK 3.23b).

12. Chiang, *Lao-tzu* 11, p. 63; Ch'ien Mu, *Chuang-tzu*, Ta tsung shih, p. 54 (SPTK 3.15b).

13. Chiang, *Lao-tzu* 27, p. 184. There is an interesting discussion of the "light within" in Kaltenmark, pp. 79–83.

14. Ch'ien Mu, *Chuang-tzu*, Ch'i wu lun, p. 17 (SPTK 1.34a). Cf. the later *Chuang-tzu* passage "All things are to him [the sage] as One"; *ibid.*, Tse yang, p. 211 (SPTK 8.45a).

15. Chiang, *Lao-tzu* 51, p. 316. I follow Chiang's commentary in interpreting [a]*wu* as "species." He speaks of it as "each kind of living thing different in form." He takes [e]*shih* as the "environment" in which a thing dwells.

16. *Ibid.*, 10, p. 62. It seems important to me to bring out by the word "to" or "in order to" the idea that the sagely ruler, like Tao, acts disinterestedly in nourishing the people.

17. Ch'ien Mu, *Chuang-tzu*, T'ien ti, p. 93 (SPTK 5.9a). Kimura Eiichi holds that in Taoist thought, since things cannot exist separately from the Absolute, the nature (*seishitsu*) of each thing, including man, is in some sense a nature given from the Absolute. Man's nature ob-

tains only one aspect of Tao, and is imperfect; but by knowing Tao well, one can reach the point of "supreme *te*" (*shang te*), i.e., of qualitatively improving one's nature. Kimura says that *te* in some cases denotes this "nature," which is good. See Kimura, pp. 578–80. His remarks, though made largely with reference to the *Tao-te ching*, are intended to be applicable to other Taoist works as well. What he refers to as "nature" I would call "principle of life"; qualifying it as "good" is questionable.

18. Ch'ien Mu, *Chuang-tzu*, Keng sang ch'u, p. 193 (SPTK 8.17a).

19. Chiang, *Lao-tzu* 28, pp. 189–91.

20. Kuo Mo-jo, *Kuan-tzu chi chiao*, Hsin shu A.36, pp. 642–43. Having got the essence of Tao, then one has *te*.

21. Note the following statements: "What is *te* which does not manifest itself in bodily form? [It is like placid water,] . . . internally maintained and externally not overflowing." Ch'ien Mu, *Chuang-tzu*, Te ch'ung fu, p. 44 (SPTK 2.40b). "Now you and I both roam [i.e., find our true being] inside form, and yet you seek my true state outside of form." *Ibid.*, p. 42 (SPTK 2.35a).

22. *Shih-san-ching*, Vol. I, Ch. 8, Hsi tz'u B.1, p. 74. Although in detailed Taoist cosmological discussions Tao is distinguished from "Heaven" and "earth" as something prior, in actual usage the latter, when combined as *t'ien-ti*, often denoted the former. They seem to do so in this case. An example of one of the rare early passages that speak of Heaven's *te* in the extended sense of "kindness" is Karlgren, *Odes*, Yü wu cheng 1, p. 140.

23. Chiang, *Lao-tzu* 10, p. 62 and 51, p. 319. The same phrase appears in both chapters. It perhaps would be more appropriate to take the sage as the subject of *sheng erh pu yu*, etc., in the former case, and Tao as subject in the latter. Regarding the former case, Chiang Hsi-ch'ang says that the sage "lets the people come into existence and grow by themselves, lets them work and rest at will, and he doesn't manage or concern himself with them." "Nourishing" had positive and negative aspects to it. In part, the people would be nourished by *Tao* when not interfered with.

24. Ch'ien Mu, *Chuang-tzu*, T'ien ti, p. 93 (SPTK 5.9a).

25. See Note 20 above.

26. Ch'ien Mu, *Chuang-tzu*, Keng sang ch'u, p. 193 (SPTK 8.17a).

27. *Ibid.*, Ta tsung shih, p. 57 (SPTK 3.20b).

28. *Ibid.*, Yü yen, p. 229 (SPTK 9.13b). Translation is from Giles, p. 267. This is one of the chapters in the Tsa-p'ien that Wang Shu-min considers authentic.

29. *Ibid.*, Ch'i wu lun, p. 14 (SPTK 1.29b) and Yü yen, p. 229 (SPTK 9.13a–b).

30. E.g., Wang Yin-lin, Yen Fu, and Chang Ping-lin, all quoted in Ch'ien Mu, *Chuang-tzu*, p. 8.

31. "The myriad things come into existence due to it"; Chiang, *Lao-tzu* 34, p. 224.

32. I think that this notion is expressed in a passage that most commentators have had difficulty explaining: "Heaven and Earth are not humane; they consider the myriad things as straw dogs." (*Ibid.*, 5, p. 33.) An explanation of "straw dogs" (*ch'u kou*) is given in *Tao-te ching chiang-i*, p. 22. It referred to special grasses used in sacrifices for burning valuables. Straw is ordinary and cheap, yet it is used in ceremonies along with things of great cost; hence it symbolizes the ultimate sameness of all things. Heaven and Earth regard all things as straw dogs, i.e., as equally valuable. The passage means that although Heaven and Earth in producing all things are not being purposefully benevolent (*jen*), they do treat everything as of the same importance, their concern reaching even to what in human eyes is the most humble and unworthy of attention. A passage helpful for understanding "are not humane" occurs in the *Mencius*, where we learn that Shun naturally "followed the path of humanheartedness and duty; he did not pursue humanheartedness and duty"; *Mencius* iv.A.19.2. Shun did not purposely use *jen* and *i* to aid the people, but the result of his actions was naturally in accord with *jen* and *i*.

33. Ch'ien Mu, *Chuang-tzu*, Ying ti wang, p. 61 (SPTK 3.28b).

34. Hou, p. 326.

35. Many writers have tried to maintain that Tao actually meant no more than the various changes of matter (*ch'i*), with no implication of an internal principle that determined the changes. Two factors contradict this view: first, Tao was definitely viewed as logically prior to *ch'i* (it "existed before *ch'i*"); second, Tao was distinguished from the constantly changing *ch'i* by being unchanging and formless. *Tao-te ching* 25 clearly states that Tao does not change, and the same fact is stated in the *Chuang-tzu*. The ideal of the changeless amid change is reflected in the Taoist portrait of the sage, of whom it is said that although life and death (changes) are momentous occurrences, they cannot change his True Ruler; see Ch'ien Mu, *Chuang-tzu*, Te ch'ung fu, p. 39 (SPTK 2.30a). Tao is spoken of as the "Producer of Changes" (*tsao hua che*); *ibid.*, Ta tsung shih, p. 55 (SPTK 3.17b). A passage in the *Hsün-tzu*, reflecting Taoist ideas, says that we can know what happens in changes ([b]*kung* or *so i ch'eng*) but cannot know the formless cause of them ([d]*shih* or *wu hsing*); Wang Hsien-ch'ien, *Hsün-tzu*, T'ien lun, p. 206 (SPTK 11.17a). The distinction between the formless principle of change and the *ch'i* that actually changes holds whether one is dis-

cussing the entire universe or a single thing. The *Chuang-tzu* says, "What they loved in their mother was not her form but what directs her form"; Ch'ien Mu, *Chuang-tzu*, Te ch'ung fu, p. 43 (SPTK 2.39a). In many passages, of course, the distinction was not clearly made; it is hard to draw a line between the things that change and the principle of change itself.

36. Chiang, *Lao-tzu* 5, p. 33.

37. For Lao Tzu on this matter, see Note 10.

38. Chiang, *Lao-tzu* 12, p. 67 and 3, p. 21.

39. "Therefore the sagely man has that in which his mind roams (Tao), and knowledge is an obstacle"; Ch'ien Mu, *Chuang-tzu*, Te ch'ung fu, p. 45 (SPTK 2.42a). I take [a]*nieh* as [b]*nieh*. "I forget how old I am and forget duties [i.e., right and wrong]"; *ibid.*, Ch'i wu lun, p. 22 (SPTK 1.46a).

40. *Ibid.*, Ch'i wu lun, p. 11 (SPTK 1.25b).

41. Mori, p. 2.

42. Ch'ien Mu, *Chuang-tzu*, Te ch'ung fu, p. 45 (SPTK 2.42b). A little further he defines [b]*ch'ing*, applicable to this passage, as follows, "What I mean by *ch'ing* is not letting man's loves and hates inwardly harm his body."

43. *Ibid.*, Jen chieh shih, p. 39 (SPTK 2.31a).

44. "I have freed myself from my body," answered Yen Hui. "I have discarded my reasoning powers. And by thus getting rid of body and mind, I have become One with the Infinite." *Ibid.*, Ta tsung shih, p. 60 (SPTK 3.26b); translation is from Herbert Giles, p. 85.

45. Ch'ien Mu, *Chuang-tzu*, Ch'i wu lun, p. 10 (SPTK 1.23a). The expression *chen chün*, meaning the same as *chen tsai*, occurs further along in the text.

46. "What they loved in their mother was not her form but what directs her form [i.e., the True Ruler]"; *ibid.*, Te ch'ung fu, p. 43 (SPTK 2.39a).

47. *Ibid.*, Te ch'ung fu, p. 40 (SPTK 2.32a).

48. "Because of what he knows as a result of his unitary knowledge, his mind never dies"; *ibid.*, Te ch'ung fu, p. 40 (SPTK 2.32b). "When you receive the Tao taking form within you, you don't change but last until the end"; *ibid.*, Ch'i wu lun, p. 11 (SPTK 1.24b). See also *ibid.*, Ta tsung shih, p. 53 (SPTK 3.13b).

49. *Ibid.*, Ma t'i, p. 71, and T'ien ti, p. 101 (SPTK 4.12b and 5.20b).

50. *Ibid.*, Ma t'i, p. 71 (SPTK 4.12b).

51. *Ibid.*, Shan hsing, p. 126, and Tse yang, p. 215 (SPTK 6.8a and 8.52a).

52. *Ibid.*, Ch'u ch'ieh, p. 78 (SPTK 4.25b).
53. *Ibid.*, Shan hsing, p. 126 (SPTK 6.7b).
54. *Ibid.*, T'ien ti, p. 101 (SPTK 5.20b); translation is from Herbert Giles, p. 109.
55. *Ibid.*, P'ien mu, p. 69 (SPTK 4.7a).
56. *Ibid.*, Shan hsing, p. 127 (SPTK 6.10a).
57. *Ibid.*, P'ien mu, p. 69 (SPTK 4.7a).
58. Mori, p. 4.
59. Ch'ien Mu, *Chuang-tzu*, T'ien ti, p. 93 (SPTK 5.9a).
60. There are numerous examples in texts of all schools in which [e]*hsing* seems to have denoted something physical. Mencius said, "The body and appearance are the Heavenly *hsing*." (*Mencius* vii.A.38. I take *se* as "appearance.") In the *Chuang-tzu* one learns that joined toes and extra fingers are superfluous to *hsing* (Ch'ien Mu, *Chuang-tzu*, P'ien mu, p. 67 [SPTK 4.1a]), and that hoofs and hair belong to the *hsing* of horses (*ibid.*, p. 71 [SPTK 4.10b]). The same work remarks that *hsing* results from the combination of bodily form ([b]*hsing*) and spirit (*shen*). There are certain specific references to *hsing* as containing "body." For example, in the *Li chi yüeh chi* is the statement that "men have a *hsing* characterized by body ["blood and *ch'i*"] and intelligence" (*Shih-san-ching*, VI, Chüan 38, Yüeh chi, p. 307); this attribute was to be repeated often in statements of the components of *hsing*. The Ch'ing dynasty commentator Tai Chen spoke of *hsing* being separated from the *yin/yang* and Five Elements as "blood and *ch'i*" with intelligence. (Tai Chen, B, 6a; the term *hsüeh ch'i* first appears in *Analects* xvi.7.) Katō Jōken traces the physical aspect of *hsing* to *sheng*, which he feels had the same physical connotation. *Hsing* written with a female radical originally meant "sameness of blood" (*t'ung hsüeh*). The character designated female children and grandchildren born of a daughter's marriage into another house, just as the *sheng* with a male component designated male children and grandchildren so born. Both were considered *t'ung sheng*, i.e., *t'ung hsing* or *t'ung hsüeh* (Katō, p. 32).

Chapter 6

1. Wang, *Hsün-tzu*, Cheng ming, p. 274 (SPTK 16.2a).
2. See Ch. 5, n. 23.
3. Chiang, *Lao-tzu* 3, p. 24.
4. *Ibid.*, 1, p. 6, and 37, p. 241.
5. *Ibid.*, 7, p. 43.
6. *Ibid.*, 22, p. 153.
7. *Ibid.*, 19, p. 119, and 18, p. 114.
8. *Ibid.*, 20, p. 130. Man is "blank as a piece of uncarved wood; yet

receptive as a hollow in the hills. Murky as a troubled stream"; *ibid.*, 15, p. 92. (Translation is from Waley, *The Way and Its Power*, p. 160.) Chiang would interpret *tun* as *shun hou* ("genuine"). Being genuine as an uncarved block means that no bad external influences can be "carved" upon you; being hollow means that you can receive and contain anything bad or good (tolerance); the last phrase may refer to the ability to live with society's murky elements as well as its good ones.

9. The term "blankness" comes from *Tao-te ching* 15.

10. Ch'ien Mu, *Chuang-tzu*, Ch'i wu lun, p. 15 (SPTK 1.31a).

11. There are various ways of expressing this. In *ibid.*, T'ien hsia, p. 278 (SPTK 10.37b) is the phrase "above he roams with the creator."

12. *Ibid.*, Te ch'ung fu, p. 44 (SPTK 2.40a–b). In the interpretations of this difficult passage I follow the commentary of Wang Shu-min.

13. *Ibid.*, Ying ti wang, p. 62 (SPTK 3.30b).

14. *Ibid.*, Ta tsung shih, p. 55 (SPTK 3.17a).

15. *Ibid.*, Ta tsung shih, p. 66.

16. Chiang, *Lao-tzu* 10, p. 58.

17. Ch'ien Mu, *Chuang-tzu*, Chih pei yu, p. 181 (SPTK 7.55b). External adaptation is described in Chiang, *Lao-tzu* 15, p. 90, in the phrase beginning "Attentive as a guest . . ."; the commentator says that the phrase "Who is able, in this murkiness, to purify his heart gradually by quietness?" (*ibid.*, p. 93) refers to the sage externally blending with the dirt of human society but internally having an intelligence that goes far above it. Since all customs are equally changing products (the rim of the wheel) of the Tao, which is always the same (the pivot of the wheel), one should follow whatever custom one encounters, and blend with any situation (*yü chu yung*); see Ch'ien Mu, *Chuang-tzu*, Ch'i wu lun, p. 16 (SPTK 1.30a).

18. *Ibid.*, Chih pei yu, p. 173 (SPTK 7.43a). Translation is from Giles, p. 210.

19. *Ibid.*, Chih lo, p. 139 (SPTK 6.32a).

20. Wang, *Hsün-tzu*, T'ien-lun, p. 206 (SPTK 11.17a). Reference is made to the "harmony" of the *yin* and *yang ch'is* in Chiang, *Lao-tzu* 42, p. 280. *Ch'i* is said to be a thing found in each individual in *ibid.*, 6, p. 40. Reference to the two opposing *ch'is* in the individual appears in Ch'ien Mu, *Chuang-tzu*, Ying ti wang, p. 62 (SPTK 3.15a).

21. *Ibid.*, Te ch'ung fu, p. 39 (SPTK 2.31a). Ch'ien Mu comments, "then sounds and colors disappear and are all blended together as one."

22. *Ibid.*, Te ch'ung fu, p. 44 (SPTK 2.40b).

23. *Ibid.*, Hsü Wu-kuei, p. 207 (SPTK 8.39b). The commentator Hsi T'ung says that [a]*yang* ("to roast") is borrowed for [b]*yang* ("to nourish").

24. *Ibid.*, Ying ti wang, p. 64 (SPTK 3.34a). Ch'ien Mu says that

the *t'ai ch'ung* is "the most empty, most harmonious, having no inclination [from the center]."

25. *Ibid.*, Jen chien shih, p. 30 (SPTK 2.13a).

26. *Ibid.*

27. Chiang, *Lao-tzu* 41, p. 272. The valley is empty and lowly, that to which water flows, says the commentator.

28. Plato, *Timaeus* 90c–e, in Cornford, *Plato's Cosmology*, p. 354.

29. Chiang, *Lao-tzu* 12, p. 65. Translation is from Waley, *The Way and Its Power*, p. 156.

30. *Ibid.*, 37, p. 240.

31. Ch'ien Mu, *Chuang-tzu*, T'ien hsia, p. 276 (SPTK 10.35a).

32. E.g., see Chiang, *Lao-tzu* 27, p. 183.

33. See *Chuang-tzu*, Ying ti wang p'ien.

34. Ch'ien Mu, *Chuang-tzu*, Ying ti wang, p. 63 (SPTK 3.31b).

35. *Ibid.*, Ta tsung shih, pp. 53, 56 (SPTK 3.13a and 3.19b).

36. *Ibid.*, K'o i, p. 123 (SPTK 6.4a).

37. *Ibid.*, Ta sheng, p. 145 (SPTK 7.3a).

38. *Ibid.*, Ying ti wang, p. 61 (SPTK 3.28a–b). Elsewhere we learn that "princes among men are inferior to Heaven"; *ibid.*, Ta tsung shih, p. 57 (SPTK 3.22a). Plato spoke of the prenatal condition as the "time when we were not yet man," meaning that the true self is not the embodied soul alone; see Taylor, p. 138, n. 1.

39. Chiang, *Lao-tzu* 55, p. 335. This same usage occurs in the *Lieh-tzu* and *Chuang-tzu*. In the latter the phrase appears as *ho ch'i te*; Ch'ien Mu, *Chuang-tzu*, Ta sheng, p. 145 (SPTK 7.3a). Wang Shu-min says *ho* should be *han*.

Chapter 7

1. *Shih-san-ching*, VI, Yüeh chi, ch. 37, p. 299.

2. Ch'ien Mu, *Chuang-tzu*, Jen chien shih, p. 32 (SPTK 2.16b–17a). The *ming* here clearly indicates that the sentiment is innate. The commentator Liu Hsien-hsin remarks: "The *ming* that Chuang Tzu speaks of is the same as the [e]*hsing* of which Mencius speaks. Mencius takes the individual as his basic concept and so repeatedly speaks of *hsing*. Chuang Tzu takes the cosmos as basic and so repeatedly speaks of *ming*."

3. Karlgren, *Documents*, Wen hou chih ming 2, p. 80.

4. *Ibid.*, K'ang kao 20–21, p. 42.

5. *Analects* iv.2. The expression [b]*an jen* appears in the phrase "... cultivates himself and by this makes tranquil all the people" (*Analects* xiv.45).

6. This complex matter is specifically discussed in *Mencius* ii.A.2.

7. *Ibid.*, vii.B.35.

8. "It [vast *ch'i*] is produced by the accumulation of acts of duty"; *ibid.*, ii.A.2.15.

9. One way in which the mind can be moved in thought is by fear; see the comment of Chao Hsün on *ibid.*, ii.A.2.1 in Chao Ch'i, I, iii.

10. In the *Tao-te ching* is the phrase *hsin shih ch'i yüeh ch'iang*; Chiang Hsi-ch'ang has interpreted this as meaning, "If the mind tolerates the *ch'i* [doing as it pleases], this means the *ch'i* will dominate the mind." See Chiang, *Lao-tzu* 55, p. 343.

11. The passage *fan wan-wu i tse mo pu hsiang wei pi* (in Wang Hsien-ch'ien, *Hsün-tzu*, Chieh pi, p. 259 [SPTK 15.2a]) means that if someone directs attention to two objects rather than one, the two cannot help being mutually obscuring. Dubs distorts the meaning by translating *ᶜi* as "unorthodox"; see Dubs, *Hsuntze*, p. 260.

12. Wang, *Hsün-tzu*, Chieh pi, p. 269 (SPTK 15.13b).

13. The former kings established the rules of proper conduct and the duties "in order to cultivate men's desires"; *ibid.*, Li lun, p. 231 (SPTK 13.1a).

14. *Ibid.*, Fu kuo, p. 113 (SPTK 6.1b).

15. "Therefore he made his mind the ruler and carefully controlled it"; *ibid.*, Chieh pi, p. 260 (SPTK 15.3a).

16. *Ibid.*, Ch'üan hsüeh, p. 12 (SPTK 1.15b); translation is from Dubs, *Hsuntze*, p. 41.

17. Chiang, *Lao-tzu* 16, p. 99.

18. *Ibid.*, 37, p. 242.

19. Ch'ien Mu, *Chuang-tzu*, Ch'i wu lun, p. 15 (SPTK 1.31a).

20. *Ibid.*, Ta tsung shih, p. 55 (SPTK 3.16a).

21. *Ibid.*, Te ch'ung fu, p. 11 (SPTK 1.24b).

22. *Great Learning* 6.1.

23. Wang Hsien-ch'ien, *Hsün-tzu*, Chieh pi, p. 269; translation is from Dubs, *Hsuntze*, pp. 273–74.

24. *Doctrine of the Mean* 26.4.

25. *Mencius* iv.A.12.2; and Legge, xx.18, p. 413.

26. *Ibid.*, 22, pp. 415–16.

27. Wang, *Hsün-tzu*, Chieh pi, p. 262 (SPTK 15.5b–6a). Translation is a revised version of that found in Dubs, *Hsuntze*, p. 265. The meaning of the first phrase is that Tao accounts for all natural changes.

28. Wang, *Hsün-tzu*, Chieh pi, p. 265 (SPTK 15.9a). Translation is a revised version of that found in Dubs, *Hsuntze*, p. 268.

29. Wang, *Hsün-tzu*, Chieh pi, p. 266 (SPTK 15.11a).

30. Ch'ien Mu, *Chuang-tzu*, Hsiao yao yu, p. 5, and Jen chien shih, p. 30 (SPTK 1.13b and 2.13b).

31. *Ibid.*, Ying ti wang, p. 62 (SPTK 3.30b).

32. The text says, "His *yin* and *yang ch'i* were disordered"; *ibid.*, Ta tsung shih, p. 54 (SPTK 3.15a).

Chapter 8

1. For a discussion of the negative legacy from the past, as determined by Chinese Communist writers, see Donald J. Munro, "Chinese Communist Treatment of the Thinkers of the Hundred Schools Period," *China Quarterly*, Oct.–Dec. 1965, pp. 132–37.

2. Chou, p. 28. Chou Yang was purged in the Spring of 1966, early in the Great Proletarian Cultural Revolution; but his remarks on "humanism" are typically Maoist. Mao's own remarks on the subject appear, among other places, in *Talks at the Yenan Forum on Art and Literature.*

3. Chou, p. 33.

4. Another characteristic of the cultivated individual in both Confucian and Taoist thought was "selflessness," a sense of union of self with something beyond. As was said, the Chinese idea also carried the notion of "unselfish," in that the person who is conscious of the union is unselfish in deeds. This ideal, unlike tranquility and harmony, has fared much better in Communist theory. It continued important in almost all Chinese philosophical schools after the Chou. (There are exceptions. Religious Taoism, for example, often stressed the search for personal bodily immortality.) For a Neo-Taoist like Wang Pi (A.D. 226–49), selflessness comes from understanding that one has an eternal role to play as part of a cosmic pattern of things, which gradually unfolds from "original substance" (*pen-t'i*) into "actuality" (*yung*). The Neo-Taoist sage who "returns to the origin" (*fan pen*) loses his selfishness in his lifetime, as does the Buddhist Arhat or the Ch'an seeker after Buddhahood. In the Neo-Confucian thought of Chu Hsi (A.D. 1130–1200), the "union of Heaven and man" comes through knowing all (*ko wu*, or "investigating things") and loving all (*jen*, or "humanheartedness"). People often have selfish desires and isolate themselves from other people and things because of illusions caused by impurities in their material constitution (*ch'i*). By "investigating every blade of grass and every shrub," one can end the false separation of self from others. Since the principles of all things are in the individual as in a microcosm, the more one studies other things (i.e., their principles), the more he sees the unity underlying all things. The "monistic idealism" of Wang Yangming should be understood as an attempt to eliminate the "selfishness" supposedly still entailed by Chu Hsi's dualism, with its split between the individual's "mind," which knows things, and the "principles of things," which are known.

Selflessness is also an ultimate goal in Chinese Communist thought. In Confucianism the phrase "unity of man and Heaven" was sometimes used to indicate achieving the union of self and something beyond the self. Achieving that union invariably entailed the elimination of selfishness. In Chinese Communist writings, the union of the individual person's own nature (*jen-hsing*) or individuality (*ko-hsing*) with the Party Nature (*tang-hsing*) takes the place of the old "unity of man and Heaven." The Party Nature (of the Communist Party) is defined as "the highest and most concentrated expression of class (i.e., proletarian) character." One does not have to be a party member to fuse his "individuality" with the Party Nature by "purifying" his thoughts (ridding them of self-interest); see, for example, Ch'ien Tzu-an, "Lun jen-hsing tang-hsing ho ko-hsing," *Jen-min t'ieh-tao*, Oct. 24, 1957. Once the union of self with Party (i.e., with the masses) is achieved, great strength is released. On the practical side, with the disappearance of selfish interest, material incentives are unnecessary to encourage the person to work at his best.

5. Wm. Theodore de Bary (ed.), *Sources of Chinese Tradition* (New York: Columbia University Press, 1960), pp. 450–53.

6. For example, Chang Chih-tung, in charge of supervising the new Ministry of Education, said: "How can a nation be preserved? With possession of knowledge it is preserved. . . . In order to save the current situation we must begin with reform, and reform must begin with the changing of the civil-service examinations." Teng and Fairbank, p. 166. In the 1860's some officials sought to obviate rebellion by establishing "academies" or "colleges" in troubled provinces to educate the people in Confucian principles.

7. Quoted in Chow, pp. 223–24.

8. Teng and Fairbank, p. 165.

9. *The Selected Writings of Mao Tse-tung, 1927–1947* (Harbin: Tung Pei Book Co., 1948), p. 915. Quoted in Dai, p. 200.

10. *Chung-kuo ch'ing-nien pao* (China Youth Daily), July 31, 1965.

11. *Peking Review* (Peking), June 2, 1967, p. 13.

12. Ch'en Ju-i, "Fa ku-chin wan-jen" (Emulate the Perfect Men of All Ages), *Chung-kuo i-chou* (China Newsweek), No. 663 (Jan. 7, 1963), pp. 8–10.

13. Chow, p. 224.

14. Po Yeh, "Shuo li" (Persuading Through Reason), *Chung-kuo ch'ing-nien* (China Youth), No. 6 (1962), 8.

15. *Mencius*, vii.B.14 and ii.A.3. Hsün Tzu makes the point that "one who understands the nature of force does not use it" (Wang, *Hsüntzu*, Wan chih, p. 99 [SPTK 5.7a]). He says that the quickest way for a powerful state to be transformed into a politically insignificant one is for its ruler to try to conquer others by force; he will "acquire land but lose the people." In both his own state and those he seeks to conquer, the people will turn away from him.

16. Meisner, pp. 26–28. Meisner himself stresses the influence of Emerson on Li Ta-chao in connection with the thesis that the individual can shape his own environment.

17. Quoted in Dai, p. 68.

18. Wang Li, "Fa-yang kung-ch'an-chu-i ti lao-tung ching-shen" (Bringing Forth the Communist Labor Spirit), *Hung ch'i* (Red Flag), No. 12 (Nov. 16, 1958), p. 25.

19. Shih Tsun, ed., *Chung-kuo chin-tai ssu-hsiang-shih ts'an-k'ao tzu-liao chien-pien* (Source Materials for the Study of the History of Modern Chinese Thought), p. 1220; quoted in Meisner, pp. 146–47.

20. These Platonic and Aristotelian ideas entered Christianity through the influence of the Neo-Platonism of Plotinus (A.D. 205–70), Proclus (A.D. 412–85), and the Pseudo-Dionysius (fifth century A.D. monk). The Pseudo-Dionysius, in his works on *The Celestial Hierarchy* and *The Ecclesiastical Hierarchy*, speaks of the structure of the universe in terms of ranks of three and nine, from God at the top down to the lowest created things (Paul E. Sigmund, "Hierarchy, Equality, and Consent," in Pennock and Chapman, p. 135).

The question of egalitarianism in Jewish thought is also complicated. In the Old Testament is the statement, "Have we not all one father? Hath not one God created us? Why do we deal treacherously every man against his brother, by profaning the covenant of our fathers?" (*Malachi* 2:10, quoted in Abernethy, p. 33.) Biblical Hebrew has no word for equality. But it is clearly implied in the Biblical texts that men are equal before God's law and also share one progenitor in Adam (other animals were created in the plural). But neither of these kinds of equality is natural in the sense in which I have been using the term. They say nothing about empirically verifiable aspects of the human endowment with which all men are born. The closest the Hebrews came to natural equality in the sense used in this book was the idea that God endows all men with His image, the *Tselem Elohim*; at a later time, under Aristotelian influence, some Jewish scholars identified this with "reason" (Emanuel Rackman, "Judaism and Equality," in Pennock and Chapman, p. 55). Yet there is complete ambivalence on the matter of natural equality in the Hebrew works. One Talmudic source states: "The creation of the first man *alone* was to show forth the greatness of the Supreme King of Kings, the Holy One, blessed be He. For if a man mints coins from one mold, they be all alike, but the Holy One, blessed be He, fashioned all men in the mold of the first man, and not one resembles the other." *Babylonian Talmud, Tractate Sanhedrin*, 38a; quoted in *ibid.*, p. 156.

21. Pennock and Chapman, p. 138.

22. *Ibid.*, pp. 140–45.

23. *Ibid.*, p. 128.

24. See Lakoff, *Equality in Political Philosophy*.

BIBLIOGRAPHY

Abernethy, George L. The Idea of Equality. Richmond, Va.: John Knox, 1959.

Balazs, Etienne. Le Traité juridique du "Souei-Chou." Leiden: Brill, 1954.

Bodde, Derk. "On Translating Chinese Philosophic Terms," *Far Eastern Quarterly*, XIV (1955).

Boodberg, Peter. "The Semasiology of Some Primary Confucian Concepts," *Philosophy East and West*, II (Jan. 1953).

Brandt, Richard, ed. Social Justice. Englewood Cliffs, N.J.: Prentice-Hall, 1962.

Chan Wing-tsit. "The Evolution of the Confucian Concept of *Jen*," *Philosophy East and West*, IV, No. 7 (Jan. 1955), pp. 295–319.

——— A Source Book in Chinese Philosophy. Princeton, N.J.: Princeton University Press, 1963.

Chang, Carsun. The Development of Neo-Confucian Thought. 2 vols. New York: Bookman, 1957.

Chang Ping-ch'üan. Yin-hsü wen-tzu ping-pien (Third Compilation of Inscriptions from the Yin Wastes). Taipei: Chung-yang yen-chiu-yüan li-shih yü-yen yen-chiu-so, 1957.

Chao Chi-pin. Lun-yü hsin-t'an (A New Study of the *Analects*). Peking: Jen-min Ch'u-pan she, 1962.

Chao Ch'i, ed. Meng-tzu cheng-i (Orthodox Interpretation of the *Mencius*). 2 vols. Taipei: Shih-chieh shu-chü, 1956.

Chou Yang. The Fighting Task Confronting Workers in Philosophy and the Social Sciences. Peking: Foreign Languages Press, 1963.

Ch'en Meng-chia. Yin-hsü pu-tz'u tsung-shu (Comprehensive Discourse on the Divination Words from the Yin Wastes). Peking: K'o-hsüeh ch'u-pan she, 1956.

Ch'en P'an. "Ch'un-ch'iu kung-shih-yü yü t'ang shuo"(On the Saying "Kung-shih-yü yü t'ang" in the *Spring and Autumn Annals*), Li-shih *yü-yen yen-chiu-so chi-k'an* (Collected Publications of the Institute of History and Language), VII, No. 2 (1936), pp. 175–93.

Ch'en Ta-ch'i. "K'ung-tzu so shuo jen tzu te i-i" (The Meaning of the Term *Jen* as Used by Confucius), *Ta-lu tsa-chih* (Mainland Magazine), XIII, No. 12 (Dec. 1956), pp. 373–77.

Cheng, Andrew Chih-yi. Hsün Tzu's Theory of Human Nature and Its Influence on Chinese Thought. Peking: 1928.

Cheng Te-k'un. Archaeology in China, Vol. II: Shang China. Cambridge, Eng.: W. Heffer and Sons, 1960.

Ch'i Ta. "Chia-ku-wen chung ti chung shih-pu-shih nu-li" (Does *Chung* on Oracle Bones Mean "Slave"?), *Hsüeh-shu yüeh-k'an* (Academic Monthly), No. 1 (1957), p. 18.

Chiang Hsi-ch'ang, ed. Lao-tzu chiao-ku (Commentary on the *Lao-tzu*). Shanghai: Commercial Press, 1937.

Ch'ien Mu, ed. Chuang-tzu tsuan-chien (Collected Annotations on the *Chuang-tzu* [including the editor's]). Hong Kong: Tung-nan yin-wu ch'u-pan she, 1957.

——— "Chung-kuo ssu-hsiang-shih chung ti kuei-shen-kuan" (The Concept of Spirits in the History of Chinese Thought), *Hsin-ya hsüeh-pao* (Journal of New Asia College), I, No. 1 (Aug. 1955), pp. 1–43.

——— "Hsing-ming" (*Hsing-ming*), *Min-chu p'ing-lun* (Democratic Review), VI, No. 3 (Feb. 1955).

——— Ssu-shu shih-i (Explanation of the Four Books). Taipei: Chung-hua wen-hua ch'u-pan shih-yeh wei-yüan hui, 1957.

Ch'ien-shou-t'ang so-ts'ang Yin-hsü wen-tzu (Inscriptions from the Yin Wastes Kept by the Ch'ien-shou-t'ang). Shanghai: Kuang-ts'ang hsüeh-ch'en, 1918.

Ching-chi chuan-ku (Comprehensive Explanations on the Classics). 4 vols. Taipei: Shih-chieh shu-chü, 1956.

Chu-shu chi-nien i-cheng (Verification of the Chronology of the Bamboo Books). Taipei: I-wen yin-shu-kuan, n.d.

Ch'ü Wan-li, ed. Shang-shu shi-i (Explanation of the *Shang-shu*). Taipei: Chung-hua wen-hua ch'u-pan shih-yeh wei-yüan hui, 1956.

Cornford, Francis M. From Religion to Philosophy. New York: Harper, 1957.

——— Plato's Cosmology. London: Routledge and Kegan Paul, 1937. New York: Humanities Press, 1956.

Creel, Herrlee G. Confucius, the Man and the Myth. New York: John Day, 1949.

——— "Shih t'ien" (Explaining the Term *T'ien*), *Yenching Journal of Chinese Studies*, XVIII (Dec. 1935), pp. 59–71.

DeWitt, Norman W. Epicurus and His Philosophy. Minneapolis: University of Minnosota Press, 1954.

Dubs, Homer H. "The Archaic Jou Religion," *T'oung Pao*, XLVI (1958).

——— "Mencius and Sun-dz on Human Nature," *Philosophy East and West*, VI (1956).

———, trans. The Works of Hsuntze. London: Probsthain, 1928.

Fan Hsiang-yung, ed. Ku-pen chu-shu chi-nien chi chiao-ting pu (A Supplementary Collation and Explanation of the Chronology of the

Ancient Text Bamboo Books). Shanghai: Hsin-chih-shih ch'u-pan she, 1956.

Fang Chün-i. Chui-i-chai i-ch'i k'ao-shih (A Study and Interpretation of Bronze Vessels by Chui-i-chai). Shanghai: Commercial Press, 1935.

Forke, Alfred, trans. Lun-Heng. 2 vols. New York: Paragon, 1962.

——— The World Conception of the Chinese. London: Probsthain, 1925.

Fu Szu-nien. Fu Meng-chen hsien-sheng chi (Collected Works of Mr. Fu Meng-chen), Vol. III: Hsing-ming ku-hsün pien-cheng (Analysis of Ancient Teachings about *Hsing* and *Ming*). N.p., n.d. Probably published about 1940.

Fung Yu-lan. History of Chinese Philosophy. 2 vols. Princeton, N.J.: Princeton University Press, 1952.

Giles, Herbert A., trans. Chuang Tzu. London: Allen and Unwin, 1961.

Giles, Lionel. Taoist Teachings. London: John Murray, 1925.

Gould, John. The Development of Plato's Ethics. Cambridge, Eng.: Cambridge University Press, 1955.

Graham, A. C. The Book of *Lieh-tzu*. London: John Murray, 1960.

Granet, Marcel. Chinese Civilization (Trans. Kathleen E. Innes and Mabel R. Brailsford). New York: Knopf, 1930.

Hamilton, Edith, and Huntington Cairns. The Collected Dialogues of Plato. New York: Bollingen, 1961.

Hou Wai-lu. Chung-kuo ssu-hsiang t'ung-shih (General History of Chinese Thought), Vol. I: Ku-tai ssu-hsiang (Ancient Thought). Peking: Jen-min ch'u-pan she, 1957.

Hsü Cho-yun. Ancient China in Transition. Stanford: Stanford University Press, 1965.

Hsü Chung-shu. "Chin-wen ku-tz'u shih-li" (Terms and Forms of the Prayers for Blessing in the Bronze Inscriptions), *Li-shih yü-yen yen-chiu-so chi-k'an*, VI, No. 1 (1936), pp. 1–44.

——— "Shuo tsun-i" (Explaining *Tsun* and *I*), *Li-shih yü-yen yen-chiu-so chi-k'an*, VII, No. 1 (1936), pp. 67–78.

Hu Hou-hsüan. "Shih 'yü-i-jen'" (Explaining "I the One Man"), *Li-shih yen-chiu* (Historical Studies), No. 1 (1957), pp. 75–78.

——— Yin-tai feng-chien chih-tu k'ao (Study of the Yin Feudal System), n.p., 1944. Ts'e 1 of Chia-ku-hsüeh Shang-shih lun-ts'ung (Collected Discussions on Shang History Based on Oracle Bone Studies).

Hu Shih. The Development of the Logical Method in Ancient China. Shanghai: Oriental Book Co., 1928.

Huang Chang-chien. "Meng-tzu hsing-lun chih yen-chiu" (A Study of Mencius' Theory of *Hsing*), *Li-shih yü-yen yen-chiu-so chi-k'an*, XXVI (June 1955), pp. 227–308.

Ikeda Suetoshi. "Kijikō-shina ni okeru soshin suhai no gensho keitai" (A

Study of the Character *Kuei*—The Initial Form of Worshipping Ancestral Spirits in China), *Hiroshima daigaku bungakubu kiyō*, No. 10 (1956).

——— "Konpaku kō—Sono kigen to hatten" (A Study of the Characters *Hun* and *P'o*—Their Origin and Development), *Tōhō shūkyō* (Eastern Religions), I, No. 3 (July 1953).

——— "Sai teiten" (Explaining *Ti* and *T'ien*), *Hiroshima daigaku bungakubu kiyō* (Bulletin of the Department of Literature of Hiroshima University), No. 3 (1953), pp. 23–42.

Itō Michiharu. "Bokuji ni mieru sorei kannen ni tsuite" (Concerning the Concept of Ancestral Spirits in Oracle Inscriptions), *Tōhō gakuho* (Eastern Journal), XXVI (1956).

Jaeger, Werner W. Paideia: The Ideals of Greek Culture, Vol. I: Archaic Greece and The Mind of Athens (translated by Gilbert Highet). Oxford: Blackwell, 1965.

Juei Senno. "Toko no gyoso" (The Character of *Te*), *Kenkyū kiyō* (Research Bulletin), II (1960).

Jung Keng. Chin-wen pien (Collection of Bronze Inscriptions). Peking: K'o-hsüeh ch'u-pan she, 1959.

Kaizuka Shigeki. Kyōto jinbun kangaku kenkyūjō kokotsu moji (Oracle Bone Inscriptions Kept by the Kyoto University Institute for Humanistic Studies). Kyoto: Jinbun kangaku kenyūjō, 1960.

——— Kodai In teikoku (The Ancient Yin Imperial State). Tokyo: Misuzu shobo, 1957.

——— "Rongo ni arawareta ningen tenkei toshite no kunshi" (The *Chün-tzu* Who Was the Model of Man in the *Analects*), *Toyoshi kenkyū* (Studies in Oriental History), X, No. 3 (July 1948), pp. 141–54.

Kaltenmark, Max. Lao Tseu et le taoïsme. Paris: Editions du Seuil, 1965.

Kanaya Osamu. Junshi (*Hsün-tzu*). Tokyo: Iwanami shoten, 1962.

——— " 'Junshi' no bunkengaku teki kenkyū" (A Textual Study of Hsün-tzu's Work), *Nihon gakushiin kiyō* (Bulletin of the Japanese Academy), IX, No. 1 (Mar. 1951).

——— "Ko-Mo no mei ni tsuite" (Concerning *Ming* According to Confucius and Mencius), *Nippon chūgoku gakkai hō* (Journal of the Japanese Sinological Society), VIII (1956).

——— "Koshi no shukyoteki tachiba" (Confucius' Religious Standpoint), *Shukan Toyogaku* (Collected Publications of Oriental Studies), VI (Sept. 1961).

——— "Sōshi tenka hen no imi" (On the Meaning of the T'ien-hsia Chapter of the *Chuang-tzu*), *Bunka* (Culture), XVI, No. 6 (Nov. 1952).

——— "Yokubō no ari kata—Junshi no shosetsu o megutte" (The Ideal Manner of Desiring—On Hsün-tzu's Views), *Bunka*, XV, No. 2 (Mar. 1951).

———, ed. Moshi (*Mo-tzu*). 2 vols. Tokyo: Asahi Shinbunsha, 1956.

Karlgren, Bernhard. The Book of Documents. Published in book form, reprinted from *BMFEA*, XXII (1950).

——— The Book of Odes. Stockholm: Museum of Far Eastern Antiquities, 1950.

——— "Contributions à l'analyse des caractères chinois," *Asia Major, Hirth Anniversary Volume* (1921).

——— "Glosses on the Book of Documents," *BMFEA*, No. 20 (1948).

——— "Glosses on the Book of Odes," *BMFEA*, No. 16 (1950).

——— "Grammata Serica," *BMFEA*, No. 12 (1940).

——— "Grammata Serica Recensa," *BMFEA*, No. 29 (1957).

Katō Jōken. Shina kodai kazoku seido kenkyū (Study of China's Ancient Clan System). Toyko: Iwanami shoten, 1940.

Kent, George William. Seven Terms of the Chou-Han Traditional Ethics. Unpublished Ph.D. dissertation, Department of Oriental Languages, University of California at Berkeley, 1961.

Kimura Eiichi. Rōshi no shin kenkyū (New Study of the *Lao-tzu*). Tokyo: Kankozo bunsha, 1959.

Ku Chieh-kang and Lo Ken-che. Ku-shih pien (Analysis of Ancient History), Vol. VII: Lun ku-shih ch'uan-shuo yen-pien chih kuei-lu hsing (On the Laws of the Evolution of Legends in Ancient History). Shanghai: K'ai-ming shu-tien, 1941.

Kuo Mo-jo. Chin-wen ts'ung-k'ao (Comprehensive Studies on Bronze Inscriptions), Vol. I: Chou i-ming chung chih ch'uan-t'ung ssu-hsiang (A Study of Traditional Thought Revealed in Chou Bronze Inscriptions); Sect. 3, Tao-te ssu-hsiang (Ethical Thought). Peking: Jenmin ch'u-pan she, 1954.

——— Hsien-Ch'in t'ien-tao kuan chih chin-chan (The Development of the Concept of Heavenly Way in the Pre-Ch'in Period). Shanghai: Commercial Press, 1936.

——— Liang-Chou chin-wen tz'u ta-hsi t'u-lu (A General Systematic Illustrated Record of the Bronze Inscriptions of the Two Chous). Peking: K'o-hsüeh ch'u-pan she, 1957.

——— Nu-li chih shih-tai (The Slave-System Period). Shanghai: Hsinwen-i ch'u-pan she, 1952.

——— Yin-ch'i ts'ui-pien (Compilation of Yin Inscriptions). Tokyo: Bunkyūdo shoten, 1937.

——— Yin-Chou ch'ing-t'ung ch'i ming-wen yen-chiu (A Study of Inscriptions on Yin and Chou Bronzes). 2d ed., revised. Peking, 1961.

——— et al., eds. Kuan-tzu chi-chiao (Collected Studies on the *Kuan-tzu*). 2 vols. Shanghai: K'o-hsüeh ch'u-pan she, 1956.

Kuo-yü Wei Chao chu (*Kuo-yü* with Annotations by Wei Chao). Taipei: I-wen yin-shu kuan, n.d.

Kuroda Genji. "K'i" (*Ch'i*), *Tōhō shūkyō*, I, Nos. 4–5 (Jan. 1954).

Lakoff, Sanford A. Equality in Political Philosophy. Cambridge, Mass.: Harvard University Press, 1964.

Latham, R. E., trans. Lucretius, *The Nature of the Universe.* London: Penguin Classics, 1951.

Lau, D. C. Lao Tzu Tao Te Ching. Baltimore: Penguin, 1963.

——— "Theories of Human Nature in Mencius and Shyuntzyy," *Bulletin of the School of Oriental and African Studies*, XV (1953).

——— "The Treatment of Opposites in Lao Tzu," *Bulletin of the School of Oriental and African Studies*, XXI, No. 2 (1958).

Legge, James. The Chinese Classics. Vol. I: Confucian Analects, The Great Learning, The Doctrine of the Mean. Vol. II: The Works of Mencius. Vol. V. The Ch'un Ts'ew with the Tso Chuen. Hong Kong: Hong Kong University Press, 1960.

Li Hsiang-yin. "Kao-tzu 'jen-nei i-wai' shuo ti chieh-shih" (An Explanation of Kao-tzu's saying "*Jen-nei i-wai*"), *Hsüeh-shu chi-k'an* (Academic Quarterly), V, No. 1 (Sept. 1956), pp. 10–16.

Li Tsung-t'ung. Chung-kuo ku-tai she-hui shih (History of Ancient Chinese Society). 2 vols. Taipei: Chung-hua wen-hua ch'u-pan shih-yeh wei-yüan hui, 1954.

Li Tu. "Hsien-Ch'in shih-ch'i chih t'ien-ti-kuan" (Concepts of *T'ien* and *Ti* in the Pre-Ch'in Period), *Hsin-ya shu-yüan hsüeh-shu nien-k'an* (New Asia College Academic Yearly), No. 3 (1961), pp. 1–65.

Li Ya-nung. Yin-ch'i chih hsü-pien (Supplementary Edition of Yin Inscriptions). Shanghai: Chung-kuo k'o-hsüeh yüan, 1950.

Liang Ch'i-ch'ao. Hsien-Ch'in cheng-chih ssu-hsiang shih (A History of Pre-Ch'in Political Thought). Shanghai: Commerical Press, n.d.

Liang Shu-jen, ed. Hsün-tzu yüeh-chu (Concise Notes on the *Hsün-tzu*). 2 vols. Taipei: Shih-chieh shu-chü, 1958.

Liao, W. K., trans. The Complete Works of Han Fei Tzu. London: Probsthain, 1959.

Liebenthal, Walter, trans. The Book of Chao. Peking: Catholic University of Peking, 1948.

Liu Pao-nan, ed. Lun yü cheng-i (Orthodox Commentary on the *Analects*). Taipei: Shih-chieh shu-chü, 1956.

Lo Chen-yü. San-tai chi-chin-wen-ts'un (A Collection of Bronze Inscriptions from the Three Dynasties). N.p., n.d.

Lu Szu-mien. Hsien-Ch'in shih (History of the Pre-Ch'in Period). Hong Kong: T'ai-ping shu-chü, 1962.

Ma Hsü-lun. Chuang-tzu t'ien-hsia-p'ien shu-i (On the Meaning of the T'ien-hsia Chapter of the *Chuang-tzu*). Shanghai: Lung-men lien-ho shu-chü, 1958.

Masubuti Tatsuo. Chūgoku kodai no shakai to kokka (The Ancient Chinese Society and State). Toyko: Kōbundō, 1960.

McKeon, Richard. *Introduction to Aristotle.* New York: Modern Library, 1947.

Meisner, Maurice. Li Ta-chao and the Origins of Chinese Marxism. Cambridge, Mass.: Harvard University Press, 1967.

Mori Mikisaburo. "Sōshi ni okeru sei no shisō—Yōsei setsu to kyorakei sugi to no hōga" (The Concept of *Hsing* in the *Chuang-tzu*—The Origins of the "Nourish Life" Theory and Epicureanism), *Tōhō Gaku* (Eastern Studies), XVIII (1959).

Needham, Joseph. Science and Civilization in China. 5 vols. Cambridge, Eng.: Cambridge University Press, 1954.

Ogura Yoshihiko. "Saden ni okeru ha to toku—Toku gainen no keisei to tenkai," (Hegemony and Virtue in the *Tso chuan*—The Formation and Development of the Concept of *Te*), in *Chūgoku kodaishi kenkyū* (Study of Ancient Chinese History). Tokyo: Yoshikawa kōbundan, 1960.

Pennock, J. Roland, and John W. Chapman. Nomos IX: Equality. New York: Atherton, 1967.

Richards, I. A. Mencius on the Mind. London: Kegan Paul, Trench, Trubner, and Co., 1932.

Sargent, Galen E. "Le Débat entre Meng-tseu et Siun-tseu sur la nature humain," *Oriens Extremis*, III, No. 1 (1956).

Shang ch'eng-tsu. Yin-ch'i i-ts'un (Supplementary Collection of Yin Inscriptions). Nanking, 1933.

Shih Ming. "Tu 'Hsin-chung-kuo k'ao-ku shou-huo'" (On reading *New China's Archaeological Harvest*), *Li-shih yen-chiu*, No. 3 (1962), pp. 160–65.

Shih-san-ching chu-shu (Commentaries on the Thirteen Classics): Vol. I, Chou-i cheng-i (Orthodox Commentary on the *Chou-i*); Vol. VI, Li-chi cheng-i (Orthodox Commentary on the *Li-chi*); Vol. VIII, Ch'un-ch'iu kung-yang chuan chu-shu (Commentary on the Kung-yang Commentary of the *Spring and Autumn Annals*), Taipei: Ch'i-ming shu-chü, 1959.

Shima Kuniyo. Inkyo bokuji kenkyū (Inscriptions from the Yin Wastes). N.p.: Chūgokugaku kenkyūkai, 1958.

Shirakawa Shizuka. "Kinbun tsushoku ichi" (General Explanation of

Bronze Inscriptions, No. 1), *Hakutsura bijitsukan* (White Crane Art Society), July 1962.

——— "Meimon koshaku" (The Pien Ch'iang Bronze Bell), *Ritsumeikan bungaku* (Ritsumeikan University Literature), No. 165 (1957).

Ssu-pu ts'ung-k'an (Comprehensive Collection of the Four Categories). Shanghai: Commerical Press, 1929.

Tai Chen, "Meng-tzu tzu-i shu-cheng" (Explanation of Terms in the *Mencius*), *Chih hai*, XVII: n.p., n.d.

T'ang Chün-i. "Hsien-Ch'in ssu-hsiang chung chih t'ien-ming-kuan" (The Concept of *T'ien-ming* in Pre-Ch'in Thought), *Hsin-ya hsüeh-pao*, III, No. 2 (1957), pp. 1–33.

——— "Meng Mo Chuang Hsün chih yen hsin shen-i" (On the Meaning of *Hsin* as Discussed by Mencius, Mo Tzu, Chuang Tzu, and Hsün Tzu), *Hsin-ya hsüeh-pao*, I, No. 2 (1956), pp. 29–81.

Tao-te-ching chiang-i (Lectures on the *Tao-te-ching*). Taichung, Taiwan: Tzu-yu ch'u-pan she, 1958.

Taylor, Alfred Edward. Plato: The Man and His Work. Cleveland: World, 1952.

Ting Fu-pao, ed. Shuo-wen chieh-tzu ku-lin (A Collection of Explanations on the *Shuo-wen chieh-tzu*). Taipei: Commercial Press, 1959.

Tung Tso-pin, ed. Chung-kuo wen-tzu (Chinese Characters). 4 vols. Taipei, 1961.

T'ung Shu-yeh. Ch'un-ch'iu shih (A History of the Spring and Autumn Period). Hong Kong: T'ai-p'ing shu-chu, 1962.

Vlastos, Gregory. Plato's Protagoras. New York: Liberal Arts Press, 1956.

Waley, Arthur, trans. The Analects of Confucius. London: Allen and Unwin, 1938.

——— The Way and Its Power. London: Allen and Unwin, 1934. New York: Macmillan, 1957.

Wang Hsien-ch'ien, ed. Hsün-tzu chi-chieh (*Hsün-tzu* with Collected Annotations). Taipei: Shih-chieh shu-chü, 1957.

Wang Hsien-shen, ed. Han Fei-tzu chi-chieh (*Han Fei-tzu* with Collected Annotations). Taipei: I-wen yin-shu-kuan, n.d.

Wang Kuo-wei. Ch'ien-shou-t'ang so-ts'ang Yin-hsü wen-tzu k'ao-shih (Explanations of Inscriptions from the Yin Wastes Kept by the Ch'ien-shou-t'ang). Shanghai: Kuang-ts'ang hsüeh-ch'en, 1919.

Wang Shu-min. Chuang-tzu chiao-shih (Collation and Explanation of the *Chuang-tzu*). N.p., n.d.

Watson, Burton, trans. Mo Tzu: Basic Writings. New York: Columbia University Press, 1963.

Wen I-to. Wen I-to ch'üan-chi (Complete Works of Wen I-to), Vol. I: Ku-tien hsin-i (New Interpretation of Ancient Terms). N.p.: K'ai-ming shu-tien, n.d.

Wilson, John. Equality. London: Hutchinson, 1966.

Wu K'ang. Lao-chuang che-hsüeh (On the Philosophy of Lao-tzu and Chuang-tzu). Taipei: Commercial Press, 1958.

Wu Shih-fen. K'uei-ku lu chin-wen (A Selection of Bronze Inscriptions). N.p., 1896.

Wu Ta-cheng. K'o Chai chi ku-lu (A Collection of Ancient Inscriptions by K'o Chai). Shanghai: Commercial Press, 1930.

Yü Hsing-wu. Shuang Chien-i chi chin-wen hsüan (Selections of Bronze Literature by Shuang Chien-i). Peking, 1932.

——— *Shang-Chou chin-wen lu-i* (Supplementary Records of Shang and Chou Bronze Inscriptions). Peking: K'o-hsüeh ch'u-pan she, 1957.

INDEX